FRONTIERS IN DEVELOPMENTAL PSYCHOLOGY RESEARCH:
JAPANESE PERSPECTIVES

FRONTIERS IN DEVELOPMENTAL PSYCHOLOGY RESEARCH
Japanese Perspectives

JAPAN SOCIETY OF DEVELOPMENTAL PSYCHOLOGY

Supervising editors:
*Shizuo Iwatate, Masuo Koyasu,
and Koichi Negayama*

HITUZI
SYOBO

Copyright © Japan Society of Developmental Psychology 2016
First published 2016

Editor: Japan Society of Developmental Psychology
Supervising editors: Shizuo Iwatate, Masuo Koyasu,
and Koichi Negayama

All rights reserved. Except for the quotation of short passages
for the purposes of criticism and review, no part of this publication may be reproduced, stored in a retrieval system, or
transmitted in any form or by any means, electronic, mechani-
cal, photocopying, recording or otherwise, without the written
prior permission of the publisher.

In case of photocopying and electronic copying and retrieval
from network personally, permission will be given on receipts
of payment and making inquiries. For details please contact us
through e-mail. Our e-mail address is given below.

Hituzi Syobo Publishing
Yamato bldg. 2F, 2-1-2 Sengoku Bunkyo-ku Tokyo,
Japan 112-0011

phone: +81-3-5319-4916 fax: +81-3-5319-4917
e-mail: toiawase@hituzi.co.jp
http://www.hituzi.co.jp/
postal transfer 00120-8-142852

ISBN 978-4-89476-798-0
Printed in Japan

MESSAGE

The Japan Society of Developmental Psychology (JSDP) was founded in 1989. Since then, we have welcomed not only many researchers but also those who are involved in practical businesses relating to human development. Today, we have over 4,200 members.

The JSDP promotes the results of research on human development based on broad views and methods through its annual conference, as well as by publishing the *Japanese Journal of Developmental Psychology* four times a year. In addition, a newsletter is produced three times a year, and information about new studies is sent twice a month via email, to keep our members informed about the latest research.

In the practical field, we have established a system to license clinical developmental psychologists who specialize in support of human development (2001), as well as operating the Japanese Organization of Clinical Developmental Psychologists. Aiming to internationalize our studies, we hold international workshops every year, inviting eminent developmental psychologists from overseas. Recently, we launched a system in cooperation with the Developmental Psychology Section of the British Psychological Society to provide keynote speakers for each other's conferences.

This volume, published on the occasion of the 31st International Congress of Psychology held in Yokohama in July 2016, supports the above-mentioned JSDP activities. Here, Japanese developmental psychologists introduce the latest knowledge and theoretical frameworks in this field. We hope this book will contribute to the advancement of research in developmental psychology and the clinical practice based on it, while promoting international activities of our Society in the future.

Finally, we would like to thank Shinji Satake, Masuo Koyasu, Shizuo Iwatate, and Koichi Negayama of the JSDP Publishing Committee as well as Isao Matsumoto, president of Hituzi Shobo Publishing, for their kind cooperation.

Kazuo Hongo, President
Japan Society of Developmental Psychology
March 2016

PREFACE

The founding principle of the Japan Society for Developmental Psychology (JSDP) is to advance both scientific research and practical activities in harmony. Membership has now reached approximately 4,200. Recently, promoting the internationalization of research by emphasizing research exchange activities with scholars from various nations has become one of the important activities of the Society. One of the most successful activities is the exchange program with the British Psychological Society's Developmental Section. Since 2010, each society has sent a keynote speaker to the other's annual conference. Now, the most important issue for the JSDP is to prepare a means for members to publish articles in English. To date, members have been relying mainly on American and British journals to publish in English because the JSDP has only one journal, which accepts articles only in Japanese. This volume therefore is a new development in this program. The Publishing Planning Board of the JSDP decided to publish a book in English to introduce the work of Japanese developmental psychologists and to show recent trends in developmental psychology in Japan. In addition, the Board has decided that the book should be published before the 31st International Congress of Psychology (ICP2016) in Yokohama, Japan, in 2016.

The members of the Editorial Board are, in alphabetical order, Shizuo Iwatate, Masuo Koyasu, and Koichi Negayama. The psychologists the Board asked to contribute papers to this volume are some of the

vii

most prominent and accomplished developmental psychologists in their respective fields. The articles have been assembled in two sections: overviews of the fruits of Japanese developmental psychology research and cutting-edge research of developmental psychology in Japan. Each article has been carefully reviewed by the Editorial Board and the Advisory Board.

The Board members greatly appreciate the extensive contributions of Kazuo Hongo, Shinji Satake, and the members of the editorial staff of Hituzi Shobo Publishing.

Shizuo Iwatate
Masuo Koyasu
Koichi Negayama
March 2016

CONTENTS

MESSAGE	v
PREFACE	vii
EDITORIAL BOARD	xii
ADVISORY BOARD	xiii
CONTRIBUTORS	xiv

1 Achievements of Developmental Psychology in Japan

Keiko Kashiwagi   3
Demographic Psychology:
The Combination of a Super-Aging Society and a Low Birth Rate

Koichi Negayama   19
Childrearing (*Kosodate*) in Japan with
Special Reference to Mutual Mother-Child Negativity

Masuo Koyasu   33
Cognitive Development Research in Japan:
Past, Present, and Future

Shizuo Iwatate and Keiko Nakamura   47
Research on Language Development in Japan:
Focusing on Acquisition of Grammar,
Polite Language, and Gender-Based Linguistic Forms

Jun Nakazawa   63
Japanese Research on Emotion

Masahiro Nochi   81
Qualitative Research in Japan

Masumi Sugawara, Satoko Matsumoto, and Atsushi Sakai 97
Developmental Psychology in Japan:
Developmental Follow-up Studies

2 Frontiers of Developmental Psychology in Japan

Yasuyo Minagawa and Sho Tsuji 113
Cerebral Lateralization of Speech Processing
Assessed with Near Infrared Spectroscopy:
Typical and Atypical Development

Noriko Toyama 129
Young Children's Cross Mind-Body Awareness

Nobuyuki Fujimura 149
Conceptual Understanding in Childhood

Hideki Okabayashi 165
Getting Older, Getting Happier?
Self-regulation and Age Trends in Well-being in Japan

Atsushi Senju 189
Atypical Social Cognition in Autism Spectrum Disorders

Junichi Yamamoto and Atsuko Matsuzaki 203
Effectiveness of a Nursery School Teacher
Training Program in Providing Interventions and
Supports for Children with Developmental Disorders

Etsuko Haryu and Sachiyo Kajikawa 221
Japanese Children's Use of Function Morphemes
during Language Development

Miki Kakinuma and Kayoko Uemura   237
Communicative Behavior of ASD and
Typically Developing Children in Japan and China

Makiko Naka   251
Where Developmental Psychology Meets the Law:
Forensic Interviews with Witnesses
and Alleged Child Victims

INDEX   265

EDITORIAL BOARD

Shizuo Iwatate
Japan Women's University

Masuo Koyasu
Konan University

Koichi Negayama
Waseda University

ADVISORY BOARD

Juko Ando
Keio University

Takeshi Asao
Nara Women's University

Hiroshi Fujino
Tokyo Gakugei University

Toru Goshiki
Ryukoku University

Harumi Kobayashi
Tokyo Denki University

Hidetsugu Komeda
Kyoto University

Ai Mizokawa
Sugiyama Jogakuen University

Takashi Muto
Shiraume Gakuen University

Masako Myowa
Kyoto University

Nobuko Nakashima
Niigata University

Masayuki Ochiai
Otemon Gakuin University

Sachiko Ono
Shirayuri University

Hiroko Sakagami
Aoyama Gakuin University

Miki Sakamoto
Kobe University

Toshiaki Shirai
Osaka Kyoiku University

Tadashi Suzuki
Shirayuri University

Noboru Takahashi
Osaka Kyoiku University

CONTRIBUTORS

Nobuyuki Fujimura
Ph.D.; Cognitive Development, Conceptual Understanding
Graduate School of Education, The University of Tokyo, Tokyo
Email: hge01342@nifty.ne.jp
http://www.p.u-tokyo.ac.jp/english/graduate-programs/curriculum-development

Etsuko Haryu
Ph.D.; Language and Cognitive Development
Graduate School of Education, The University of Tokyo, Tokyo
Email: haryu@p.u-tokyo.ac.jp
http://researchmap.jp/read0187961/?lang=english

Shizuo Iwatate
Ph.D.; Language Development
Department of Psychology, Japan Women's University, Kawasaki
Email: siwatate@fc.jwu.ac.jp
http://www2.jwu.ac.jp/kgr/jpn/ResearcherInformation/ResearcherInformation.aspx-?KYCD=00006165

Sachiyo Kajikawa
Ph.D.; Language Development
College of Arts and Sciences, Tamagawa University, Tokyo
Email: kajikawa@lab.tamagawa.ac.jp
http://www.tamagawa.jp/graduate/brain/staff/labs/kajikawa.html

Miki Kakinuma
Ph.D.; Social Cognitive Development
Faculty of Comparative Developmental Psychology, Nippon Veterinary and Life Science University, Tokyo
E-mail: kakinuma-miki@nvlu.ac.jp
http://tlo.nms.ac.jp/researcher/1306.html

Keiko Kashiwagi
Ph.D.; Personality Development,Gender, Family Psychology
Tokyo Woman's Christian University,Professor Emeritus,Tokyo
Email: k.kashi@hb.tp1.jp

xiv

Masuo Koyasu
Ph.D.;Cognitive Development
Faculty of Letters, Konan University, Kobe
Email: HGB03675@nifty.com

Satoko Matsumoto
Ph.D.; Environmental Psychology
Institute for Education and Human Development, Ochanomizu University, Tokyo
Email: matsumoto.satoko@ocha.ac.jp

Atsuko Matsuzaki
M.A.; Clinical Developmental Psychology, Applied Behavior Analysis
Keio Advanced Research Center, Keio University, Tokyo
Email: matsuzakiatsuko@gmail.com

Yasuyo Minagawa
Ph.D.; Developmental Cognitive Neuroscience
Department of Psychology, Keio University, Tokyo
Email: minagawa@flet.keio.ac.jp
http://duallife.web.fc2.com/i/next.html

Makiko Naka
Ph.D.; Psychology and Law, Cognitive Development
Graduate School of Letters, Hokkaido University, Sapporo
Email: mnaka@let.hokudai.ac.jp
http://cogpsy.let.hokudai.ac.jp/~nakalab/index-english.html

Keiko Nakamura
Ph.D.; Developmental Psychology
Faculty of Languages and Cultures, Meikai University, Chiba
Email: kei@aya.yale.edu

Jun Nakazawa
Ph.D.; Social and Emotional Development
Faculty of Education, Chiba University, Chiba
nakazawa@faculty.chiba-u.jp
http://www.e.chiba-u.jp/~nakazawa/

Koichi Negayama
Ph.D.; Developmental Human Ethology
Faculty of Human Sciences, Waseda University, Saitama
Email: negayama@waseda.jp
https://sites.google.com/site/negayamawsd/home

Masahiro Nochi
Ph.D.; Clinical Psychology
Graduate School of Education, The University of Tokyo, Tokyo
Email: mnochi@p.u-tokyo.ac.jp
http://researchmap.jp/read0061460

Hideki Okabayashi
Ph.D.; Life-span Developmental Psychology
Department of Psychology, School of Humanities, Meisei University,Tokyo
Email: okabaya@psy.meisei-u.ac.jp
http://www.iag.meisei-u.ac.jp/meuhp/KgApp?kyoinId=ygggyyyyykm

Atsushi Sakai
Ph.D.; Developmental Psychology
Graduate School of Humanities, Tokyo Metropolitan University, Tokyo
Email: sakai-atsushi@tmu.ac.jp
http://www.comp.tmu.ac.jp/psychology/

Atsushi Senju
Ph.D.; Developmental Social Neuroscience
Centre for Brain and Cognitive Development, Birkbeck, University of London, London
Email: a.senju@bbk.ac.uk
http://www.cbcd.bbk.ac.uk/people/scientificstaff/atsushi

Masumi Sugawara
Ph.D.; Developmental Psychopathology
Human Science Division, Faculty of Core Research, Ochanomizu University, Tokyo
Email: sugawara.masumi@ocha.ac.jp
http://www.ocha.ac.jp

Noriko Toyama
Ph.D.; Cognitive Development
Faculty of Human Sciences, Waseda University, Saitama
Email: toyama@waseda.jp
http://www.waseda.jp/fhum

Sho Tsuji
Ph.D.; Language Development
Départment d'Etudes Cognitives, Ecole Normale Supérieure, Paris
tsujish@gmail.com
https://sites.google.com/site/tsujish/home

Kayoko Uemura
Ph.D.; Development of Language and Communication Skills
Faculty of Human Studies, Bunkyo Gakuin University, Tokyo
Email: kuemura@bgu.ac.jp
http://www.u-bunkyo.ac.jp/faculty/staff/3809.html

Junichi Yamamoto
Ph.D.; Clinical Developmental Psychology, Applied Behavior Analysis
Department of Psychology, Keio University, Tokyo
Email: yamamotj@flet.keio.ac.jp
http://www.flet.keio.ac.jp/~yamamotj/

1 Achievements of
Developmental Psychology in Japan

Demographic Psychology:
The Combination of a Super-Aging Society and a Low Birth Rate

Keiko Kashiwagi

Japan is referred to as "a super-aging society with a low birth rate" both by politicians and the media. Indeed, Japan has a low birth rate and a long life expectancy; the total fertility rate is extremely low, and the life expectancy for both men and women ranks among the world's top three. These demographic parameters have an extremely big impact on the human mind, particularly the development of the mind—a central issue of developmental psychology.

However, developmental psychology has not paid full attention to the effects of these demographic factors on psychological development. The condition of an aging society with a low birth rate that exists in Japan is observed in few other countries. Despite the fact that these societal conditions massively affect the Japanese people—their purpose in life, identity, and family relationships between husband and wife and parent and child—, there has been very little research that focuses on these as significant environmental factors. The need to study such issues as "demographic psychology" has been discussed (Kashiwagi, 2001), and, this chapter reviews the main issues arising from this demographic change in japan.

1. LONGEVITY IS THE "FATHER" OF LIFESPAN DEVELOPMENTAL PSYCHOLOGY

Today, "development" refers not only to children's development and the process of becoming an adult. It is now recognized as a life-long process that continues from birth to death. In the days when the average life expectancy was 50 to 60 years, developmental research studied the period up to adulthood, and consigned the rest to perceptual psychology, social psychology, and other fields. So, child psychology and adolescent psychology were considered sufficient to understand human development. That has changed greatly due to the prolongation of the lifespan. Longevity has created a life stage after reaching adulthood that is longer than ever, and this change has brought another long stage of life that cannot be categorized simply as "adulthood." These require development of life-long studies. Lifespan developmental psychology from birth through death is, thus, the outcome of the demographic change caused by the great prolongation of life. That is, prolongation of life as a demographic change has shifted the subject and perspectives of developmental psychology. Although Japan is one of the fastest aging nations with a significantly low birth rate, Japanese have not contributed to the birth of lifespan developmental psychology and have not played a leading role in this field of research. This suggests a certain lack of sensitivity to societal changes on the part of Japanese psychological researchers.

2. IMPACT OF LONGEVITY AND THE LOW BIRTH RATE ON PSYCHOLOGICAL DEVELOPMENT

The demographic state of "prolonged life expectancy and low birth rate" has had a massive impact on psychological development, as described below.

2.1 *Demographic Revolution More Important than Declining Number of Children*

The declining number of births is publicized widely as a problem and a matter of great concern, but what deserves more attention are the "demographic revolution" and "reproductive revolution." Scientifically controlling reproduction, specifically pregnancy and birth, has now become possible. This is the result of progress in medical science and technology, and it also reflects the pro-birth control attitude of the public (Tsuge, 1999; Ogino, 2008). The phenomenon of declining number of children is not recent. In the past, many children were born, but the majority of them did not survive. Mozart, the great composer, who lived approximately 200 years ago, sired six children in his nine-year marriage. However, four died prematurely, and only two survived. The distinct difference in decline in the number of children between the present and the past is that what was once accidental is today a matter of choice. In other words, childbirth has been changed from a "given" to a "decision." This is called the demographic/reproductive revolution.

This phenomenon has changed the value of children to their parents and their feelings toward and care for their children. The phenomenon has altered the quantity and quality of parents' investment in parenting, discipline, and education of their children. Japanese people have long thought of children as treasures; yet if children were still treasures worth more than anything today, the birth rate would not be low. This clearly shows an alteration in the value of children.

To date, studies have focused on the value of children on an abstract and conceptual level (Hoffman & Hoffman, 1973; Trommsdorff & Nauck, 2005). However, the current condition of permitting children to "be made" has enabled the subject to be studied on an objective behavioral level. Kashiwagi and Nagahisa's study (1999) is one of the pioneer studies on the value of children, and remains one of the few valuable resources in this field. Their study demonstrates changes in the reasons why people have children. The common reasons given by the older generation (now in their 60s), such as "it is normal to have children after marriage" and "it is our responsibility to produce the next generation," have been diminished in the younger generation (now in their 40s). Instead, more reasons such as "I can now start a new chapter of my life" or "I have financial stability now" are given (Figure 1). This shows that children are no longer an absolute treasure that is greater than anything. The value of children seems to have become somewhat relative—whose value a person measures in comparison to other activities in his/her life.

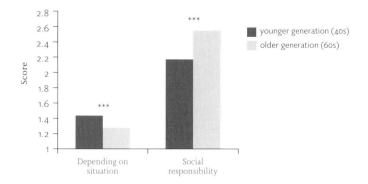

Figure 1 Reasons why people of two different generations have children
*** $p<.001$ Source Kashiwagi & Nagahisa (1999).

3. Longevity with Declining Number of Children and Women's Identity/Purpose in Life

The relativized value of children is associated with changes in women's identity and purpose in life. Prior to this modern period, the purpose of a woman's life was to give a birth, raise children, and do vast amounts of housework. Her life expectancy was also coterminous with the time she finished her role as a mother—she probably died not too much after the marriage of her youngest child.

Motherhood was a women's life in premodern Japan. Women were not expected to live as individuals. However, this life no longer exists in our society today; after raising a small number of children, a woman is left with 20 to 30 years of life that she is now entitled to live not as a mother but as an individual. This time remaining as an individual has led her to question how she can live her life with happiness, which also guides her to question her identity as an individual. Being a good mother, spouse, and housekeeper is no longer her source of psychological fulfillment, and these roles alone no longer give substantial meaning to her life. However, her dissatisfaction and frustration are greatly increased because no chance is provided for her to live as an individual and choose her own life not merely as someone's mother or someone's wife. She is prevented from living a life that develops her own skills and expresses her own abilities. Consequently, this condition conflicts with women's identity and creates dissatisfaction and frustration. Over the past 30 years, there has been a change in answers to the question "Which self is important to me?" by married women with children. Along with this change, the importance of "myself as an individual" has gained a more prominent attention, while that of "myself as a mother" has subsided.

The demographic revolution, by which childbirth has become a choice and not something natural/inevitable, has prompted the reconstruction [construction?] of women's not-a-mother life and identity. Furthermore, women's hesitation about having children and the lower birth rate may have been impacted by this revolution. The demographic revolution of longevity combined with the low birth rate has greatly affected women's psychological development (Kashiwagi, 2001).

4. LONGEVITY COMBINED WITH LOW BIRTH RATE AND MOTHER'S CHILDREARING ANXIETY

Over the past 30 years, anxiety about rearing children has become prevalent among mothers in Japan (Ohinata, 1988). Childrearing anxiety refers to the irritation, worry, and discontent with the job of childcare, her children, and herself, in spite of her love for the children and her wish to be a good mother. This phenomenon in Japanese mothers is remarkable and could be considered a direct outcome of modern society. The factors and background behind this phenomenon may have arisen from the fact that Japanese have not fully digested the social conditions of prolonged life expectancy combined with the low birth rate and have not adjusted their lifestyles to those new conditions. This is evident when we look at what types of mothers have the highest childrearing anxiety. An enormous amount of research on childrearing anxiety reveals that there are two factors that reinforce the anxiety.

The first factor is the mother's unemployment—the difficulty of being a full-time worker. The idea that childrearing should be performed by a mother has been positively or negatively prevalent in Japanese society, and it affects women's behavior. This is shown by a high number of women—over 60 percent—who quit their jobs after childbirth. However, these women are the mothers who have the highest likelihood of developing childrearing anxiety (Kosaka & Kashiwagi, 2007).

The second factor in childrearing anxiety is the absence of the father (mother's spouse) in childrearing (Figure 2).

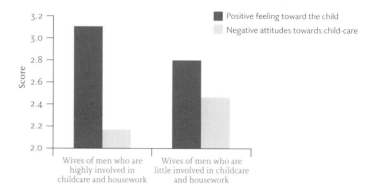

Figure 2 Mothers' feelings about children and childcare by extent of fathers' involvement in childcare and household
Source Kashiwagi & Wakamatsu (1994).

When a wife leaves work after childbirth, her husband becomes the breadwinner of the family. As a result, all the housework and childrearing is left to the wife, and the woman starts to lack time for herself. Her life becomes all about being a mother and a wife. Although the gender division of labor that "men work outside and women work at home" has lost its suitability due to societal changes, the idea still seems to strongly dominate people. This is the fundamental reason why mothers' child-anxiety occurs in Japanese society.

5. Background of Fluctuating Identity: Feminization of Labor and Future Perspectives

A question of why a life as only a mother and wife causes childrearing anxiety should be recognized in terms of the feminization of labor (also mechanization/computerization) in addition to the extreme changes in the life-course due to the prolongation of life and the low birth rate. Labor historically depended on the brawn of strong men (thus, the workforce was called "manpower"); however, that situation changed with mechanization and computerization, which have opened the doors for women to be employed and earn their own income, enabling them to live independently. Nonetheless, it is not just due to the money. Employment opportunities have enabled women to realize that they can utilize their own abilities and be appreciated for their contributions. Today, the majority of women have experienced paid work. Yet, this is why they suffer from difficulties when they experience life as only a mother/wife after retiring from work to give birth. Then the loss of such experience and of opportunities to grow as an individual becomes depressing.

In addition, humans do not live in the present moment. We look to the future and imagine how we should be and what we want to become, and we try to cultivate ourselves to achieve this (Shirai, 1997). This is unique to human beings. Even if a woman loves her children and thinks childrearing is very important, when she looks to the future, she cannot ignore her "remaining time." She then thinks seriously about how she can utilize that time meaningfully, and evidently does not come up with an easy answer. This becomes a source of irritation and anxiety.

6. MIDDLE-AGE DIVORCE; DISSATISFACTION WITH HUSBAND AND DETERIORATION OF HAPPY MARRIAGE

The irritation and anxiety of women after childbirth is also linked to dissatisfaction with husbands when they notice a gap between them. When a woman realizes that her husband, whose age, education, and abilities are similar to hers (a superior-subordinate relationship between husband and wife is almost non-existent in love-based marriages), has maintained his life unchanged after childbirth, she realizes the difference between them. This may lead to dissatisfaction.

Research unanimously confirms that husbands show higher satisfaction with their marriage and spouse than wives (Sugawara & Takuma, 1997; Inaba, 2002). However, in the background lie the unequal division of household tasks and the lack of an intimate relationship between husband and wife that becomes noticeable after childbirth. In many cases, couples compromise or just keep up appearances; they play their nominal role as husband or wife—the husband works and earns money and the wife does housework and childrearing. They simply act as husband and wife on the surface, though they lack psychological intimacy (Utsunomiya, 2004). The predominance of divorce in middle-aged couples in recent years could be due to women's decision to not compromise in the prolonged period after the husband's retirement and the wife's completion of childrearing and due to their decision to commit to a new life. A substantial percentage of middle-aged divorce is initiated by wives. This appears to be the result of the wives' dissatisfaction with their spouses and the fact that the "remaining time" is more strongly recognized by the women.

Historically, a marriage meant living and growing old together, despite some discontent, until death parts the couple. Today, however, this no longer applies. Because being parted by death is a long way in the future, it has become unbearable and/or undesirable to live an unhappy life for such a long time. The prolonged life expectancy may make it more difficult to stay together till parted by death. In this sense, the prolongation of life expectancy has brought a new family crisis.

7. A Personal Resource Investment Strategy in a Career Plan

Childbirth and childrearing are an investment of one's own resources, including time, money, and psychological and physical energy. The recent reasons for women's decision to have a child, such as "Because I can start a new chapter of my life" or "Because I am not busy with my work now," indicate an attitude of allocating personal resources by evaluating the value of children in comparison to other aspects of life.

Nonetheless, this resource allocation seems to be inadequate in many cases. Objectively designing countermeasures by tackling the issues regarding resource investment means career planning. When this investment allocation fails, time and psychological/physical energy are consumed only by childrearing, and investment in her own life becomes nearly impossible. Further, women come to realize problems and experience discontent. Such discontent may stem, for example, from the fact that the husband, also a parent, is living his life unaffected by childbirth or from the fact that the woman has been alienated from a world where she could live and be treated as an individual after childbirth. The discontent and anxiety that comes from being a good mother, wife, and homemaker but with no sense of feeling alive, is a result of this career plan that failed to adequately capture the importance of living as an "individual." Career planning, thus, is required to thoroughly take her entire lifetime into consideration, including not only marriage, childbirth, and childrearing, but also employment.

8. Social Changes and Changes in Men

Yet, what about men? Regardless of the social condition of longevity with a low birth rate and the feminization of labor, the majority of men are workers who derive satisfaction from the expectation that men work. With such conditions, Japanese men who become fathers but decline to do childcare (Kashiwagi, 2013) tend to fail in constructing an identity as a parent (Ishii-Kuntz, 2013). Moreover, many men lack the maturity to live daily life independently as a result of leaving the housework and childcare to their wives. Longevity means an extended post-retirement period. Today, peoples' lives are not coterminous with their work, which implies that the "men are to work" lifestyle no longer functions adequately. However, men's unawareness of that reality causes them to become useless at home as "over size dust". This in turn causes "at-home husband stress syndrome" among the wives.

In contrast to this majority, there are an increasing number of men who have developed an equal relationship with their spouse by putting equal importance on both work and home (Ohno, 2008, 2012). These men are gradually recognizing the social reality of longevity with the declining number of children and that labor/breadwinning is no longer exclusive to men. The emergence of such men not possessing traditional "manliness" should be studied as a change in Japanese men.

In recent years, there has been an increase in both men and women who exhibit both male (such as strong, assertive, rational) and female (such as gentle, meek, submissive) characteristics (Azuma & Ogura, 1984; Azuma & Ogura, 2000; Shimonaka, Nakazato, & Kawaai, 2003), called androgyny. They tend to have the highest self-esteem (Figure 3). In this aging society with the low birth rate, both men and women are required to take the caregiving role while working outside the home. For this reason, the combining of both male and female characteristics is both necessary and promising.

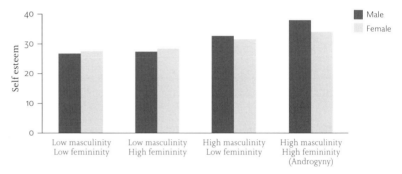

Figure 3 Self esteem by gender type (Japanese university students)
Source Azuma & Ogura (1984).

9. The "Virtue" of Filial Piety Is Threatened by Longevity and the Low Birth Rate: The Other Impact of Longevity on the Parent-Child Relationship

Longevity combined with the declining number of children has had a massive impact on the parent-child relationship. The sixtieth birthday was specially celebrated as *Kanreki* in Japan because in the past not many would have reached that age. Today, however, seventieth and even eightieth birthdays are not rare. Thus, elderly parents experience the longest parent-child relationship when their children are already adults. In the past, the misfortune of parents' death before completion of their childrearing was not rare; however, children today tend to have a new struggle. Due to longevity combined with the low birth rate, the children themselves are quite old when the parents become aged. The burden of long-term care for their parents is imposed on them. This situation has brought massive psychological, physical, and economic burdens to both parents and children, and leads to conflict between them and/or between siblings.

Care for parents has long been considered a "natural duty of children" and a good custom, though such ideas have decreased and are dominated by an idea that describes such care as "inevitable due to poor official government systems for the aged" (Figure 4).

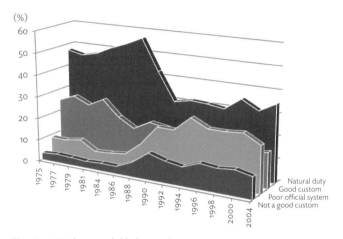

Figure 4 Changing attitudes toward elderly parent care
Source Mainichi News Population Issue Investigation Committee (2005).

The demise of filial piety (Fukaya, 1995) is not because Japanese have become callous or because parent-child relationships have collapsed. The longevity that people had long desired has ironically brought about a condition that is hardly auspicious. It is not unusual that a middle-age woman who has provided long-term care for her parents or her husband's parents suffers from physical and psychological distress and has problems with work and the relationship with her husband. Such situations are caused by a breakdown of resource allocation between care for one's parents and one's own life, making a death something to look forward to. This is an issue that anyone may face in an aging society with a declining number of children.

Cases of abandonment of elderly mothers in India were critically reported (August 19, 2013 *Asahi Shimbun* Morning Edition). However, because longevity is progressing even more rapidly in Japan than India (and anywhere else in the world), such incidents cannot be considered someone else's problem. We are facing an urgent need to take prudent actions to develop parent-child relationships beyond the abstract idea that filial piety is important.

10. Breakdown of the "Feminization of Care Work": Readiness and Sympathy for the Increasingly Important Care Work

The current feeling that longevity is a mixed blessing has created issues regarding care work. These issues have evolved around the extended life expectancy, hence the extension of the duration of care work, and the declining number of children combined with the "feminization" of care work. This feminization of care work burdens women, such as wives, daughters, and daughters-in-law, with the nursing work. Male participation in care work, such as childrearing, household labor, and nursing care, which can be called feminization of care, is extremely low in Japan (Figure 5).

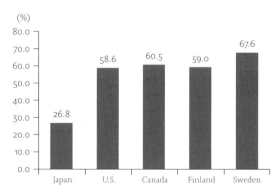

Figure 5 Proportion of men to women who devote time to caregiving in major countries
Source Statistics Bureau, Ministry of Internal Affairs and Communications (2011).

For a long time, it was quite common for women to retire from their careers to provide nursing care. It is only recently that men have finally been pressured into balancing both work and nursing care. Nonetheless, because the men have been exempted from household chores since childhood and have not contributed to housework or childrearing even after marriage, they may not necessarily be capable of managing nursing tasks. Care work requires a readiness and empathy to understand another person's situation and his/her needs, and caregivers need to relate to patients responsively. Theses abilities may not have been fostered in men who have lived in a work world that emphasizes planning-execution-results and efficiency. Abuse in family-oriented nursing care has been increasing, and the perpetrators of such abuse are highly likely to be men—husbands, sons, and grandsons. This is probably because these men have not developed the readiness and sympathy to perform care work.

11. RETHINKING THE PARENT-CHILD RELATIONSHIP: INDEPENDENCE OF CHILDREN/INDEPENDENCE OF PARENTS

The parent-child relationship once considered natural was that parents nurture children when the children are young and the children look after the parents when the parents become old. However, due to the longevity of parents and the declining number of children, this relationship is becoming imbalanced because the circulation of resources between parents and children is no longer functioning as it once did. This condition calls for a shift to a Western style parent-child relationship, in which the parents stop investing in their children after they achieve independence and the parents do not expect investment from their children in return. A shift to this Western style seems to be occurring. Many members of the parental generation proclaim, "I do not wish to have my children to look after me," and an increasing number of these parent generation couples, who have children, are moving voluntarily into nursing homes; these are a part of the shift. Thus, this change deserves attention as an aspect of recent developments of social change in Japanese life and the family.

As such changes occur, Japanese cannot overlook their tendency to invest excessively in their children for an overly long time, involvement that is both psychological and/or economic. This links to the strong

Japanese ideology of affection and wish to do everything one can, which reinforces the trend toward excessive investment in a few children. A typical case of this is the parasite singles phenomenon (Yamada, 1999), in which adult children cohabit with their parents and depend on them for household services (Miyamoto, 2004). The fact that childrearing is solely the mother's responsibility and the lack of an intimate husband-wife relationship cultivates this overly long and excessive involvement in children, and causes the parents to miss the opportunity to terminate the role of parent. This interferes both with the child's independence from the parents and the parent's independence from their child. Japanese need to rethink parent-child relationships, which have already become inadequate in the demographic condition of prolonged lifespans and the declining number of children.

REFERENCES

Azuma, K., & Ogura C. (1984). *Psychology of Sex role*. Dai nihon Tosho.

Azuma, K., & Ogura C., eds. (2000). *Gender no shinrigaku* [The psychology of gender]. Tokyo: Waseda University Publishing Department.

Fukaya, M. (1995). *Oyako no shuen* [The demise of filial piety]. Tokyo: Reimei Shobo.

Hoffman, L. W., & Hoffman, M. L. (1973). The value of children to parents. In Fawcett J. T. (ed.), *Psychological perspectives on population*. New York: Basic Books.

Inaba, A. (2002). *Kekkon to distress* [Marital Status and Psychological Distress in Japan]. *Japanese Sociology Review*, 53, 69–84.

Ishii-Kuntz, M. (2013). *"Ikumen"gensho no shakaigaku* [Sociology of "child caring men": In search of realizing fathers' involvement in child rearing]. Kyoto: Minerva Shobo.

Kashiwagi, K. (2001). *Kodomo to iu kachi: Shoshika jidai no josei no shinri* [The value of children: Psychology of women in an age of declining birth rates]. Tokyo: Chuko Shinsho.

Kashiwagi, K. (2013). *Otona ga sodatsu joken: Hatatsu shinrigaku kara kangaeru* [The conditions of adult development: The developmental psychology approach]. Tokyo: Iwanami Shoten.

Kashiwagi, K., & Nagahisa H. (1999). *Josei ni okeru kodomo no kachi: Ima naze kodomo wo umuka?* [The Value of Children for Women: Why have a child now?] *The Japanese*

Journal of Educational Psychology, 47, 170–179.

Kashiwagi, K., & Wakamatsu M. (1994)."*Oya to naru*"*koto ni yoru Jinkaku hattatsu: Shogai hattatsuteki shiten kara oya o kenkyu suru kokoromi* ["Becoming a Parent"and Personality Development: A Lifespan Developmental View]. *The Japanese Journal of Developmental Psychology*, 5, 72–83.

Kashiwagi, K., & Takahashi, K.(in press) *Jinko no Shinrigakue*. Chitose Press

Kosaka, C., & Kashiwagi, K. (2007). *Ikujiki josei no shirou keizoku / taishoku o kiteisuru yoin* [Influences on women's decisions to continue work vs. discontinue employment to raise children]. *The Japanese Journal of Developmental Psychology*, 18,45–54.

Mainichi News Population Issue Investigation Committee, ed. (2005). *Jinko gensho shakai no miraigaku* [Changing family norms among Japanese women in an era of lowest-low fertility].Tokyo: Ronsosha.

Miyamoto, M. (2004). *Post seinenki to oyako senryaku:Otona ni naru imi to katachi no henyo* [Post-adolescence and parent-child strategies: Transformation in the meaning and form of becoming an adult].Tokyo: Keiso Shobo.

Ogino, M. (2008). "*Kazoku keikaku*" *e no michi:Kindai Nihon no seishoku o meguru seiji* [The road to "family planning": The politics around reproduction in modern Japan]. Tokyo: Iwanami Shoten.

Ohinata, M. (1988). *Bosei no kenkyu* [Research on Motherhood]. Tokyo: Kawashima Shoten.

Ohno, S. (2008). *Ikujiki dansei no seikatsu sutairu no tayouka:* "*Kasegite yakuwari*" *ni kodawaranai atarashii dansei no shutsugen* [Emerging varieties of life style in married men: The new type of being free from "the sole provider role."] *The Japanese Journal of Family Psychology*, 22, 107–118.

Ohno, S. (2012). *Ikujiki dansei ni totte no katei kanyo no imi: Dansei no seikatsu sutairu no tayosei ni chumoku shite* [Men's commitment to family reconsidered: Focus on the diversity of lifestyle as a work/life balance]. *The Japanese Journal of Developmental Psychology*, 23, 287–297.

Shimonaka, Y., Nakazato, K., & Kawaai, C. (2003). *Ronenki ni okeru seiyakuwari to shinriteki tekiou*[Gender roles and psychological adaptation in old age]. *Social Gerontology*, 31, 3–11.

Shirai, T. (1997). *Jikanteki tenbo no shogai hattatsu shinrigaku* [Time prospecs of lifespan developmental psychology]. Tokyo: Keiso Shobo.

Statistics Bureau, Ministry of Internal Affairs and Communications (2011). *Heisei 23 nen shakai seikatsu kihon chosa* [Report of the 2011 Survey on time use and leisure activities].

Sugawara, M., & Takuma, N. (1997). *Fufukan no shinmitsusei no hyoka* [Evaluation of intimacy between husband and wife]. *Psychological Diagnostics Quarterly*, 8,155–166.

Trommsudorff, G. & Nauck, B.(Eds.) (2005). *The value of children in cross-cultural perspective: Case studies from eight societies.* Lengerich: Pabst Science Publishers.

Tsuge, A. (1999). *Bunka to shiteno seishoku gijutsu:Funin chiryo ni tazusawaru ishi no katari* [Reproductive technology as culture: As told by a doctor engaged in fertility treatment]. Tokyo: Shoraisha.

Yamada, M. (1999). *Parasaito shinguru no jidai* [The age of parasite singles]. Tokyo: Chikuma Shobo.

Utsunomiya, H. (2004). *Koreiki no fufu kankei ni kansuru hattatsu shinrigakuteki kenkyu* [Developmental psychology research on husband-wife relationship in old age]. Tokyo: Kazama Shobo.

Childrearing (*Kosodate*) in Japan with Special Reference to Mutual Mother-Child Negativity

Koichi Negayama

There has been a significant shift in Japan, as elsewhere, towards parents having fewer children and therefore greater parental investment in each child. The dramatic decrease in child mortality over the last century or so has been one cause of this. The rise of *risshin shusse-shugi* (careerism) and the commercialization of education have also been major factors. Motherhood was especially promoted in Japan during the period 1910–1930 along with the development of the urban nuclear family, and again during the period of rapid economic growth in the 1960s (Ohinata, 1990).

The shift described above has increased a responsibility and a burden in childrearing among the Japanese mothers. This chapter focuses on the characteristics of the current Japanese childrearing with a special reference to mutual negativity between mother and child and their autonomy at the situation of infant feeding and weaning.

1. TOPICS AND TRENDS IN PREVIOUS RESEARCH

There has been a particular increase in interest in childrearing in recent decades. A search using Kikuzo II Visual through the Tokyo and Osaka editions of the national newspaper *Asahi Shimbun* from 1879 to the present shows that articles with the word *kosodate* (childrearing) in the headline almost never appeared until 1970. Then, there were 135 such articles during the 1970s, followed by a major upsurge (1,419 articles in the 1990s and 2,986 in the 2000s).

How has the academic world reacted to the increasing interest in child-rearing in Japan? The academic publications on *kosodate* in Japanese that appeared in major psychological journals after 1950 were counted in the database PsychINFO using the keywords "childrearing," "childcare," and "parenting." The publication trends in two languages, Japanese and English, were found to be surprisingly similar: both remained low until the 1960s and then rapidly increased. It is worth noting that the period roughly corresponded to a wider increase of interest in children, women, and the family (the International Women's Year in 1975, the International Year of the Child in 1979, and the International Year of the Family in 1994, respectively).

In spite of the similarity in the trends of publication in Japanese and English, there was a considerable difference in the ratios of different types of caregivers mentioned in the keywords and abstracts of the studies. Ratios of publications mentioning each type of caregiver are shown in Figure 1. No data are shown for Japanese publications for the 1950s and 1960s because of the extremely limited number of publications mentioning these words. The most remarkable difference was the frequent mentioning of the words "mother(s)" and "maternal" by Japanese researchers (left graph) in comparison with researchers of other countries (right graph), strongly suggesting a greater interest in motherhood in Japan.

It is of note that the Equal Employment Opportunity Law (Danjo Koyo Kikai Kinto Ho) came into effect in Japan in 1986. Many Japanese mothers prefer to take leave from their workplace when their children are young, and come back to work afterwards (the so-called "M-shaped labor force curve"; Ministry of Health, Labour and Welfare, 2015).

Figure 2 shows the ratios of the different topics of the Japanese articles on childrearing from the 1970s to 2013. The topics are classified into five categories based on the keywords and abstracts: "Child" (e.g., "personality," "eating," and "language"); "parent-child relationship (positive or neutral)" (e.g., "parental attitude," "parental role," and "attachment"); "parent-child relationship (negative)" (e.g., "childcare stress," "work-family conflict," and "scolding"), "care-support" (e.g., "social support," "marital relations," and "support by spouse"); and "clinical" (e.g., "disorder," "disability," and "crime").

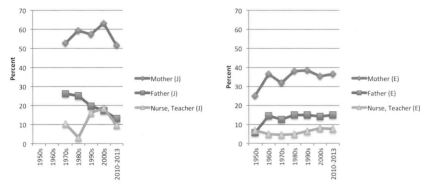

Figure 1 Main caregivers in the studies retrieved from PsychINFO (Japanese left and English right).

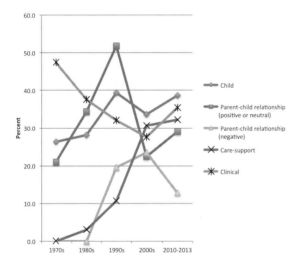

Figure 2 Ratio of topics of papers on childrearing in Japanese classified by the title, keywords, and abstracts in PsychINFO.

What is most interesting is the rapid increase in the mention of both negative parent-child relationships and care-support from the 1980s onwards. Japanese mothers are very often torn between the desire to remain in the workforce and the desire to stay in the home to care for their children. This suggests that the increase in articles on childrearing from the 1970s is a reflection of an ambivalent attitude towards motherhood in Japanese society. The mother-child relationship consists of a combination of positivity and negativity, and consideration of negativity is necessary for a holistic understanding of the relationship. The self-image as a mother is in fact known to be negative among Japanese mothers (Negayama, Norimatsu, Barratt, & Bouville, 2012), and their typically strong inclination toward motherhood is now being questioned (Kashiwagi, 2010). To get a more detailed understanding of the Japanese mother-child relationship, I will examine Japanese studies on infant feeding by mothers as a typical example of mother-infant communication.

2. INFANT FEEDING AND UNDERSTANDING JAPANESE MOTHERHOOD

Feeding is a task with both biological and social functions. It is necessary for an infant mammal to be fed milk and then to be weaned. At the same time, feeding and weaning are highly social or interpersonal activities. There is evidence that issues concerning feeding and weaning are associated with the above-mentioned ambivalence towards motherhood. The infant's age, the weaning process, and a perceived insufficiency of breast milk are the reasons cited most frequently for stopping breastfeeding by Japanese mothers (Yamaguchi & Tanabe, 2012). The mothers in the study who reported insufficiency of breast milk or illness weaned their infants earlier than those citing other reasons (e.g., infant's age and character). Japanese mothers mentioned milk insufficiency more frequently as a reason for weaning than French and American mothers (Negayama, Norimatsu, Barratt, & Bouville, 2012).

For Japanese mothers, weaning is an important part of their maternal role, of coming to understand their infant, and develop their role as a mother (Nakata, Murai, & Emori, 2013). Solid food is first provided by caregivers, and infants gradually participate more actively in the process of feeding. Mothers support and prompt infants to eat on their own by putting food on a spoon and leaving it on the plate for the infants to take by him-/herself.

2.1 Culture and feeding

Feeding involves the child's participation in a cultural activity and cultural learning with the mother's support (Toyama, 2008; Toyama & Muto, 1990). Toyama detailed interactions between Japanese mothers and 1- to 3-year-olds at lunchtime (Toyama, 2008). The 3-year-olds ate almost independently, but one-third of the 2-year-olds were still helped by their mothers. The mothers often talked to the children during the meals, and eating manners were a major topic of comment. The mothers also sought to teach the child by manipulating the situation, by changing the spatial arrangements of foods and utensils, for example.

Infants' autonomy in eating starts with spontaneous manipulation as well as through mothers' support with utensils (Shizawa & Shizawa, 2009). In the transitional stage, from being fed passively to autonomous food-taking, different types of maternal assistance, such as passing a food-loaded spoon to the infant, and partial participation of the infant, such as pulling the spoon toward him-/herself, are reported (Kawata, Tsukada-Jo, & Kawata, 2005).

Interestingly, infants' rejection of mothers' feeding attempts and self-assertion markedly increased after the appearance of the infant's offering food to the mother (Kawata, Tsukada-Jo, & Kawata, 2005). Mothers became less empathetic and increased their talking, trying to check the infants' intention. Kawata et al. interpreted these findings as a sign of infants' differentiating between self and other and coming to understand themselves as distinct subjective agents (Kawata, Tsukada-Jo, & Kawata. 2005).

A study of child day nurseries found that in spite of a steady increase in self-feeding, the use of utensils first increased but then decreased slightly in the latter half of the second year (Kawahara, 2006). This flexibility was interpreted as an outcome of the development of the child's self.

Japanese infants at a day nursery used their hands more often and were more autonomous in feeding than French infants at the early stages of the development of feeding (Norimatsu, 1993). In spite of the infants' early autonomy, Japanese adults remained close to the infants, whereas in France the amount of adult physical intervention and closeness decreased rapidly after 12 months. Greater involvement by Japanese mothers after the infants' attainment of self-feeding—more frequent empathetic mouth movement and persistence of feeding attempts—was also found in comparison with British mothers (Negayama, 1998–1999).

2.2 *Conflict and rejection*

Feeding is often a source of conflict between mother and child. Fukuda (2003) observed mealtime interaction between 4- and 5-year-olds and their parents in the home. Children often reacted negatively to a prompt to eat by the parents, and a stronger prompt increased the intensity of the negative response of the child.

Kawahara (2004) observed toddlers' refusal to eat and their professional caregivers' interventions at lunchtime. Refusal was initially a simple reaction to the caregiver's offering food, but later, refusal as a result of food choosiness increased. The caregivers employed verbal encouragement to the more advanced children, showing that the feeding situation involves reading and manipulating the other's intentions by both caregivers and infants.

To understand Japanese mothers' ambivalence about motherhood, it is important to note that Japanese mothers engage in persistent attempts to feed their child and these are often met with the infants' refusal (Negayama, 1993). Kawata (2009) correctly pointed that what is refused is not food itself but the intention of the feeder or the manner of feeding.

Kawahara and Negayama (2014) compared toddlers' negative interactions during feeding with caretakers in the home and at a day nursery. At less than 19 months, both passive eating and refusal to eat were more frequent during feeding at home than at the nursery. At 19 months children refused to eat in the way offered, but food previously refused was often accepted when a caretaker added a positive meaning to the food such as a comment that carrot is rabbits' favorite. This type of refusal by the child is the same as that reported by Yamada (1982) as a special type of strong cry intended as a protest against what is done to him or her. Yamada described it as a result of the violation of "tsumori" (image of intention or plan), and interpreted this as a sign of self-other differentiation.

The duration of co-sleeping is positively correlated with the duration of breastfeeding (Lindenberg Artola, & Estrada, 1990). Night-time breastfeeding is a burden for mothers, and the above-mentioned conflicts in feeding look similar to bedtime difficulty as they both can be a conflict between mother and infant over the amount of maternal care provided. Among parents of 12 predominantly Asian and five predominantly Caucasian countries/regions, Japanese parents felt much greater difficulty when they put children to bed (Mindell, Sadeh, Wiegand, How, & Goh, 2010). Together with a closer sleeping arrangement between Japanese parents and children (e.g., Caudill & Plath, 1966; Katayama, 2010), this strongly suggests an ambivalence in Japanese mothers between the motivations to be with the infant and to be away from them.

---

3. NEGATIVITY AND AUTONOMY

Mother-offspring interactions during feeding have both positive and negative aspects, and child negativism (Wenar, 1982) and the resulting mother-child conflict seem profoundly related to the above-mentioned negativity in the relationship.

Child negativity can be viewed as developmentally appropriate behavior where it is a reaction to an intrusive mother who threatens the autonomy of the self-as-agent (Wenar, 1982). Japanese mothers usually take children's negativism and noncompliance as a sign of the normal development of the self in 2.5-year-olds (Ujiie, 1997). At the same time, they would like their children to be self-inhibited and obedient to them. Ujiie interpreted this as the mothers' having an expectation that their children will develop an empathic understanding of what is expected and required of them. On the other hand, American mothers expect non-compliance to encourage freedom and self-reliance in children, which Ujiie (1997) calls assertive autonomy.

Child-rearing in everyday life is filled with conflict between demanding children and disciplining parents. A positive component is required in parenting for the offspring's care and protection, and a negative component is necessary for the offspring's discipline and development of autonomy. Mother-infant relationships are more interdependent, and participation by the father in child care is less frequent in Japan than in the United States (Barratt, Negayama, & Minami, 1993). The societal expectation that Japanese mothers stay in the home when their children are young might make the relationship more difficult.

Studies have repeatedly demonstrated two distinct styles of parenting (e.g., Conroy, Hess, Azuma, & Kashiwagi, 1980; Kochanska, Kuczynski, & Radke-Yarrow, 1989; Raphael-Leff, 1993; Saito & Uchida, 2013): regulator or authoritarian (appealing to authority and power) and facilitator or authoritative (appealing to empathy and autonomy). Japanese parenting is the latter type. Japanese mothers place greater reliance on affective ties to gain compliance, which encourages the internalization of parental norms in children (Conroy, Hess, Azuma, & Kashiwagi, 1980). For the Japanese, a good child is one who understands the parent's expectation and corrects their own behavior accordingly (Azuma, 1994).

As noted above, Japanese mothers have been reported to have a poor self-image as mothers, viewing themselves as being less competent in and less satisfied with their parenting than they would like (Bornstein et al., 1998; Negayama, Norimatsu, Barratt, & Bouville, 2012; Takahama, Watanabe, Sakagami, Takatsuji, & Nozawa, 2008; Ujiie, 1997). Overall, Japanese mothers relied more on their children's competence in autonomy than on their own control of the relationship. Such a strategy by Japanese parents, of disciplining children to comply with them not by authority but by empathy, may facilitate the child's negativism. Japanese mothers expect children to behave harmoniously with wishes. Children's disobedience conflicts with the mothers' expectation and irritates the mothers.

Japanese mothers are expected to have a sense of strong responsibility for child care (Ohinata, 1990), which confronts children's negativity and amplifies their irritation. Experiencing negative feelings in reaction to their child's misbehaviors is a strong source of stress in Japanese mothers. Mother-toddler negativity is a way of reaching a solution by mutual adjustment and compromise (Sakagami, 2003, 2005). Rejection and disobedience by the child may lead to the mother reflecting on her childcare, and this may be a Japanese way of coming to understand the mother-child relationship and establish adequate distancing, guided by the child. American parents interpret children's negativity in a different way: they respect the child's autonomy and feel positive about their negativity (Ujiie, 1997).

3.1 Negativity in mothers

Japanese mothers often adopt the special procedure of *dannyu* (sudden weaning) in which mothers draw a cute face on the breasts and then refrain from offering their infant the breast from a scheduled day on (Negayama, 2011). The infant may protest by crying, but will normally accept the situation in a few days if the scheduled day of weaning is set according to proper judgment of the infant's readiness. Mothers introduce solid food, but at the same time autonomy is also sought from the infant by refusal of passive feeding by the mother. The weaning struggle between Japanese infants and their mothers is consequently hard (Negayama, 1993, 1998–1999). The harshness of the rejection is ameliorated by the drawing of a cute face on the breasts.

A Japanese mother's negative behavior occurs to control the infant's untidy eating, not to counter his/her overdependency (Norimatsu, 1993). Feelings of anger are also triggered by improper eating by children (Noguchi & Ishii, 2000). Sugano (2001) reported mother's negative feelings toward children when the children are noncompliant or show inappropriate behaviors for the child's age. Children are not simply passive receivers of care but are active manipulators of their parents.

Sugano (2001) suggests that negative feelings are provoked by the discrepancy between the mother's expectations and the child's behavior, and that a reorganization of the mother-child relationship is triggered by the negativity. The mothers' negativity may result in the promotion of the infants' autonomy. Parenting actually encompasses a struggle between parents and children for mutual autonomy.

3.2 Mutuality of negativity as weaning

Mothers and infants constantly monitor each other's states dynamically and interact to achieve an appropriate level of mutual autonomy and distance, which varies by moment, situation, age, gender, and culture. Negativity on the part of the infant sometimes provokes irritation and anger in the mother, which results in negativity and withdrawal of care by the mother. In this case, the infant's negativity is a trigger that reorganizes the relationship, and the result might be interpreted as child-driven autonomy. Where mothers are too intrusive, such negativity on the part of the child could be adaptive for regaining a balance.

The weaning conflict model by Trivers deals with the negativity of mothers (Trivers, 1974). The spontaneous withdrawal of maternal care may cause negativity in the children in turn, and play an important role in the mother's ability to assess the offspring's current level of dependency (Bateson, 1994). Thus negativity exists on both sides, and each partner's negativity may serve to reorganize the relationship, which is a continuing process of mutual adjustment involving both positive and negative behaviors. The parent-child relationship with such mutuality can be called companionship, and a process of mutual negativity dynamically linking each with the other is *kowakare* (Negayama, 2011). Keller et al. (2009) describe two different parenting styles: distal (face-to-face interaction and object stimulation) and proximal (body contact and body stimulation) styles. Japanese mothers and infants engage in more physical contact than their U.S. counterparts (Rothbaum, Pott, Azuma, Miyake, & Weisz, 2000), and are obviously classified as the proximal type. Bodily contact is unique as a communicative modality in its reciprocity based on the mutually shared experience of the same intensity and timing of touch (Negayama, 2011). A proximal parenting style provides plenty of opportunities to experience reciprocity. The mothers' negativity seems to be important and adaptive for such relationships.

Childrearing is a dynamic process of adjustment by children and mothers (and fathers as well) to being together with and apart from each other. Japanese mothers are culturally biased to devote themselves to their children, and their childrearing style increases the probability of coming up against the child's negativity.

Negativity is not only shown by direct mother-child conflict but also by allomothering, i.e., care given by those other than the mother. Human childcare is unique in the intervention of complex allomothering systems of objects (e.g., toys), persons (e.g., fathers), and institutions (e.g., daycare centers) as a socio-cultural interface between infant and mother to promote mutual autonomy (Negayama, 2011). The allomothering system is one of mild negativity in the sense of making a space between the mother and the child. We should also think about this kind of negativity when trying to capture a broader view of Japanese childcare.

References

Azuma, H. (1994). *Nihonjin no shitsuke to kyoiku: Hattatsu no Nichibei hikaku ni motozuite* [Education and socialization in Japan: A comparison between Japan and the United States]. Tokyo: Tokyodaigaku Shuppankai.

Barratt, M. S., Negayama, K., & Minami, T. (1993). The social environments of early infancy in Japan and the United States. *Early Development and Parenting*, 2, 51–64.

Bateson, P. (1994). The dynamics of parent-offspring relationships in mammals. *TREE*, 9, 399–403.

Bornstein, M.H., Haynes, OM., Azuma, H., Galperin, C., Maital, S., Ogino, M., Painter, K., Pascual, L., Pecheux, M.-G., Rahn, C., Toda, S., Venuti, P., Vyt, A., & Wright, B. (1998). A cross-national study of self-evaluation and attribution in parenting: Argentina, Belgium, France, Israel, Italy, Japan, and the United States. *Developmental Psychology*, 34, 662–676.

Caudill, W., & Plath, D.W. (1966). Who sleeps by whom? Parent-child involvement in urban Japanese families. *Psychiatry*, 29, 344–366.

Conroy, M., Hess, R.D., Azuma, H., & Kashiwagi, K. (1980). Maternal strategies for regulating children's behavior: Japanese and American Families. *Journal of Cross-cultural Psychology*, 11, 153–172.

Fukuda, K. (2003). The relationship between parents' prompting of children to eat and children's emotions: A family systems view. *Japanese Journal of Developmental Psychology*, 14, 161–171. (in Japanese with English summary)

Kashiwagi, K. (2010). Allomothering o habamu bunka: Naze "hahanote-de" ga Heranainoka? [Culture blocking allomothering: Why is the idea of rearing by mothers' own hand not reduced?] In: K. Negayama & K. Kashiwagi (Eds.), *Hito no kosodate no shinka to bunka: Allomothering no yakuwari o kangaeru* [Evolution and culture in human child care: Considering the role of allomothering], (pp. 163–181). Tokyo: Yuhikaku.

Katayama, S. (2010). A study on mother's consciousness of the sleeping style of her children. *Journal of Architecture and Planning, AIJ*, 75, 17–23. (in Japanese with English summary)

Kawahara, N. (2004). Toddlers' refusal behaviors and caregivers' intervention at lunchtime: An analysis of interaction patterns. *Research on Early Childhood Care and Education in Japan*, 42, 112–120. (in Japanese with English summary)

Kawahara, N. (2006). Development of eating with tool in toddlers. *Japanese Journal of Applied Psychology*, 31, 98–112. (in Japanese with English summary)

Kawahara, N., & Negayama, K. (2014). Negative toddler-caretaker interactions during feeding at home and nursery mealtimes. *Journal of Child Health*. (in Japanese with English summary)

Kawata, M. (2009). *Shoku no naka no moho katei to jita-kankei no keisei* [The process of imitation in eating and formation of self-other relationships]. *Baby Science*, 9, 24–36.

Kawata, M., Tsukada-Jo, M., & Kawata, A. (2005). Infant self-assertiveness and maternal coping behavior: A longitudinal study from 5 to 15 months of age. *Japanese Journal of Developmental Psychology*, 16, 46–58. (in Japanese with English summary)

Keller, H., Borke, J., Staufenbiel, T., Yovsi, R., Abels, M., Papaligoura, Z., Jensen, H., Lohaus, A., Chaudhary, N., Lo, W., & Su, Y. (2009). Distal and proximal parenting as alternative parenting strategies during infants' early months of life: A cross-cultural study. *International Journal of Behavioral Development*, 33, 412–420.

Kochanska, G., Kuczynski, L., & Radke-Yarrow, M. (1989). Correspondence between mothers' self-reported and observed child-rearing practices. *Child Development*, 60, 56–63.

Lindenberg, C.S., Artola, R.C., & Estrada, V.J. (1990). Determinants of early infant weaning: A multivariate approach. *International Journal of Nursing Studies*, 27, 35–41.

Mindell, J.A., Sadeh, A., Wiegand, B., How, T.H., & Goh, Y.T. (2010). Cross-cultural differences in infant and toddler sleep. *Sleep Medicine*, 11, 274–280.

Ministry of Health, Labour and Welfare (2015). *Hataraku josei no jokyo* [Condition of working women] Retrieved from www.mhlw.go.jp/koyoukintou/josei-jitsujo/dl/14b.pdf

Nakata, H., Murai, F., & Emori, Y. (2013). The process of maternal role attainment through the performance of giving baby food: A qualitative research into the maternal role for the later period of weaning. *Japanese Journal of Maternal Health*, 54, 69–77. (in Japanese with English summary)

Negayama, K. (1993). Weaning in Japan: A longitudinal study of mother and child behaviours during milk- and solid-feeding. *Early Development and Parenting*, 2, 29–37.

Negayama, K. (1998-1999). Feeding as a communication between mother and infant in Japan and Scotland. *Annual Report of Research and Clinical Center for Child Development*, 22, 59–68.

Negayama, K. (2011). *Kowakare*: a new perspective on the development of mother-offspring relationship. *Integrative Psychological and Behavioral Science*, 45, 86–99.

Negayama, K., Norimatsu, H., Barratt, M., & Bouville, J.-F. (2012). Japan–France–US comparison of infant weaning from mother's viewpoint. *Journal of Reproductive and Infant Psychology*, 30, 77–91.

Noguchi, K., & Ishii, T. (2000). Emotional feeling and coping behavior of mothers with infants and toddlers. *Journal of Child Health*, 59, 102–109. (in Japanese whith English summary)

Norimatsu, H. (1993). Development of child autonomy in eating and toilet training: One- to three-year-old Japanese and French children. *Early Development &*

Parenting, 2, 39–50.

Ohinata, M. (1990). *Nihon shakai no hensen to bosei* [Change in Japanese society and motherhood]. *Human Mind*, 30, 85–91.

Raphael-Leff, J. (1993). Facilitators and regulators: Two approaches to mothering. *British Journal of Medical Psychology*, 56, 379–390.

Rothbaum, F., Pott, M., Azuma, H., Miyake, K., & Weisz, J. (2000). The development of close relationships in Japan and the United States: Paths of symbiotic harmony and generative tension. *Child Development*, 71, 1121–1142.

Saito, Y., & Uchida, N. (2013). Discipline style and picture-book reading among sharing and authoritarian mothers. *Japanese Journal of Developmental Psychology*, 24, 150–159. (in Japanese with English summary)

Sakagami, H. (2003). Adaptation of mothers to children's negativism and self-assertion: The development of mothers and toddlers. *Japanese Journal of Developmental Psychology*, 14, 257–271. (in Japanese with English summary)

Sakagami, H. (2005). *Kodomo no hankoki ni okeru hahaoya no hattatsu: Hoko kaishiki no boshi no kyohenka katei.* [Maternal development at the stage of children's negativism: A process of mutual change in mothers and toddlers]. Tokyo: Kazama Shobo.

Shizawa, M., & Shizawa, Y. (2009). Development of eating behavior in infants and the effect of feeding by mother during introduction of solid food. *Journal of Child Health*, 68, 614–622. (in Japanese with English summary)

Sugano, Y. (2001). The effects of a mother's negative feelings toward her child on the mother-child relationship. *Japanese Journal of Developmental Psychology*, 12, 12–23. (in Japanese with English summary)

Takahama, Y., Watanabe, T., Sakagami, H., Takatsuji, C., & Nozawa, S. (2008). The transformation process of the mother-child system during toddlerhood: The relationship between a mother's framework and a child's negativism. *Japanese Journal of Developmental Psychology*, 19, 121–131. (in Japanese with English summary)

Toyama, N. (2008). Mother-toddler lunchtime interaction at home: Collaborative organization of meals as cultural activities. *Japanese Journal of Developmental Psychology*, 19, 232–242. (in Japanese with English summary)

Toyama, N., & Muto, T. (1990). Mother-toddler interaction in a meal time. *Japanese Journal of Educational Psychology*, 38, 395–404. (in Japanese with English summary)

Trivers, R. L. (1974). Parent-offspring conflict. *American Zoologist*, 14, 249–264.

Ujiie, T. (1997). How do Japanese mothers treat children's negativism? *Journal of Applied Developmental Psychology*, 18, 467–483.

Wenar, C. (1982). On negativism. *Human Development*, 25, 1–23.

Yamada, Y. (1982). Expressions of request and rejection and the emergence of self in infancy. *Japanese Journal of Educational Psychology*, 30, 38–48. (in Japanese with English summary)

Yamaguchi, K., & Tanabe, K. (2012). The difference in the mother's reasons for weaning by age and nutrition of their children at weaning. *Japanese Journal of Maternal Health*, 53, 65–72. (in Japanese with English summary)

Cognitive Development Research in Japan:
Past, Present, and Future

—

Masuo Koyasu

While it is true that the Latin-derived term *cognition* is synonymous with *knowing*, cognition entails various processes of knowing: knowing through perception, knowing through memory, knowing through imagination, knowing through reasoning, knowing through language, and so on. Furthermore, cognitive development in children can be manifested as intelligence and achievement yet also includes problems of mental retardation and disability. It is thus apparent why research on cognitive development is a fundamental theme of developmental psychology. This chapter will consider the history of Japanese cognitive development research alongside the evolution of the formal education system, review the characteristics and issues of present-day cognitive development research, such as follow-up studies and theory of mind research, and also the direction of cognitive development research that should be done in the years ahead.

1. BEGINNING OF FORMAL EDUCATION AND ESTABLISHMENT OF PSYCHOLOGY

Academic interest in the development of children may be traced back to the book *Emile, or On Education* by the Swiss philosopher Jean-Jacques

Rousseau (1712–1778), which was based on the insight that children are not smaller adults but exhibit a unique process of growth, and described the need for an educational system that supports and assists that growth process. Yet education at the time was only available to the few—children of wealthy families taught at home by tutors or governesses, apprentices taught a trade or a technique by craftsmen, and children receiving instruction at schools attached to churches, for example—and it was not until the latter half of the nineteenth century that government-supported formal education was established. Public schools for children aged five to twelve years were not established in the United Kingdom (England and Wales), for example, until the Elementary Education Act was passed in 1870. And it was not until much later that compulsory tuition-free education was fully implemented in the U.K. when the Education Act of 1918 was passed in the aftermath of World War I.

The modern education system in Japan began with the Education System Order (*Gakusei*) of 1872, followed seven years later by the Ordinance of Education (*Kyoiku-rei*) of 1879, which addressed various issues associated with the earlier law. Here we note that Japan was not far behind the West in establishing a formal education system.

Modern psychology also got its start this same year of 1879 when Wilhelm Wundt (1832–1920), a German physiologist and philosopher, set up the first formal laboratory for psychological research at the University of Leipzig. Meanwhile, on the other side of the Atlantic, William James (1842–1910), a professor at Harvard University, also made the transition from physiology to psychology. He authored two famous books—*The Principles of Psychology* in 1890 and *Pragmatism: A New Name for Some Old Ways of Thinking* in 1907—and continued to promote psychology and the philosophical tradition of pragmatism throughout his life.

---

2. BEGINNING OF DEVELOPMENTAL PSYCHOLOGY

The American psychologist Stanley Hall (1844–1924) is widely credited as being the father of developmental psychology. Inspired to pursue psychology by Wundt's book *The Principles of Physiological Psychology*, he studied under James at Harvard, which awarded Hall the first doctorate in psychology in 1878. Then Hall went abroad to study directly under Wundt in Leipzig. Hall was installed as the first president of Clark University in 1888, and became the first president of the American Psychological Association in 1892.

John Dewey (1859–1952), the prominent American philosopher of pragmatism and education, studied first under Hall at Johns Hopkins University graduate school, then took a teaching position and set up an experimental school at the University of Chicago. In 1899 he published *The School and Social Progress*, and in 1904 took a teaching position in the philosophy department of Columbia University, a position he would hold for close to half a century. In 1916, Dewey published *Democracy and Education: An Introduction to the Philosophy of Education*, a popular book that is still in print.

In Japan, the distinction of father of psychology is bestowed on Yujiro Motora (1858–1912). Motora studied English at Doshisha Eigakko (English Academy), the predecessor of Doshisha University, and then had an opportunity to travel to the U.S. where he attended John Dewey's lectures. In 1890, Motora joined the Faculty of Letters at the Imperial University of Japan, precursor to the University of Tokyo, and in 1893 began offering the first courses in psychology, ethics, and logic in Japan.

Also closely associated with the emergence of developmental psychology in Japan is Matataro Matsumoto (1865–1943), whose research focused on intelligence and ability. After graduating from the Imperial University of Japan, Matsumoto studied under Wundt at Leipzig. After returning to Japan, he was appointed professor of psychology at Kyoto Imperial University (now Kyoto University), and in 1913 succeeded to Prof. Motora's chair at Tokyo Imperial University (University of Tokyo). In 1927, Matsumoto founded and became the first president of the Japanese Psychological Association.

One can see from this brief review that Japan kept abreast of world developments in instituting formal education and in establishing psychology and developmental psychology as academic disciplines.

3. Development of intelligence testing

Public education opened new opportunities to countless children brought into the system, but serious difficulties were encountered when trying to apply a uniform curriculum across the board to all students. Developmental differences due to age as well as developmental variation among individual children of the same age were a challenge, and solving these problems was a key factor in the emergence of developmental psychology. The development of intelligence testing was one effort to deal with this challenge.

France introduced a compulsory education system in 1881, but management of children who could not keep up with the regular curriculum posed a major challenge. The French psychologist Alfred Binet (1857–1911) was commissioned by the education authorities to come up with a solution, and together with the physician Théodore Simon (1873–1961) created the Binet-Simon intelligence scale in 1905. This was the world's first practical intelligence test. The Binet test incorporated a wide range of questions from simple everyday ploblems regarding the denominations of coins and age and gender of the testees to problems involving memory, calculation, and reasoning. The questions were then arranged in order of easiest to hardest, and sets of questions were defined as appropriate for different age ranges. The success of this test is attributed to the fact that the same questions were not given to all the students, but rather were flexibly varied depending on the age of the testees and their ability to answer the questions.

Alfred Binet died prematurely, and Binet and Simon's intelligence scale was not readily adopted in France. However, it was developed in the United States and other countries around the world. This started with the creation of the Stanford-Binet intelligence scale in 1916 by the Stanford University psychologist Lewis Terman (1877–1956). Key innovations of Terman's intelligence test included the development of a more practical test by incorporating the concept of the intelligence quotient (IQ) and expansion of the goal of identifying not only children with subnormal mental abilities but also gifted children with better than normal mental abilities.

The Binet test was first introduced to Japan through an article by psychiatrist Koichi Miyake (1876–1954) that was published in a medical journal in 1908. Meanwhile, Yoshihide Kubo (1883–1942), a graduate of the Psychology Department at Tokyo Imperial University, studied abroad under Stanley Hall at Clark University, then came back to Japan and developed a Japanese version of the Binet test. A fully standardized Japanese version of the Binet test, the Suzuki-Binet Intelligence Test, was published in 1930 by Harutaro Suzuki (1875–1966). Suzuki graduated from Shiga Normal School and was later awarded a Ph.D. by Kyoto University. In addition, Kan'ichi Tanaka (1882–1962), who studied at Kyoto Imperial University and under Matsumoto at Tokyo Imperial University Graduate School, published the Tanaka-Binet intelligence test in 1947. These two individual tests of intelligence—the Suzuki-Binet test and the Tanaka-Binet test—have served for decades as the two authoritative intelligence tests in Japan.

4. PIAGET'S RESEARCH IN COGNITIVE DEVELOPMENT

The Swiss developmental psychologist Jean Piaget studied intelligence under Théodore Simon and focused particular attention on the developmental process of children's cognition at research institutes in Switzerland and France. It was during that time that Piaget established his genetic epistemology in which he classified the cognitive development of children from age 0 to 15 into four stages: the sensorimotor stage, the preoperational stage, the concrete operational stage, and the formal operational stage. Piaget originally believed that formal operational thinking was largely acquired between the ages 11 and 15, but follow-up research did not confirm this hypothesis. Indeed, a good number of college students have yet to develop formal operational thinking. In 1972, Piaget argued that the developmental order from the concrete operational stage to the formal operational stage is stable, but that there are big individual differences in the timing of transitions from one stage to the next, and that there are cases where it is necessary to keep developmental stage concepts and aptitude differentiation concepts in synch (Piaget, 1972).

Piaget published prolifically from the early 1920s to his death, but nearly all of his research was published in French, so he had little impact on the English-speaking world before World War II. Eventually, Piaget and his cognitive developmental theory became widely known, especially in the United States, through the publication in 1963 of John Flavell's (1928–) book *The Developmental Psychology of Jean Piaget.*

Piaget's writings became familiar in Japan before World War II through study of Piaget's writings in the original French by Kanji Hatano (1905–2001) and his associates. Hatano was a graduate of the Tokyo Imperial University Psychology Department, where he studied child psychology, the psychology of writing styles, and other psychology-related themes before becoming president of Ochanomizu University, Tokyo. One of Hatano's sons, Giyoo Hatano (1935–2006), also pursued psychology as an undergraduate and graduate student at the University of Tokyo. Giyoo Hatano was a well-known professor at Keio University and other themes of universities, where he conducted world-class research on conceptual change and other cognitive development (e.g., Hatano & Inagaki, 1994).

After World War II, Japanese researchers on cognitive development were influenced by Piaget's theory and research until the 1980s. They wrote many research papers on such topics as egocentrism, conservation, and formal operational thinking. Since then, Piaget's individualistic approach to development has been criticized due to its lack of perspective on the social and emotional aspects of development.

5. Psychology of children with special needs

The most fundamental issue when applying a uniform curriculum across large populations of children is how to deal with the special educational needs of variously handicapped children. The term "handicapped children" in this context refers to children whose physical or mental development has been impeded or disrupted partially or wholly as a result of genetics, illness, accident, or some other cause.

In surveying the history of education of disabled or handicapped children, a classic case that immediately comes to mind is that of Helen Keller (1880–1968). Keller overcame severe disabilities to obtain a first-rate higher education, and devoted her life to social welfare activities.

When she was a year and a half old, Keller contracted an illness that left her deaf, blind, and unable to speak. Blessed with a remarkably dedicated tutor by the name of Anne Sullivan (1866–1936), Keller was educated both socially and intellectually, attended schools for the blind, and was finally admitted to Radcliffe College (Harvard University's coordinate institution for female students when Harvard was an all-male school) in 1900. As Keller became older, she developed a special fondness for Japan and visited the country on three separate occasions.

In Japan, the first school for the blind and deaf was the Kyoto Institute for the Blind and Dumb established by Kyoto municipal authorities in 1878. In other words, Japan had established an institution to educate the blind and deaf before Helen Keller was born. Schools for the blind and the deaf were institutionally separated after the enactment of the Imperial Decree on Schools for the Blind and Deaf in 1923, and schools were set up to deal with both disabilities in all prefectures across Japan, comparable to regular elementary and middle schools. Note that in 1922, the year before this decree went into effect, there were already 78 schools for the blind and deaf scattered across Japan (National Institute of Special Needs Education; http://www.nise.go.jp/cms/13,3288,54,245.html).

The Japanese Association of Special Education was founded in 1963 as an academic association focused solely on scientific research in the area of special needs education in Japan. The first president of the Association was Mantaro Kido (1893–1985). After graduating from Tokyo Imperial University, Kido was a professor at Hokkaido University before taking over as President of Hokkaido University of Education. Kido was actively involved in many different areas of psychology and education, published *Early Childhood Education Theory* (in Japanese) in 1939, and in the chaotic aftermath of World War II, set up an early childhood school for young children who had never had the opportunity to attend a regular school.

6. FOLLOW-UP STUDIES

A follow-up study offers a way of identifying phenomena thought to be relevant to the various factors involved in the development of intelligence, personality, and other factors. The term follow-up study originally referred to a study conducted after a certain period of time to determine how the effects on a target population—say, a group at risk from a disaster or harmful effects of a medicine, or a group subjected to an educational or medical treatment program—had changed over the period. However, in a broader sense, the term is used to describe an investigation of a group's developmental change over a fairly long period of time without such preconditions.

We observed earlier that one of Terman's primary motives in developing the Stanford-Binet intelligence scale was to measure the intelligence of gifted children, and he spent the latter half of his life conducting follow-up studies of the intellectually gifted children that he had identified. In the early 1920s, Terman et al. contacted the families of some 1,528 individuals (ranging in age from three to twenty-eight years) in San Francisco, Los Angeles, and other cities in California with IQ scores of 135 and above, and these were the participants of his follow-up studies. There are obvious problems with his sampling—the majority of the participants were Caucasian, middle class, and lived in cities, and there were more males than females—but this was typical of early follow-up studies.

When the participants in a follow-up study are born during a defined period and share a common characteristic or experience growing up, the group is called a "cohort." For example, if a population graphed by age shows a sharp decline in numbers at a certain age, if the decline cannot be attributed to the "age effect" of increased mortality due to aging, it is likely the result of a "period effect" such as a war or a disease that occurred during a particular period of time. Thus, varying survival rates experienced at a certain age due to war or pestilence are called "cohort effects," and analyses to determine whether such effects exist are called "cohort analyses."

---

7. LONGITUDINAL STUDIES

Developmental research methodology can be broadly divided between studies such as cross-sectional studies and follow-up studies, which identify developmental change or developmental mechanisms of different populations classified by age, and longitudinal studies, which track actual developmental changes in individuals or populations over long periods of time. Because data derived from longitudinal studies are based on the same population, conclusions have a high degree of certainty, but such studies take a long time to complete and are extremely costly. Research involving both a longitudinal method and a cross-sectional method is ideal, but this requires substantial research funding and human resources, which for all practical purposes must be underwritten by an established research institution supported by the government.

Japan's development since the Meiji Restoration was inspired by the goal to "catch up and overtake" the advanced countries of the West. Some have promoted this national ambition more aggressively than others, but there is a general feeling that Japan's national motivation has diminished somewhat in recent years. For example, this is reflected in the fact that fewer Japanese students are going abroad to study. Having a keen interest in the differential in funding to conduct large-scale research projects between Japan and other countries, I attended a preconference workshop at the International Society for the Study of Behavioral Development Conference held in Melbourne, Australia, in 2006. At this event, I was really struck by the vast amounts of money spent by countries around the world (U.S., U.K., Canada, Australia, and Norway) as the participants described long-term projects that were in progress with several million dollars.

For example, Canada's National Longitudinal Study of Children and Youth, started in 1994, examines 22,831 children every two years. Or consider the UK Millennium Cohort Study launched in the year 2000 that tracks 18,818 children in 398 towns and other locations all across the U.K. at nine months, three years, five years, and seven years after birth. Another example is the Longitudinal Study of Australian Children launched in 2003 that surveyed about 5,000 people with infants less than one year old and another 5,000 people with children between the ages of four and five every other year over a seven-year period.

Turning to Japan, the NHK Broadcasting Culture Research Institute launched a Better Broadcasting for Children Project in 2002 that ran for 12 years. From a randomized sample of 6,000 babies born in Kawasaki City on the outskirts of Tokyo in 2002, a follow-up study tracked children in 1,368 households willing to participate in the study, and examined the video media viewing habits and development of mind and body once a year for 12 years. The project brought together a team of experts in different fields—pediatrics, developmental psychology, social psychology, cultural anthropology, and media studies—that scientifically studied the effects of different types of media (television, video, video games, computers, etc.), different types of programming on parent-child relationships, as well as childrearing practices, language, cognitive abilities, socialization, and other factors.

Findings for the first six years of the study (the halfway point) were posted on the NHK Broadcasting Culture Research Institute's website under the title "Television and Japanese Children: A Longitudinal Study from Zero to Twelve, Interim Report from Zero to Five" (http://www.nhk. or.jp/bunken/english/reports/pdf/report_11040102.pdf).

I was involved in the Better Broadcasting for Children Project from the initial planning stage. This large-scale project achieved significant results, but it would be desirable to pursue further work as a national longitudinal study of children with government backing and support.

Indeed, there is a unique project under way in Japan right now that is supported by substantial funding from the national budget. This is the National Assessment of Academic Ability, better known as the National Achievement Test, organized and implemented by the Ministry of Education, Culture, Sports, Science and Technology. Started in 2007, this mass achievement test has been administered every April to all students in their final year of elementary school (6th graders) and final year of middle school (9th graders). Since 2012, the test has covered three subject areas—mathematics, Japanese language, and science—and each subject area is divided into two parts: Part A consists of questions to test the students' knowledge of the subject matter, and Part B consists of questions to test the students' ability to use the knowledge in each area. The test serves as an assessment of students' academic ability and also the learning and living environment of children and students. The actual amount budgeted to carry out the survey and analyze the results for fiscal 2013 was 5.4 billion yen. While this grant is really sufficient only to carry out the testing, the project has been relentlessly criticized for not doing enough to raise the academic performance of students. From a psychological perspective, the fact that the survey has remained a cross-sectional study within a single year is also problematic. A great deal of information can be obtained through a longitudinal study that demonstrates the changes in cognitive development that occur between the 6th and 9th grades. The sampled data is more than adequate for the survey to achieve its intended purpose without having to test every child and student across the nation.

8. THEORY OF MIND RESEARCH

In addition to the cost differential for large-scale research projects, there was another event that I was keenly interested in. During my stay at the University of Oxford (U.K.) as a visiting scholar sponsored by the Japanese Ministry of Education in 1994, I attended an international symposium at the University of Sheffield on *Theories of Theories of Mind* (Carruthers & Smith, 1996). I was struck by the richness of the content and potential of this topic. At the same time, I was also acutely aware that "theory of mind" had been developed and elaborated for over ten years in the West, yet was practically unknown in Japan, and I felt some sense of urgency about introducing this subject in Japan. I set to work exploring theory of mind as soon as I returned to Japan, and published a number of books and studies including "Review of the research on theory of mind" (Koyasu & Kinoshita, 1997) in the *Japanese Psychological Research* in 1997, I edited a special issue of the *Japanese Psychological Review* focusing on theory of mind in 1997, and in the year 2000, Iwanami Publishers Co. published *Theory of Mind: The Science of Reading the Mind* (Koyasu, 2000) and Yuhikaku Publishing Co. published *When Young Children Encounter Mind: Mixed Age Daycare from a Developmental Psychology Perspective* (Koyasu, Hattori, and Goshiki, 2000). Since this outpouring of information on theory of mind, I remain very much committed to the subject today.

In collaboration with Charlie Lewis (Lancaster University, U.K.), I continued to explore the development of theory of mind, with particular emphasis on discovering how false belief understanding and executive functions are different in Japanese and British preschoolers (Lewis, Koyasu, Oh, Ogawa, Short, & Huang, 2009). The notion that Japanese children's understanding of theory of mind shows over a year's delay compared with their Western peers continues to be accepted as an established theory. Working with a sample of 87 Japanese and 81 British preschoolers, my collaborators and I found that Japanese lagged behind the British young children only on the deceptive box (Smarties) test but not on the unexpected transfer (Sally-Anne) test. However, regression analyses revealed that while the data conformed to the prevailing findings that executive function predicted false belief understanding for the British young children, no such links were found in the Japanese data. In other words, while a tendency toward slower development of theory of mind was confirmed for young Japanese children despite the level of executive functions, this can probably be attributed to the tendency of Japanese parents to anticipate and plan ahead to prevent their children from failing.

9. ACADEMIC PSYCHOLOGY-RELATED ASSOCIATIONS IN JAPAN

The three main Japanese academic societies that attract most researchers interested in cognitive development are the Japanese Psychological Association (JPA) established in 1927 with about 7,700 members, the Japanese Association of Educational Psychology (JAEP) established in 1959 with approximately 6,600 members, and the Japan Society of Developmental Psychology (JSDP) established in 1989 with roughly 4,300 members. The JPA is a broad-based organization that covers a wide range of psychology-related research. The JAEP has a more practical orientation with emphasis on research relating to schools and education. The JSDP specializes specifically in the area of developmental psychology. I served as President of the JSDP for six years from 2008 to 2014. The JSDP has an exchange program with the Developmental Section of the British Psychological Society (BPS). The JSDP and its British counterpart have also exchanged keynote speakers at the annual conferences held in each country since 2010.

One challenge for developmental psychology in Japan is the dissemination of domestic research to the international community. There are currently two psychology journals published in English in

Japan—*Japanese Psychological Research* (impact factor 0.379) published by JPA and *Psychologia* (impact factor 0.09) published by Kyoto University—but there are no English language journals relating specifically to developmental psychology published in Japan. This means that Japanese developmental psychologists wanting to publish in English must submit their manuscripts to developmental psychology journals in the United States or United Kingdom. The number of papers in the area of cognitive development by Japanese authors published in foreign journals is quite limited, so getting our research out to an international audience is a growing issue.

10. CONCLUSIONS

In decades past, Japan was always quick to exploit and follow up on cutting-edge trends in cognitive development research from around the world, but this tendency has abated since the 1980s. Currently, we cannot point to any great surge in original cognitive development research coming out of Japan. There is thus a compelling need for Japan's developmental researchers to put their efforts into original research while staying well informed about the latest cognitive development trends in other parts of the world. From graduate school on, young developmental researchers in Japan are clearly capable of doing research that is on a par with world standards. They are quite capable of making presentations at international conferences, and even publishing papers in the leading foreign psychology journals is within their grasp. Yet above all, the most important thing for pursuing cognitive development research is to maintain affection for children, an abiding sense of surprise and wonder at children, and a spirit of inquiry and curiosity to unlock the secrets of children's cognitive development.

REFERENCES

Carruthers, P., & Smith, P. K. (Ed.) (1996). *Theories of Theories of Mind*. Cambridge, UK: Cambridge University Press.

Flavell, J. H. (1963). *The Developmental Psychology of Jean Piaget*. New York: D. Van Nostrand.

Hatano, G., & Inagaki, K. (1994). Young children's naive theory of biology. *Cognition*, 50, 171–188.

Koyasu, M., & Kinoshita, T. (1997). Review of the research on "theory of mind." *The Japanese Journal of Psychology*, 68, 51–67. (in Japanese with an English abstract).

Koyasu, M. (2000). *Theory of Mind: The Science of Reading the Mind*. Tokyo: Iwanami Publishers Co. (in Japanese).

Koyasu, M., Hattori, K., & Goshiki, T. (2000). *When Young Children Encounter "Mind": Mixed Age Daycare from a Developmental Psychology Perspective*. Tokyo: Yuhikaku Publishing Co. (in Japanese).

Lewis, C., Koyasu, M., Oh, S., Ogawa, A., Short, B. & Huang, Z. (2009). Culture, executive function and social understanding. In Lewis, C. & Carpendale, J. I. M. (Eds.), *Social Interaction and the Development of Executive Function* (pp. 69–85). Monograph in the series New Directions in Child and Adolescent Development, 123. San Francisco: Jossey Bass.

National Institute of Special Needs Education; http://www.nise.go.jp/cms/13, 3288,54,245.html

Piaget, J. (1972). Intellectual evolution from adolescence to adulthood. *Human Development*, 15(1), 1–12.

Research on Language Development in Japan: Focusing on Acquisition of Grammar, Polite Language, and Gender-Based Linguistic Forms

—

Shizuo Iwatate and Keiko Nakamura

Research on language development in Japan includes a wide range of approaches and topics. On the one hand, some of the current research is being actively conducted in a manner closely linked to Western research, such as Etsuko Haryu's research on word meaning in this volume (Haryu & Kajikawa, 2016). However, such studies are sporadic and the number is insufficient. On the other hand, there are many other noteworthy studies that delve into specific aspects of Japanese language acquisition, such as acquisition of grammar, vocabulary, and pragmatics. Readers interested in Japanese language acquisition may refer to journal articles and chapters from edited volumes (e.g., Clancy, 1985; Hakuta, 1982; Imai & Haryu, 2007; Imai et al., 2008; Nakayama, Mazuka, Shirai, & Li, 2006), as well as collections of papers from academic conferences (e.g., *Japanese / Korean Linguistics, Studies in Language Sciences: Papers from the Annual Conference of the Japanese Society for Language Sciences*) written in English, or academic articles and books in Japanese (e.g., Imai & Haryu, 2007; Ito, Tahara, & Park, 1991; Iwatate & Inaba, 1987; Kobayashi & Sasaki, 1997, 2008; Morikawa, 2006; Murata, 1984).

In this chapter, we will introduce several areas of research on language development in Japan. Conventionally, we would attempt to describe research on language development in a wide range of areas, such as phonology, morphology, syntax, semantics, lexicon, and pragmatics. However, due to page limitations, we will focus mainly on research conducted by the authors. The topics selected all illustrate distinctive characteristics of the acquisition of Japanese that differ from the acquisition of other languages, such as English. In Section 1, we will introduce three studies on the acquisition of grammar; in Section 2, we will describe one study on the acquisition of polite language; and in Section 3, we will focus on one study on the acquisition of gender-based linguistic forms.

1. RESEARCH ON THE ACQUISITION OF GRAMMAR

The idea that language is not random but rule-governed has been the basic understanding of many people who study language since the emergence of Noam Chomsky's (1957) generative grammar. In the same manner, many researchers of language development proceed from the basic understanding that language acquisition involves the acquisition of various rules. Classic examples include the idea that there is a distinct form of grammar in children's language (Brown & Fraser, 1964; Iwatate, 1994), Slobin's (1985) classic concept of the "language-making capacity," which explains the process of language acquisition with given principles, and the theory of "language learnability" developed by Pinker (1984) and Wexler (1982). In this chapter, we would like to introduce examples of studies that illustrate the kinds of rules acquired by children being raised in a Japanese language environment. We will not discuss the controversy regarding whether these rules are innate or learned via input from the language environment (Braine, 1994; Iwatate, 2006). This is because the authors think that understanding actual language development is the fundamental point of departure for research.

1.1 *Study 1: Errors in use of the particle "no"*
In Japanese, there are numerous postpositional particles that follow nouns. In particular, there are more than 10 particles, such as *ga* and *o*, that are grammatically important. Such particles are used for various functions, such as expressing the argument structure of verbs and nouns and indicating the modification of nouns by nouns. Regarding noun modification, in Japanese, there are two forms used to modify a noun: (1)

the form using the particle *no*, with a noun modifying a noun (e.g., *Inoue Mao no shashinshu* "(the) collection of photographs of Mao Inoue") and (2) the form not using the particle *no*, with an adjective modifying a noun (e.g., *kiiroi biitoru* '(the) yellow beetle'). Native Japanese speakers use, these two forms naturally. However, nonnative speakers, even with high levels of Japanese proficiency, make the following kinds of errors:

(1) *yasui no kamera* (unnecessary particle *no* is included)
cheap *no* camera
"cheap camera"

Errors like these are called "particle *no* errors," and they are made not only by nonnative speakers, but also by toddlers in the early stages of language development. For example, the children K and R, studied by Yokoyama (1990), made the following utterances around the age of 2:

(2) *ookii no sakana* (unnecessary *no* is included; K, age 1;8)
big *no* fish
"(a) big fish"

(3) *marui no unchi* (unnecessary *no* is included; R, age 2;0)
round *no* poo
"round poo"

According to Yokoyama (1990), errors such as these have been described in many studies and are common in toddlers who are acquiring Japanese. However, there is insufficient research on the developmental process of how and why such errors occur. Consequently, Yokoyama collected the verbal utterances of Child K and Child R from ages 0;10 until 2;11 in order to examine the incorrect usage of the particle *no* and related expressions. As a result, the following points emerged. First, the correct use of adjectives modifying nouns appears in the latter half of age 1 and continues to be used, without disappearing. Secondly, the incorrect use of adjectives modifying nouns appears one to three months after the first appearance of the correct usage and is used alongside the correct form. This incorrect use emerges particularly frequently until ages 2;3 to

2;4. However, after this age, its use declines and at the same time, self-correction appears. Incorrect usage does not appear with all adjectives, but is limited to a narrow range. Furthermore, incorrect usage disappears completely between the ages of 2;6 and 3;6. One important thing to note is that approximately one month before the appearance of incorrect usage, the correct "noun-*no*-noun" form (modification of a noun with a noun) appears.

The developmental patterns of Child K and Child R are summarized in Figures 1 and 2. The left-pointing arrow indicates the emergence of the form, while the right-pointing arrow indicates its disappearance. The solid line indicates use of the form.

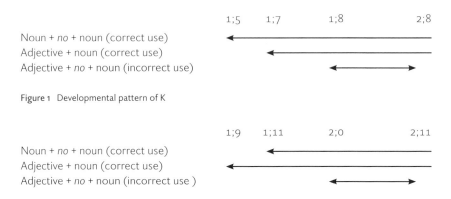

Figure 1 Developmental pattern of K

Figure 2 Developmental pattern of R

Yokoyama, based on the above findings, explained that the incorrect use of particle *no* occurred due to overgeneralization of modification rules of nouns by nouns. In addition, thinking that incorrect usage should also occur with adjectival nouns and verbs that do not require *no*, such as adjectives in adjective-noun constructions, Yokoyama analyzed the utterances of K and R. As expected, there were several incorrect uses such as the following, which appeared around age 2.

(4) *hen na no uta* (example of adjectival noun, incorrect use, K, age 1;11)
    strange *no* song
    "strange song"

(5) *o-sakana hakobu no reitooko* (example of verb, incorrect use, R, age 2;0)

fish carry *no* freezer/cooler

"freezer to carry fish"

Yokoyama's research is a classic example of rule-governed learning in language development. However, emphasizing only this point will lead to overlooking an important aspect of language development. Here, note the following additional points: (1) incorrect use emerges after correct use, (2) incorrect use can co-exist with correct use, and (3) incorrect use only appears for a limited range of words.

In Western research, it has been commonly observed that incorrect use emerges after correct use, but the last two points failed to gain attention until Tomasello's longitudinal research (Tomasello, 1992). Around the same time as Tomasello's publication, Iwatate (1992) focused on these points, demonstrating the idea of generalizing "from local rules to global rules."

The acquisition of irregular conjugation by English-speaking children is often introduced as an example of "incorrect use lagging behind correct use." For example, according to Slobin (1971), the order of acquisition of the past tense form "did" is (1) the stage of correct usage, "he did it," followed by (2) the stage of incorrect usage "he doed it," and lastly, (3) the stage of correct usage.

1.2 *Study 2: Development of transitive verb argument structure (Child J)*

Longitudinal research on the development of transitive verb argument structure in Japanese reveals interesting patterns (Iwatate, 1981, 1994). Argument structure refers to "the fixed relationship that individual verbs have with modifiers, mainly nouns." For example, the transitive verb *taberu* "to eat" forms a frame construction with two central clauses, "subject" (the case particle *ga* is postpositioned) and "object" (the case particle *o* is postpositioned). The word order in the clause is flexible in adult Japanese, but when there is no special condition, it tends to follow the word order subject + object. In addition, there are two points regarding the acquisition of argument structure. First, the number of argument structures used in one sentence increases: one-word utterances become two-word and then three-word utterances. Secondly, the number of types of modifying arguments increases.

Here is a concrete example: A child who can only say *tabeta* 'ate' learns to add an object and say *ringo tabeta* (Object + Verb) "apple ate" and later learns to add a subject and say *o-uma ringo tabeta* (Subject + Object + Verb) "horse apple ate." Then, how did the argument structure of child J develop? In order to explain this, Iwatate selected and analyzed five transitive verbs. The period of investigation lasted from ages 2;1 until 2;8. The criterion for the five verbs was "verbs with which the subject and the object appeared in the same sentence by the end of the data collection period." Table 1 illustrates the types and frequencies of sentence structures with the verb *taberu* "to eat," while Table 2 illustrates the types and frequencies of sentences structures with the verb *kaku* "to write/draw" by month. In addition to arguments with Subject and/or Object, arguments using the postpositional particle *ni* were also used or implied, so such arguments are referred to as "Ni." Non-argument forms such as adverbs, are referred to as "open." The other two selected verbs rarely appeared in spontaneous speech, so they were omitted from the analysis. The word orders of the arguments of the three verbs were as follows:

(6) Argument structure of the verb *taberu* "to eat": Subject + Object + Verb (see Table 1)
(e.g., *Aki-chan kore tabenai-tte yo*. Aki-chan says she won't eat this.)

(7) Argument structure of the verb *tsukuru* "to make": Ni + Subject + Object + Verb
(e.g., *Yatchan mo ojichan fusen tsuku[run]no*. (For) *Yatchan* (child's name), old man (the researcher) is going to make (a) balloon.)
Ni: Utterance with postpositional particle *ni* attached or implied

(8) Argument structure of the verb *kaku* "to write/draw": Ni +Object + Subject + Verb (see Table 2)
(e.g., *yatchan booru okaachan kaita no*. (For) *Yatchan* (child's name), Mommy drew (a) ball.)

52

Table 1 Word order of the verb "eat"

				Age							
	Word Order			2;1	2;2	2;3	2;4	2;5	2;6	2;7	2;8
			Verb	2	1	4	8	4	1	3	6
		Object	Verb	1	1	9	7	4	1	4	6
	Open		Verb	2	2	3	2	4			4
Subject			Verb	1		1	2		1	2	
	Open	Object	Verb			1	4			1	
Subject		Object	Verb					5	1	3	2
Subject	Open		Verb					3	1		

Note   Open: a non-argument (e.g., adverbs)

Table 2 Word orders of the verb "write/draw"

					Age							
		Word Order			2;1	2;2	2;3	2;4	2;5	2;6	2;7	2;8
				Verb				14		1		
			Subject	Verb			4	6		2		
		Object		Verb				37	9			3
	Open			Verb			5	5			3	3
Ni				Verb					3			
		Object	Subject	Verb			1			4		1
	Open	Object		Verb				1	1			
Ni		Object		Verb					1			1
	Open		Subject	Verb				1				
				Verb	Open			1				

Note   Ni: with postpositional particle "ni" attached or implied   Open: a non-argument (e.g., adverbs)

From the word order in examples (6) to (8), we can see the following: first, the three verbs are similar in that they are used with a fixed word order; secondly, the three verbs are similar in that they appear at the end of the utterance. The word order of subject and object for the verbs "to eat" and *tsukuru* "to make" are the same, but differ for the verb *kaku* "to write/ draw." What is important about this is that these three transitive verbs, which would be expected to have the same word order of arguments in adult language, do not have the same word order in J's language before age three. This is consistent with the phenomenon explained by Tomasello's (1992) "verb island hypothesis."

1.3 *Study 3: Argument structure of transitive verbs in five children*

Case study analyses of the utterances of five children older than Child J in Study 2 also provide insights into the argument structure of transitive verbs (Iwatate, 1994). The ages of the five children are listed in Table 3. The youngest children are Child Y and Child J at age 2;5, while the oldest child is Child T at age 3;9. Child J is the same as the target child in Study 2, and in this study, data were collected twice (at ages 2;5 and 3;5). The criteria for the analyzed verbs were "verbs with which a Subject and Object appeared in the utterance in the last month of data collection." Child Y was the participant with the smallest number of verbs with six types, while Child F had the most verbs with 12 types.

Table 3 Word orders of five children

Child (sex)	Y (female)	A (female)	F (female)	J (male)	J (male)	T (male)	
			Age				
Word Order	2;5	2;7	3;7	2;5	3;6	3;9	Total
Subject + Object + Verb	24	11	12	6	11	15	79
Object + Subject + Verb	2	1	2	4		1	10
Subject + Verb + Object	1	3	3				7
Object + Verb + Subject	2		1	1			4
Verb + Subject + Object							0
Verb + Object + Subject			1				1

Table 3 lists the word order for Subject, Object, and Verb for all the targeted verbs. Only sentences with Subject, Object, and Verb in the same sentence were included and tallied. Therefore, many other utterances such as "Subject + Verb", "Object + Verb" and "Verb" were omitted from the analysis. Table 3 shows that a clear fixed word order of Subject + Object + Verb was apparent in the five children. However, we can see that the issue of word order is not that simple when you examine the utterance characteristics of each of the five children. In some children (Child Y, Child J at age 3;6, Child T, Child A), Subject + Object + Verb word order was found. In one child (Child F), the position of the verb was not fixed, but the word order of Subject + Object was fixed. In another child (Child J at age 2;6), the word order of Subject and Object was not fixed, but the verb was placed at the end of the utterance.

Based on Studies 2 and 3, Iwatate (1992) proposed the following hypotheses:

Hypothesis 1 (Strong Local Rules): The acquisition of verbs starts with independent acquisition of individual verbs.

Hypothesis 2 (Weak Local Rules): During the next stage, several verbs begin to share some partial commonalities.

Hypothesis 3 (Global Rules): The partial commonalities merge, and in the end, general rules are acquired.

Hypothesis 4 (Innate Constraints): From the earliest stage, there are exceptional global rules. These can be called constraints.

While the first three studies introduced in this chapter focus on grammatical development, the following two studies focus on other aspects of language development: namely, (1) pragmatic development, as seen in the acquisition of polite language, and (2) sociolinguistic development, as seen in the acquisition of gender-based forms. Both of these are aspects of the Japanese language that seem to be particularly challenging for non-native speakers of Japanese, yet acquired relatively easily by native speakers of Japanese. In addition, they highlight features of the Japanese language that differ from many other languages, and therefore, may provide insight to the acquisition of such forms across languages.

2. ACQUISITION OF POLITE LANGUAGE

Japanese is well known for its elaborate system of polite language, which is relatively complex compared to that of other languages, involving subject, object, addressee, and beautification honorifics, among other things.

In general, Japanese people seem to think that children do not have productive use of different politeness registers until they receive explicit instruction in specific social contexts such as schools and workplaces. Previous researchers reported that Japanese children master addressee honorifics (e.g., *desu*/-*masu* forms) effortlessly at an early age, while 'honorific language' (*sonkeigo*) and 'humble language' (*kenjoogo*) seem to emerge much later (see Nakamura, 2006). However, research by Nakamura (1996, 2002, 2006) shows that even young children seem to be grappling with the complexities of the Japanese politeness system.

Longitudinal research was conducted through naturalistic observations of 24 monolingual Japanese preschool children, eight 3-year-olds, eight 4-year-olds, and eight 5-year-olds (Nakamura, 1996, 2002, 2006). The children were all from middle-class Japanese families in the Tokyo metropolitan area. The data collection period continued over a minimum of one year, with several children participating for up to three years. During the monthly home visits, the target children engaged in various interactive contexts with their mothers, siblings, and close friends, including spontaneous play and snack time. Spontaneous use of polite language first emerged with conventional greetings and routine expressions, such as saying *doozo* "please" and *itadakimasu* "(I will humbly) receive (this meal)" before meals. Addressee honorifics (*teineigo*) appeared from an early age in the form of *desu*/-*masu* predicate endings and other derivative endings. Even 3-year-olds could use such forms in interactions with unfamiliar adults, such as Child T (age 3;7):

(9) *kore nan <u>desu</u> ka?* "What is this?" (pointing to something in a bag)

Furthermore, beautification honorifics, or *bikago*, were also common in the children's language, which was to be expected, as they are common in the children's input from mothers and preschool teachers. Children were often seen using words such as *o-sakana* "fish," *o-uchi* "house," and *o-shigoto* "work." However, while *teineigo* and *bikago* emerged relatively early, subject honorifics (*sonkeigo*) and object honorifics (*kenjoogo*) developed at a much slower rate. Early use of such forms was mostly limited to use in greetings and routine expressions.

Though spontaneous use of polite language was limited during casual interactions with family and friends, children exhibited their ability to use polite language in interactions with unfamiliar adults. In addition, during free play sessions, the children were encouraged to engage in different pretend play scenarios (e.g., doctor-patient, parent-child, store clerk-customer). While engaging in pretend play, children showed that they were able to use polite language forms (e.g., honorific and humble forms) that they did not usually use spontaneously in everyday interactions. This shows that although children may not spontaneously use different forms of polite language, when given the opportunity to do so (e.g., pretend play), they show that they are aware of the need to use different levels of politeness. Due to the morphosyntactic, semantic, and lexical complexity of some of the forms (i.e., honorific and humble language) and the complexity of the sociocultural concepts and underlying interpersonal relationships, children may not always be able to use the correct forms, but they do show that they are grappling with the politeness system and learning to master it from an early age (Nakamura, 2006).

Regarding the socialization of polite linguistic forms, it seems that even as early as the preverbal stage, mothers play an important role, sensitizing their children to the use of polite language forms through modeling, direct instruction, and play routines (Nakamura, 2002). In addition, as the child grows older, mothers switch to more direct forms of instruction, such as correcting the child when the child uses impolite language. However, despite the facts that parents and surrounding adults provide modeling and instruction regarding the use of polite language and children seem to show metalinguistic awareness regarding polite language, fluent usage of polite language remains a challenge for many young Japanese adults.

3. ACQUISITION OF GENDER-BASED LINGUISTIC FORMS

Compared to many other languages, Japanese is a language rich in gender-based linguistic forms with numerous forms that are gender-preferential (i.e., tend to be used more frequently by one gender compared to the other). Children learn these forms effortlessly through gender

socialization by surrounding adults and peers (e.g., Sakata, 1990). However, non-native learners often have difficulty with these forms, with
men inadvertently using forms which make them sound feminine or
women using forms which make them sound masculine.

The following study is based on the same set of data as the previous study on the acquisition of polite language (Nakamura, 1997, 2001a,
2001b). Analyses of the data revealed gender-based differences including phonological, lexical, and morphosyntactic differences, as well as
differences in conversational style. Children showed different patterns of
language usage based on their gender even in the youngest age group
(age 3). Despite the fact that the youngest children were still unable to use
proper gender labels (e.g., *otoko no ko* "boy," *onna no ko* "girl") to describe
themselves, they were already using gender-appropriate first person
pronouns (e.g., *boku* "I/me" male first-person pronoun, *atashi* "I/me"
female first-person pronoun). In addition, they were able to use gender-
appropriate sentence-final particles (e.g., *zo/ze* male emphatic particles,
kashira female particle marking uncertainty), addressee-reference terms
(e.g., *omae* and *temee* "you" male second-person pronouns), and lexical
forms (e.g., male lexical forms such as *dekkai* "big," *kusee* "stinky"). In the
following typical superhero scene, the two four-year-old boys use the
male first-person pronoun *boku* and the assertive sentence-final particle
zo, which is more commonly used by males.

(10) Child R (age 4;3): <u>*boku*</u> *wa hontoo no urutoraman sebun* <u>*da*</u>*! Shuu!*
Bakaan! Urutoraman Reo!
I'm the real Ultraman Seven! Whoosh! Bang! Ultraman Leo!

Child M (age 4;3): *iku* <u>*zo*</u>*, Ultraman Seven!*
(Here I) go, Ultraman Seven!

Boys also used bald commands, such as *mane suru na!* "don't copy me!"
and *sore kase!* "give me that" uttered by 4-year-old boys. Phonological
differences also appeared in the form of non-standard reductions used by
boys, such as *tsumaranee* instead of *tsumaranai* "boring," which is common in casual male speech.

Analyses of boys' and girls' speech during same-sex peer interactions also showed differences in conversational style. When language was compared within specific interactional contexts, boys used more commands, more threats, and more derogatory terms, challenging and arguing with their same-sex peers. On the other hand, girls' language was much more cooperative, using questions, explanations, requests for opinions and permission, as well as mitigated and indirect requests. Such findings were similar to those of previous studies conducted on American boys and girls, as seen in Sheldon (1990).

Regarding gender socialization, the influence of same-sex peers seems to be particularly strong. As early as age 3, the children preferred to play with same-sex friends and had distinct differences in their play activities (Nakamura, 2001a). Peers also were quick to notice and admonish gender-inappropriate language forms, showing a high level of metalinguistic awareness.

In addition, language use was closely related to the nature of the play context, with strongly masculine forms emerging most frequently in boys' rough-and-tumble play and pretend play involving superheroes, as compared to activities such as object construction. On the other hand, girls rarely used strongly feminine forms, with the majority of their language being gender-neutral. Feminine forms appeared during pretend play, when girls played the roles of older women, such as their mothers. This study supports the view that gender is constantly negotiated, and Japanese children learn from an early age to pay attention to contextual factors (e.g., type of play, gender of interactant) in "performing" gender in a context-appropriate manner.

REFERENCES

Braine, M. D. S. (1994). Is nativism sufficient? *Journal of Child Language*, 21, 9–31.

Brown, R. & Fraser, C. Eds. (1964). The acquisition of syntax. In U. Bellugi & R. Brown (eds.), *The acquisition of language*. Monographs of the Society for Research in Child Development, 29, No. 1, 43–79.

Chomsky, N. (1957). *Syntactic structures*. The Hague: Mouton.

Clancy, P. M. (1985). The acquisition of Japanese. In D. I. Slobin (Ed.), *The crosslinguistic study of language acquisition:* Vol. 1 (373–524). Hillsdale, NJ: Lawrence Erlbaum Associates.

Hakuta, K. (1982). Interaction between particles and word order in the comprehension and production of simple sentences in Japanese children. *Developmental Psychology*, 18, 62–76.

Haryu, E. & Kajikawa, S. (2016). Japanese children's use of function morphemes during language development. In Japan Society of Developmental Psychology (Eds.), *Frontiers in Developmental Psychology Research: Japanese Perspectives* (221–236). Tokyo: Hitsuzi Shobo Publishing.

Imai, M. & Haryu, E. (2007). *Lexicon no kochiku: Kodomo wa dono yo ni go to gainen o manande iku ka?* [The formation of the lexicon: How children learn words and concepts]. Tokyo: Iwanami Shoten.

Imai, M., Li, L. Haryu, E., Okada, H., Hirsh-Pasek, K., Golinkoff, R., & Shigematsu, J. (2008). Novel noun and verb learning in Chinese-, English-, and Japanese-speaking children. *Child Development*, 79, 979–1000.

Ito, T., Tahara, T., & Park, W. (1991). Acquisition of the Japanese accusative particle "o" as a patient marker. *Japanese Journal of Educational Psychology*, 39, 75–84.

Iwatate, S. (1981). Word order in early utterances of Japanese children. *Japanese Journal of Educational Psychology*, 29(2), 105–111.

Iwatate, S. (1992). Bunpo no kakutoku: Rokaru ruru kara gurobaru ruru e [The acquisition of grammar: From local rules to global rules]. *Gengo*, 21(4), 46–51.

Iwatate, S. (1994). *Yoji gengo ni okeru gojun no shinrigakuteki kenkyu* [Psychological research on the word order of the language of preschoolers]. Tokyo: Kazama Shobo.

Iwatate, S. (2006). Are nativism and usage-based account sufficient?: Social bio-cognition approach. *Japanese Psychological Review*, 49(1), 9–18.

Iwatate, S., & Inaba, R. (1987). Acquisition of Japanese particles "wa" and "ga" in preschool children: In relation to new and old information. *Japanese Journal of Educational Psychology*, 35, 241–246.

Kobayashi, H. & Sasaki, M. (Eds.). (1997). *Kodomotachi no gengo kakutoku* [Child language acquisition]. Tokyo: Taishukan.

Kobayashi, H. & Sasaki, M. (Eds.). (2008). *Shin-kodomotachi no gengo kakutoku* [New perspectives on child language acquisition]. Tokyo: Taishukan.

Morikawa, H. (2006). From isolated islands to a continent of grammar. *Japanese Psychological Review*, 49(1), 96–109.

Murata, K. (1984). *Nihon no gengo hattatsu kenkyu* [Japanese research on language development]. Tokyo: Baifukan Shuppan.

Nakamura, K. (1996). The use of polite language by Japanese preschool children. In D. Slobin, J Gerhardt, A. Kyratsis & J. Guo (Eds.), *Social interaction, social context and language: A festschrift for Susan Ervin-Tripp*. Hillsdale, NJ: Lawrence Erlbaum Associates, 235–250.

Nakamura, K. (1997). Gender-based differences in the language of Japanese preschool children: a look at metalinguistic awareness. In *Proceedings of the 28th Child Language Research Forum* (213-222), Palo Alto, CA: CSLI.

Nakamura, K. (2001a). Gender and language use in Japanese preschool children, *Research on Language and Social Interaction*, 34(1), 15–34.

Nakamura, K. (2001b). Peers and language: The acquisition of "male" speech forms and conversational style by Japanese boys. In M. Almgren, A. Barreña, M. Ezeizabarrena, I. Idiazabal, & Brian MacWhinney (Eds.). *Research on Child Language Acquisition: Proceedings of the 8th Conference of the International Association for the Study of Child Language*. Somerville, MA: Cascadilla Press, 504–520.

Nakamura, K. (2002). Polite language usage in mother-infant interactions: A look at language socialization. In Y. Shirai, H. Kobayashi, S. Miyata, K. Nakamura, T. Ogura, & H. Shirai (Eds.), *Studies in language sciences II* (pp. 175–191), Tokyo: Kuroshio Publishers.

Nakamura, K. (2006). The acquisition of linguistic politeness in Japanese. In M. Nakayama, R. Mazuka, & Y. Shirai (Eds.), *Handbook of Japanese psycholinguistics* (pp. 110–115). Cambridge: Cambridge University Press.

Nakayama, M., Mazuka, R., Shirai, Y., and Li, P. (2006). *The handbook of East Asian psycholinguistics: Volume 2, Japanese*, Cambridge: Cambridge University Press.

Pinker, S. (1984). *Language learnability and language development.* Cambridge: Harvard University Press.

Sakata, M. (1990). The acquisition of Japanese "gender" particles. *Language and Communication*, 11(3), 117–125.

Sheldon, A. (1990). Pickle fights: Gendered talk in preschool disputes. *Discourse Processes*, 13, 5–31.

Slobin, D. I. (1971). *Psycholinguistics.* Glenview: Scott, Foresman and Company.

Slobin, D. I. (1985). Crosslinguistic evidence for the language-making capacity. In D. I. Slobin (Ed.), *The crosslinguistic study of language acquisition*: Vol. 2 (1157–1249). Hillsdale, NJ: Lawrence Erlbaum Associates.

Tomasello, M. (1992). *First verbs: A case study in early grammatical development.* Cambridge: Cambridge University Press.

Wexler, K. (1982). A principle theory for language acquisition. In E. M. Wanner and L. R. Gleitman (Eds.), *Language acquisition: The state of the art.* Cambridge: Cambridge University Press, 288–315.

Yokoyama, M. (1990). Errors of particle "no" of young Japanese children in adjective-noun construction. *The Japanese Journal of Developmental Psychology*, 1(2), 2–9.

Japanese Research on Emotion

—

Jun Nakazawa

As developmental psychologist Seisoh Sukemune (1981, p. 242) once remarked, "The walls that refused the approach of psychologists are motivation and emotion" In other words, as psychology approached an understanding of development, it found insurmountable obstacles in these two domains. However, research on motivation has progressed in 1980s along with the development of cognitive psychology. Then, research on emotion proliferated after the 1990s in what may be called the "emotional revolution" or "affective turn" (Clough & Halley, 2007). These days, emotion is one of the hottest fields in psychology. There are three main reasons for this emotional revolution. First, people recognized that humans are not cool information-processing machines like computers. Humans have emotions, and their information processing is indeed "hot." Thus, people recognized that analysis of the interaction between cognition and emotion could lead to a fuller understanding of the human mind (Garber & Dodge, 1991). Second, the growing interest in evolutionary psychology has expanded our perspective by looking comparatively at human and animal adjustment. That is, emotion was seen as a basic common factor in both human and sub-human psychology (Panksepp, 1998; Plutchik, 1980). Third, new technologies that non-invasively record physiological and brain function have been developed. These instruments permit researchers to objectively record emotional responses and to examine the physiological background of emotions in detail (Matsumura, 2006; Whalen & Phelps, 2009).

These trends in the "emotional revolution" and "affective turn" are global, and Japanese research on emotional development reflects these changes. Although an emotion is a biological response, it is influenced by sociocultural background. It has been found that Japanese tend to repress facial expression (Ekman, 1972; Matsumoto, 2001) The examination of Japanese emotional development and its sociocultural background is indeed an interesting research theme within the field of Japanese developmental psychology. The purpose of this chapter is review the literature on emotional development research in Japan. However, due to space constraints, I will not discuss emotional intelligence, emotional dysfunctions, anger or depression, although these topics are important.

---

1. EARLY EMOTIONS

Temperament is generally defined as an individual collection of basic dispositions of activity, emotionality, attention and self-regulation. An infant's emotional expression plays a large role in its temperament. For example, Kusanagi (1993) observed the expressions of pleasure, fear, and anger by 10- to 14-month-old infants in a laboratory setting. The correlations of both smiles and fearful expressions in different situations and with different people (mother and experimenter) were high. Specifically, infants who often expressed themselves with smiles approached novel toys quickly, whereas infants with more frequent expressions of fear were slower to approach novel toys. In a related study, Sugawara, Sato, Shima, Toda, and Kitamura (1992) observed infants' fear responses to strangers at six, 12, and 18 months of age. Their longitudinal findings showed that individual differences were relatively stable (the correlation between six and 18 months was .57 and between 12 and 18 months was .60). Infants' early emotions reflect a stable basic disposition and may derive from temperament (Kagan, 1994; Rothbart & Bates, 2006).

Among the environmental influences on early emotions, we may include the proximal mothering style. In her early attachment research, Takahashi (1986) reported that Japanese infants rarely showed A-type (avoidant) attachments, while she noted many more C-type (ambivalent) insecure attachments in the Strange Situation test. The daily childrearing customs of Japanese may arouse stress at separation from mothers, and distress in infants may increase during such procedures. Aspects of infants' early emotional experience (pleasure-displeasure), emotional expression (laughter, crying), and recognition of others' emotions (mother's still face, social referencing) will be located in the emotional processes described the next section. Early emotions will be seen as being socialized into a cultural context with development.

2. EMOTIONAL PROCESSES

2.1 *Emotional experience: Understanding one's own emotions*
Emotional processes have three components: understanding one's own emotions, sending affective messages, and receiving affective messages (Halberstadt, Denham, & Dunsmore, 2001). These components occur sequentially and cyclically as we engage in continuous interaction with others. Awareness and understanding of one's own emotions is a basic experience of affect. Kikuchi (2004) examined children's understanding of their own facial expressions. He showed expressions indicating pleasure, sadness, anger, and a neutral emotional in schematic drawings of a face, illustration of a face, photos of a face, and photos of three- to six-year-old children's own faces, and asked them to choose the face expressing pleasure, sadness, and anger. The percentage of correct responses increased with age. Accuracy for both line drawings and illustrated faces were highest (93 percent), a photo of another's face (79 percent) was next, and the lowest accuracy was for a photo of the child's own face (63 percent). Children construct an emotional face schema by looking at the other person's face, and then used this schema to understand their own faces. Thus, understanding of one's own emotional facial expressions lagged behind children's understanding of others' emotions.

Kubo (2000) asked four- to six-year-old children about the events that caused others' and their own happiness, sadness, and anger. Young children in this sample could describe the events that aroused emotions in other people but had difficulty describing the events that aroused their own emotions, especially sadness and anger. According to Kubo, young children apparently had an emotionally positive bias, and they tended to focus on positive aspects more than negative aspects of events. Together, the Kikuchi and Kubo data showed that young children understand the others' emotions first, they understand their own emotions later.

2.2 *Sending affective messages*

We express emotions via the face, voice, and bodily actions. What kinds of factors influence these instruments of emotional transmission? It is well known that the facial expression is influenced by sociocultural factors. As mentioned before, compared with other populations, Japanese tend to repress facial expression (Ekman, 1972; Matsumoto, 2001). Nakazawa (2010a) compared the facial expressions of Japanese and American kindergarten children while watching an emotion-inducing video (using the Mood Induction Stimulus for Children; Cole, Jordan, & Zahn-Waxler, 1990). He reported that children in the United States showed a wider range of facial expressions than Japanese children. He also compared four- and six-year-old Japanese children's facial expressions while watching emotion-inducing videos when children were watching alone or watching in pairs. There were no differences for four-year-olds, but six-year-old children repressed their facial expressions when they watched the video with a friend. This result showed that Japanese repression of facial expression has started by age six. While constructing a database of Japanese children's facial expressions of happiness, surprise, sadness, and anger, Komatsu and Hakoda (2012) found that 11- to 13-year-old children had difficulty expressing sadness. They also found a gender difference in that girls expressed happiness well, whereas boys expressed other emotions well.

Emotion is also expressed verbally. Naka (2010) reported that verbal emotional expressions among 3- to 12-year-old children were more diverse for negative emotions than positive emotions, and that girls had a wider range of emotional expressions than boys.

These research studies found that the transmission of an affective message was influenced by developmental, cultural, and gender factors. As to variations based on gender, we need further examination of the differential evolutionary adaptive role of male and female emotional expressions (Becker, Kenrick, Neuberg, Blackwell, & Smith, 2007) and the differences between mother-daughter and mother-son emotional conversations (Fivush, Berlin, Sales, Mennuti-Washburn, & Cassidy, 2003).

2.3 Receiving affective messages

2.3.1 Understanding facial expressions

To study developmental differences in the decoding of facial expressions, Sakuraba and Imaizumi (2001) asked two- to four-year-old participants to choose the picture that represented emotions such as happiness, sadness, anger, and surprise (label-to-face matching task). The percentage of correct responses increased with age (two-year-olds = 50 percent, three-year-olds = 78 percent, 4-year-olds = 88 percent). In this study, participants were also asked to choose the picture that corresponded to a photo of a baby's emotional expression (face-to-face matching task). The percentage of correct responses of this face-to-face matching task (53 percent) was lower than for the label-to-face matching task (72 percent). Hoshino (1969) reported the correct percentage of answers the label-to-face matching task by 5-year-olds was over 90 percent and by 9-year-olds was over 95 percent. In contrast, the percentages of aged people's correct answers decrease. For example, Kumada, Yoshida, Hashimoto, Sawada, Maruhashi, & Miyatani (2011) examined the understanding of facial expressions among aged people. Using face morphing, they changed the degree of emotional expression by altering the stimulus by 100, 75, 50, or 25 percent and measured the discrimination threshold of facial emotions. There were no differences between aged people (M = 74.8 years old) and younger people (M = 20.1 years) for recognizing happiness, but thresholds for sadness, anger, disgust, and fear were higher for elderly people than for younger people. This means that older people remain sensitive to positive facial expressions and show less sensitivity to negative facial expressions. This positivity bias has adaptive implications for everyday life in that the elderly may be biased to perceive interactions with others positively.

2.3.2 Understanding vocal expressions

Vocalization is another means of transmitting emotions. This is especially true for the perception of infant emotional vocalizations as a cue in childrearing interactions. Shimura, Imaizumi, and Yamamuro (2002) presented examples of two-month-old infants' "comfort-discomfort" and "calm-surprise" vocalizations to two- to six-year-old children and asked them to choose the corresponding facial picture. For "comfort-discomfort," responses for the comfort voice were more correct than for the discomfort voice (even the two-year-olds performed at a higher than a chance level), and the percentages of correct responses increased with age. For "calm-surprise," there were no age differences and the percentage of correctness was at the chance level. "Comfort-discomfort" is an emotion that communicates an infant's needs for prompt support. Thus, cognition of the comfort-discomfort voices of infants is one base of human nurturance.

Crying is a clear signal of unhappiness in infants. Esposito, Nakazawa, Venuti, and Bornstein (2012) presented the crying of infants with autism spectrum disorder (ASD) and infants with typical development to Japanese and Italian adults. Crying by infants with ASD was perceived as an expression of distress and aroused more distress among adults than did the cries of typical infants, and there were no differences between Japanese and Italian samples in this study. One of the difficulties in raising developmentally disabled children may come from this kind of arousal of distress in caretakers. In another study by this group, the features of the ASD infant's cry were simulated artificially to examine the vocal factor that triggered adults' distress (Esposito, Nakazawa, Venuti, & Bornstein, 2014). The proportion of sound/pause, fundamental frequency, and number of utterances were manipulated in the crying of a typical six-month-old infant. Listening to these cries, adults perceived continuous crying at a high pitch as distress. These are the same features as an ASD infant's crying. When adults were also asked to estimate the age of the crying baby, females were more accurate in their perceptions than males, and parents were more correct than nonparents. As a method of emotional transmission, crying has important survival value for infants because it gets the attention of caretakers and triggers their childcaring behavior.

2.3.3 Understanding conflicting emotional information
Emotion is highly complex and it sometimes temporarily reveals

conflicting information. Asou (1987) examined the effects of psychological discrepancy (e.g., like vs. dislike) between subject and protagonist on the emotional inference of three- to five-year-old children. For example, she presented a story in which the protagonist, who dislike beetles, received a beetle from a friend. Then Asou asked the subject, who likes beetles, to choose the facial expression of the protagonist. Her three-year-old participants estimated the emotions of the protagonist from their own viewpoint (feeling positive), but five-year-old children were able to predict the protagonist's emotion from the protagonist's point of view (feeling negative). Kubo (1982) examined how children resolved the contradiction of the situation vs. the protagonist's facial expression. Young children (four to seven years old) were presented a story in which a protagonist expressed a negative face in a positive situation (e.g., the protagonist received ice cream but made a negative face), and the children were asked to describe the emotions of the protagonist and their reasons for these choices. Thinking based only on situational information or only on emotional information decreased with age, and children were able to integrate the contradictory information by six or seven years of age (e.g., "He has a stomachache" or "She wants a different flavor of ice cream"). The preschool children who could integrate the conflicting emotional information showed a higher level of prosocial behavior (Ito, 1997). Mizokawa (2007), in a similar experiment, presented a story in which the protagonist made a face that disguised his/her real emotions to four- and six-year-old children, and participants were asked to choose the protagonist's real and falsified emotions from happy, sad, and neutral faces. There were two types of motivation for the false emotions: self-defensive motivation (e.g., having a stomachache, but expressing a happy face because he wanted to play) and prosocial motivation (e.g., receiving a present she didn't like, but expressing a happy face because she did not want to hurt the gift giver). The discrimination of real emotion from falsified emotion was more accurate by the six-year-olds than the four-year-olds, more accurate for happy expressions than sad expressions, and more often based on self-defensive motivation than prosocial motivation. Self-defensive falsified sad expressions like faked crying were already understood in early childhood, and prosocial understanding of falsified emotions developed subsequently. In sum, these research results show that the understanding and integration of conflicting emotional information develops during early childhood.

3. Emotion and adjustment

3.1 *Emotional sympathy*
From an evolutionary point of view, emotion is a biological mechanism that promotes survival and adaptation to one's environment. Several researchers have examined the adaptive function of emotion. For example, emotional sympathy has a positive function for adjustment, and prosocial behavior is evoked by sympathy for the person in the negative situation. Kato, Onishi, Kanazawa, Hinobayashi, and Minami (2012) observed the behavior of two-year-old children in reaction to the crying of peers in nursery school. Toddlers displayed many prosocial behaviors (including direct behaviors such as gently stroking a crying peer's head and indirect support such as calling the teacher) for peers who rarely cried or were non-aggressive. However, they showed few prosocial behaviors in reaction to peers who cried often or were aggressive. The sympathy of two-year-olds in response to crying peers depends on the daily emotional expressions of those peers.

The consolation evoked by sympathy gives the people in a negative situation a feeling of relief. However, consolation sometimes evokes negative feelings such as anger and self-contempt. What kinds of factors affect these differences? Ogawa (2011) examined the emotions of students consoled by peers in a negative situation, e.g., being sick, failing an examination, and having trouble with friends. In all of these situations, the emotions of the student who attributed the cause of these negative events to their own ability were more negative than those of the student who attributed the events to luck or to obstruction by others. In addition, in all situations consolation by intimate friends produced more positive emotions and less repulsion than that by non-intimate friends.

The inability to read others' emotions is one of the causes of maladjustment. Katsuma and Yamasaki (2008) showed that relationally aggressive fourth to sixth graders lacked empathetic emotional ability.

Compared to less aggressive children, relationally aggressive children estimated the victim's emotion as lower (victim does not feel sad), shared the emotion with the victim less (showed less pity), and were less inclined to help the victim (did not think to encourage). However, Hatakeyama and Hatakeyama (2012) found that compared with less aggressive young children, the relationally aggressive young children (four to six years old) had the ability to perceive victims' emotions more correctly (victims may feel sad). They said that these children are effective at reading the other's emotions when showing relational aggression. Further studies are needed on the contradictions between findings on relational aggression in children. From these studies we can say that the reading of others' emotions is an important factor for adjustment.

3.2 *Feelings of envy and inferiority*

Feelings of Envy and inferiority may become important aspects of interpersonal relations. Sawada (2005) analyzed the envy of third to ninth graders and found that envy consisted of three factors: "antagonistic feelings" (hate, irritation), "anguished feelings" (agony, sadness), and "feelings of inadequacy" (frustration, discomfort). Elementary school boys in his study reported higher levels of "antagonistic feelings" than girls, especially in the ability domain (school achievement, skills, and physical ability). "Anguished feelings" increased with age, especially in unchangeable domains like athletic ability and popularity. "Feelings of inadequacy" were high, and this suggested that it would be at the core feelings of envy. The strength of each factor involved in envy depends on the contextual domain. In a similar study, Kosaka (2008) examined the relationship between feelings of inferiority and important domains of participants in junior high school, high school, and college. Junior high school students regarded intellectual abilities as an important domain, and poor achievement caused feelings of inferiority. However, high school students regarded personal attractiveness as an important domain, and physical unattractiveness caused feelings of inferiority. Meanwhile, university students regarded self-approval as an important domain, and lack of interpersonal skills caused feelings of inferiority. At the same time, university students who regarded maturity as an important domain did not have feelings of inferiority.

4. REGULATION OF EMOTION

4.1 *Early regulation of emotion*

As described in the previous section, emotions are closely linked to human adjustment and/or psychological health. Thus, regulation of emotion is important because it facilitates human adjustment. It is one aspect of self-regulation, and now has become an attractive research topic in this global field (Nakazawa, forthcoming; Philippot, & Feldman, 2004). Early emotions are influenced by temperament, and they are related to the basic components of regulation of emotion. Sakagami (1999) observed 1.5- and two-year-old children trying to open a locked toy box. Their behaviors were categorized as indicative of emotion-focused coping (asking others for comfort, self-comfort, exploration, and distraction) and problem-focused coping (exploring the box, asking mother to help). From 1.5 to two years of age, problem-focused coping behavior increased, and asking for comfort and help from the mother decreased. This suggested that children shifted to more autonomous coping during this age period. In emotion-focused coping, distracting behavior emerged. This behavior has active functions such as calming negative affect and spontaneous creation of positive affect. Kanamaru and Muto (2006) observed children's regulation of emotion in a situation where mothers took away toys from two- and three-year-olds. The behaviors at two years of age were categorized into three types: "distress continuance," "distress soothing," and "distress non-expression." Two-year-old children who expressed distress continuance and distress soothing showed "distress non-expression" at three years of age. At three years of age, "other activity," "distraction," "verbal reference to toys," and "approach to mother" behaviors increased. Thus, from 1.5 to three years of age, children's autonomic behavior increased and regulation of emotion appeared.

4.2 *Regulation of emotion in early childhood and childhood*

Regulation of emotion develops from early to middle childhood, and it becomes relevant to children's peer relations. Nakazawa and Nakazawa (2004) examined the facial expressions of kindergarten to second grade children in the United States watching an emotion-inducing video. They also collected behavior ratings from teachers in addition to peer nomination data. Children who showed frequent changes in facial expressions during inter-trial rest periods of videos were rated as less prosocial and more asocial and hyperactive by teachers, and named as friends by fewer peers. Difficulty in calming down evoked emotions may have produced inadequate social behavior and as a result led to poor relationships. In a subsequent study, Nakazawa and Takeuchi (2012) reported that young children who made negative faces when they received a disappointing gift were named as friends by fewer peers, compared with children who repressed their disappointment facially. This showed that children's inability to repress or suppress negative emotions led to difficulties in peer interactions, so that they had less acceptance by peers. In addition, children repressed their negative feelings for the gift-giver (the experimenter) more when she was present than when she was absent. Children with less peer acceptance showed expressions of negative feelings more immediately even when the gift-giver was present. Such findings showed that social factors influence young children's emotional regulation (Nakazawa, 2010a), and individual differences.

4.3 *Emotion regulation in later adolescence*

How does regulation of emotion function in adolescence? Choi and Arai (1998) reported that university students who frequently repressed negative emotions (repressed anger toward a selfish friend; behaved positively even when experiencing sad feelings) had lower satisfaction in their friendships and lower self-esteem. University students have developed emotion-regulation skills, but excessive regulation of emotion toward other people may be stressful for them. Because Japanese culture emphasizes an "interdependent construal of self" (Markus and Kitayama, 1991, p. 227), stress from excessive regulation of emotion may be frequent in Japanese adolescents.

4.4 *Strategies of regulation of emotion*

There are many ways to regulate emotion. One common strategy among adolescents is to listen to music. Matsumoto (2002) asked university students to write descriptions of sad events, in order to induce a sad mood in them. Then her participants were divided into three groups to listen to sad music, listen to happy music, or (as a control) work on a geometry problem. The listeners' sadness was unchanged if they had been only slightly sad, whereas the sad mood was weakened after listening to sad music if the listeners had felt very sad. Matsumoto concluded from this experiment that sad music compounded the students' sad mood and had a cathartic effect on the original sadness.

Another common form of regulation of negative mood is to remember positive past events. Sakaki (2005) examined the effects of recalling a positive experience to alleviate affective states. She induced a negative mood in university students, and then asked them to recall and write about some of their positive experiences. The more important the memories these participants recalled, the more positive mood they reported after the task. Sakaki (2005) interpreted this result as follows: important memories appeared to contain highly sensory and perceptual information. By recalling such informative and clear memories, students may have re-experienced past emotions vividly, and as a result increased their self-esteem and achieved a more positive mood.

4.5 *Physiological response to emotion*

In the field of emotion research, use of non-invasive physiological response measures is now commonplace. For example, infrared thermo graphy can assess sympathetic nerve activity by measuring body temperature. The first Japanese study to use infrared thermography was a study of infants by Mizukami, Kobayashi, Iwata, and Ishii (1987). They found, that the infant's forehead temperature decreased when separated from the mother. In a related study, Nakazawa (2010b) measured the tip of nose temperature of five-year-olds when watching an emotion-inducing video. Compared to children who had more positive peer nominations, children who had fewer positive peer nominations showed a greater decrease in temperature, and the decrease in temperature did not recover during an inter-trial rest period. Once a negative emotion was evoked, these children had difficulty in calming themselves down. Their continuing negative emotions may disturb subsequent smooth interactions with their peers. Near-infrared spectroscopy has also been used in Japan to assess brain functions. Such an inexpensive and convenient tool to measure emotional response is likely to be used more widely in the future, leading to other findings in the field of emotional development.

5. CONCLUSION

This chapter reviewed Japanese research on emotional development from several vantage points: early emotions, emotional processes (emotional experience, sending and receiving affective messages), emotion and adjustment, and regulation of emotion. In this final section, I consider Japanese research on emotional development in relation to aspects of Japanese culture. In the early years of life, the mother-child relationship in Japan is very close (most Japanese infants and children co-sleep with their parents). Thus, separation from the mother is quite stressful for Japanese infants. In the context of this cultural tradition of close interpersonal relationships, cooperative relationships with others and consideration for others becomes important. Japanese mothers therefore commonly use a childrearing strategy of referring to others' emotions (Azuma, 1994, e.g., when children do not eat vegetables, mothers say "that hurts the farmer" or express their own sadness). Azuma (1994) called this kind of childrearing strategy *kimochishugi* ("affectionism," p. 91). Children in this context become sensitive to reading others' emotions and learn to control expression of emotion. The result of this socialization may be seen in young Japanese children's reduced facial expression and inhibited facial expression in situations with others (friends, givers of presents, etc.). Later in development, adolescent maladjustment may actually be due to inhibition of young people's emotion due to overconsideration of others.

It is evident that most research domains in this chapter were examined in participants of specific ages and lack a lifespan development perspective. It will of course be necessary to examine the longitudinal relationship between early emotions and later emotional development in each research domain (emotional processes, adjustment, and regulation). In addition, although emotions are subject to aspects of human biology, they are also influenced by sociocultural aspects, as described in this chapter. Investigation of the influence of Japanese culture on each research domain will contribute to a more global view within the study of these research topics.

Research on emotion in Japan is progressing rapidly. In the near future, we may expect researchers to focus increasingly on the connections between psychological and physiological responses, regulation of emotion and adjustment, cognitive and emotion regulation, cool and hot executive functions, and to promote practical interventions based on the findings of regulation of emotion. A number of younger Japanese scholars are at work in these areas, and I look forward to their results.

ACKNOWLEDGEMENT

Supported by a Scientific Research Grant from the Japan Society for the Promotion of Science (#26285149). The author expresses special thanks to Dr. David W. Shwalb, Southern Utah University, for his careful reading of this chapter.

REFERENCES

Asou A. (1987). Yojiki ni okeru tasha kanjo no suisoku noryoku no hattatsu [Development of ability to inner other's emotions in preschool children]. *Japanese Journal of Educational Psychology*, 35, 33–40.

Azuma, H. (1994). *Nihonjin no shitsuke to kyoiku* [Japanese child rearing and education]. Tokyo: Tokyodaigaku Shuppankai.

Becker, D. V., Kenrick, D. T., Neuberg, S. L., Blackwell, K.C., & Smith, D.M. (2007). The confounded nature of angry men and happy women. *Journal of Personality and Social Psychology*, 92, 179–190.

Choi, K. & Arai, K (1998). Negachibu na kanjo hyoshutu no seigyo to yujin kankei no manzokukan oyobi seishinteki kenko to no kankei [Relationship between regulation of negative emotional expression, satisfaction of friendship, and mental health]. *Japanese Journal of Educational Psychology*, 46, 432–441.

Clough, P. T. & Halley, J. (Eds.), (2007). *Affective turn: Theorizing the social*. Durham, NC: Duke University Press.

Cole, P. M., Jordan, P. R., & Zahn-Waxler, C. (1990). *Mood induction stimulus for children*. Bethesda, MD: National Institute of Mental Health.

Ekman, P. (1972). Universals and cultural differences in facial expressions of emotion. In J. Cole (Ed.), *Nebraska symposium on motivation. 1971* (Vol. 19, pp. 207–283). Lincoln: University of Nebraska Press.

Esposito, G., Nakazawa, J., Venuti, P., & Bornstein, M. H. (2012). Perceptions of distress in young children with autism compared to typically developing children: A cultural comparison between Japan and Italy. *Research in Developmental Disabilities*, 33, 1059–1067.

Esposito, G., Nakazawa, J., Venuti, P., & Bornstein, M. H. (2014) Judgment of infant cry: The roles of acoustic characteristics and sociodemographic characteristics. *Japanese Psychological Research*, 57, 126–134.

Fivush, R., Berlin, L. J., Sales, J. M., Mennuti-Washburn, J., & Cassidy, J. (2003). Function of parent-child reminiscing about emotionally negative events. *Memory*, 11, 179–192.

Garber, J., & Dodge, K. A. (1991). *The development of emotion regulation and dysregulation*. New York: Cambridge University Press.

Halberstadt, A. G., Denham, S. A., & Dunsmore, J. C. (2001) Affective social competence. *Social Development*, 10, 79–119.

Hatakeyama M., & Hatakeyama, H. (2012). Kankeisei kogeki yoji no kyokansei to dotokuteki handan, shakaiteki joho shori katei no hattatsuteki kenkyu [A developmental study of empathy, moral judgment, and social information processing in preschooler's with relational aggression]. *Japanese Journal of Developmental Psychology*, 23, 1–11.

Hoshino, K. (1969). Hyojo no kanjoteki imi rikai ni kansuru hattatsuteki kenkyu [The ability to identify the affective meanings of facial expressions at successive age levels]. *Japanese Journal of Educational Psychology*, 17, 90–101.

Ito, J. (1997). Yoji no koshakaiteki kodo ni okeru tasha no kanjo kaishaku no yakuwari [Relationship between inference of feeling and prosocial behavior in preschool children]. *Japanese Journal of Developmental Psychology*, 8, 111–120.

Kagan, J. (1994). *Galen's prophecy: Temperament in human nature*. New York: Basic Books.

Kanamaru, T., & Muto, T., (2006). Jodo chosetsu purosesu no kojinsa ni kansuru 2- sai kara 3- sai eno hattatsuteki henka [The development of individual differences in emotional regulation in 2- and 3-year olds]. *Japanese Journal of Developmental Psychology*, 17, 219–229.

Kato, M., Onishi, K., Kanazawa, T., Hinobayashi, T., & Minami, T. (2012) 2- saiji ni yoru naite iru yoji e no ko-shakaiteki na hanno [Two-year-old toddlers' prosocial responses to crying peer: Social evaluation mechanisms]. *Japanese Journal of Developmental Psychology*, 23, 12–22.

Katsuma, L. & Yamasaki, K. (2008). Jido ni okeru 3 taipu no kogekisei ga kyokan ni oyobosu eikyo [The effects of three types of aggressions on empathy in elementary school children]. *Japanese Journal of Psychology*, 79, 325–332.

Kikuchi, T. (2004). Yoji ni okeru jibunjishin no hyojo ni taisuru rikai no hattatsuteki henka [Development of young children's understanding of their own facial expressions]. *Japanese Journal of Developmental Psychology*, 15, 207–216.

Komatsu, S., & Hakoda, Y. (2012). Kodomo no hyojo gazo deta beisu no kochiku to hyoka [Construction and evaluation of a facial expression database of children].

Japanese Journal of Psychology, 83, 217–224.

Kosaka Y. (2008). Jiko no juyo ryoiki kara mita seinenki ni okeru rettokan no hattatsuteki henka [Developmental changes in inferiority feelings in adolescents and young adults: Important areas of the self]. *Japanese Journal of Educational Psychology*, 56, 218–229.

Kubo, Y. (1982) Yoji ni okeru mujun suru dekigoto no episodo no kosei ni yoru rikai [Episodic understanding of conflicting events in children]. *Japanese Journal of Educational Psychology*, 30, 239–243.

Kubo, Y. (2000). Young children's view of emotions in themselves: Preschooler's reporting about their own emotional experiences. *Bulletin of Faculty of Sociology, Toyo University*, 38, 75–87.

Kumada, M., Yoshida, H., Hashimoto, Y., Sawada, K., Maruhashi, M., & Miyatani, M. (2011). Hyojo ninshiki ni okeru karei no eikyo ni tsuite [Discrimination thresholds for recognizing facial emotions: Mostly higher among the elderly]. *Japanese Journal of Psychology*, 82, 56–62.

Kusanagi, E. (1993). Nyuji no kishitsu no kozo [The structure of infant temperament: Emotional expression and the tendency to approach]. *Japanese Journal of Developmental Psychology*, 4, 42–50.

Markus, H. R., & Kitayama, S. (1991) Culture and self: Implications for cognition, motivation and self. *Psychological Review*, 98, 224–253.

Matsumoto, D. (2001). Culture and emotion. In D. Matsumoto (Ed.), *The Handbook of Culture and Psychology* (pp. 171–194). New York: Oxford University Press.

Matsumoto, J. (2002). Ongaku no kibun yudo koka ni kansuru jishoteki kenkyu [Why people listen to sad music: Effects of music on sad moods]. *Japanese Journal of Educational Psychology*, 50, 23–32.

Matsumura, K. (2006). Nyuji no jodo kenkyu: Hiseshokuho ni yoru seirigaku-teki apurochi [Research on infant emotion: Non-invasive physiological approach]. *Baby Science*, 6, 2–14.

Mizokawa, A. (2007). Yojiki ni okeru tasha no itsuwari no kanashimi hyoshutsu no rikai [Young children's understanding of false sadness]. *Japanese Journal of Developmental Psychology*, 18, 174–184.

Mizukami, K., Kobayashi, N., Iwata, H., & Ishii, T (1987). Telethermography in infant's emotional behavioral research. *Lancet*, 11, 38–39.

Naka, M. (2010). Kodomo ni yoru pojichibu, negachibu na kimochi no hyogen [Children's description of positive and negative feeling: Use of emotional words under safe and unsafe conditions]. *Japanese Journal of Developmental Psychology*, 21, 365–374.

Nakazawa, J. (2010a). Yoji ni okeru jodo seigyo no shakaiteki yoin to bunkateki yoin [Effects of social and cultural factor on differences of emotion regulation of kindergarten children: Social context comparison and the US-Japan comparison of facial expression]. *Bulletin of the Faculty of Education, Chiba University*, 58, 37–42.

Nakazawa, J. (2010b). *Yoji no jodo seigyo to nakama kankei* [Emotion regulation and peer relation in young children]. 2007-2009 reports of the Grant for Scientific Research. Developmental psychopathological research about the factors of peer adjustment during transition from kindergarten to elementary school, 20–29.

Nakazawa, J. (inprint). Serufu regyureshon [Self-regulation]. N. Tajima, S. Iwatate, & T. Nagasaki (Eds.) *Shin hattatsu shinrigaku handobukku* [New Developmental Psychology Handbook]. (pp.533-542). Tokyo: Fukumura Shuppan.

Nakazawa, J., & Nakazawa, S. (2004). Shakaiteki kodo to jodo seigyo no hattatsu [Development of social behavior and emotion regulation]. *Proceedings of the 46th Conference of Japanese Society of Educational Psychology*, 31.

Nakazawa, J., & Takeuchi, Y. (2012) Yoji ni okeru negachibu jodo no hyoshutu seigyo to nakama kankei [Regulation of facial display of negative emotion and peer relation among Japanese kindergarten children]. *Bulletin of the Faculty of Education, Chiba University*, 60, 109–114.

Ogawa S. (2011). Tasha kara no dojo ni yotte shojiru kanjo [Affect occurring in relation to sympathy from the other: Differences resulting from attributions of an event and intimacy with the other]. *Japanese Journal of Educational Psychology*, 59, 267–277.

Panksepp, J. (1998). *Affective neuroscience*. New York: Oxford University Press.

Philippot, P., & Feldman, R. S. (2004). *The regulation of emotion*. Mahwah, NJ: LEA

Plutchik, R. (1980). *Emotion: A psychoevolutionary synthesis*. New York: Harper & Row.

Rothbart, M. K., & Bates, J. E. (2006). Temperament in children's development. In W. Damon & R. Lerner (Series Eds.) & N. Eisenberg (Vol. ed.), *Handbook of child psychology: vol. 3. Social emotional and personality development* (6th. ed. pp. 96–166). New York: Wiley.

Sakagami, H. (1999). Hoko kaishi ki ni okeru jodo seigyo [Emotional regulation in toddlerhood: The development of coping behavior in a problem-solving situation]. *Japanese Journal of Developmental Psychology*, 10, 99–109.

Sakaki, M. (2005). Kanjo seigyo o sokushin suru jidenteki kioku no seisitsu [Nature of autobiographical memory that facilitates improvement of negative moods]. *Japanese Journal of Psychology*, 76, 169–175.

Sakuraba, K., & Imaizumi, S. (2001). 2-4-saiji ni okeru jodo go no rikairyoku to hyojo ninchi noryoku no hattatsuteki hikaku [Affect label comprehension and facial expression in 3- to 4-year-olds: A developmental study]. *Japanese Journal of Developmental Psychology*, 12, 36–45.

Sawada, M. (2005). Jido seito ni okeru urami kanjo no kozo to hattatsuteki henka [Envy and its emotional structure: Developmental changes in elementary and junior high school pupils, domain specificity, and grade and gender differences]. *Japanese Journal of Developmental Psychology*, 53, 185–195.

Shimura, Y., Imaizumi, S., & Yamamuro, C. (2002). Yoji ni yoru nyuji onsei no kanjosei joho no choushu tokusei [Young children's recognition of emotional aspects of 2-month-olds' vocalization]. *Japanese Journal of Developmental Psychology*, 13, 1–11.

Sugawara, M., Sato, T., Shima, S., Toda, A. M., & Kitamura, T. (1992). Nyujiki no mishiranu tasha e no osore [Fear of strangers in infancy: A longitudinal study of 6-, 12-, and 18-month-olds]. *Japanese Journal of Developmental Psychology*, 3, 65–72.

Sukemune, S. (1981). *Dokizuke to jodo* [Motivation and emotion]. Tokyo: Science Sha.

Takahashi, K. (1986). Examining the strange-situation procedure with Japanese mothers and 12-month-old infants. *Developmental Psychology*, 22, 265–270.

Whalen, P. J., & Phelps, E. A. (2009). *The human amygdala*. NY: Guilford Press.

Qualitative Research in Japan

Masahiro Nochi

"Qualitative research" is a general term referring to scientific inquiries in which data are collected, analyzed, and reported in the form of verbal descriptions, without relying on statistical procedures. It is often contrasted with quantitative research, such as experiments or surveys. Qualitative research includes ethnography, fieldwork, narrative research, document analysis, and other methods that use naturalistic observation and/or interview (both semi-structured and unstructured) to collect data about the phenomenon that interests the researcher.

However, the difference between these two forms of research is not just a matter of methodology, but of epistemology—that is, the mindset of the researcher observing the phenomena naturalistically is very different from the mindset of the researcher conducting an experiment. The former mindset involves understanding reality as having multiple meanings, reflecting on different research viewpoints, and regarding research as an active approach to the research subjects (Nochi, 2011 b). With this mindset, qualitative researchers collect data in naturalistic settings, paying attention to the meanings that the research subjects construct, taking an interest in the processes of the phenomenon, and analyzing the data inductively (Bogdan & Biklen, 2006). As a result, qualitative research can be used to create new hypotheses by capturing reality from a viewpoint that has been previously overlooked.

This chapter outlines the significance of qualitative research in Japan and traces its development. Some important findings that have contributed to the field of developmental psychology are then described. Finally, this chapter reviews the current status of qualitative research in psychology education, as well as methodological development in this inquiry, and refers to its implications for the future of qualitative research in Japan.

1. QUALITATIVE RESEARCH AS A FRONTIER OF DEVELOPMENTAL PSYCHOLOGY

In the past few decades, qualitative research has gained increasing popularity in developmental psychology and other disciplines of the social sciences. The number of research articles using a qualitative method has gradually increased in academic journals, and qualitative research has begun to be taught as a standard method of psychological investigation in many graduate schools and even some undergraduate courses. In this sense, qualitative research is a frontier in developmental psychology and related fields that allows researchers to gain new insights into developmental phenomena.

Although introduced in developmental psychology quite recently, qualitative approaches to developmental phenomena have been used for a long time. The classic works by Wallon and Vygotsky, both of whom were born in the nineteenth century, were in essence based on qualitative descriptions and analyses of their research subjects. Piaget also extensively described child behaviors in a qualitative manner, even though his research has mainly influenced quantitative research in subsequent generations (Giorgi, 2006). Asao (2013) pointed out that developmental phenomena inherently involve variation and fluctuation in the historical context, and thus categories that are universally applicable to them may not exist. Developmental inquiry, therefore, has been since its earliest stages compatible with qualitative descriptions. Thus, contemporary developmental psychology perhaps has "rediscovered" the significance of the approach often used by these classic scholars.

This rediscovery did not occur in a vacuum. In the twentieth century, social science researchers made much of qualitative descriptions in order to understand other people without imposing traditional concepts upon them. Cultural anthropologists, who had remained in their armchairs while studying other cultures before the nineteenth century, began extensive fieldwork to collect information about other cultures and to write ethnographies. In these initial forays, anthropologists were aware that their viewpoints and conceptual frameworks might not be valid for understanding other cultures. This awareness was shared by other social scientists, including sociologists. Researchers observed individuals such as criminals or immigrants, who lived in cultures similar to their own but had different values and morals. By the middle of the century, even women came to be seen as having a different viewpoint—feminists asserted that women's experiences in society might not be the same as men's. Thus, the twentieth century can be regarded as a time when "otherness" was discovered in many facets of human life (Nochi, 2013).

Under these cultural transformations, developmental psychology also changed its views on human development. Theorists began to examine developmental phenomena from a wider variety of viewpoints, as if they had found an "otherness" in what they had once seen as familiar. For example, some psychologists proposed that developmental psychology should expand its scope from childhood to the entire lifespan because an individual develops continuously from birth to death (Sigelman, 1999). In fact, a lifespan perspective on developmental psychology is easy to find when looking through introductory psychology textbooks. Development is now viewed against the background of an individual's whole life, which may show larger individual differences according to his or her life experience and self-image. Today's theorists on psychology seem to pay more attention to cultural or societal influences on human development. Rogoff (2003), for instance, believes that human development is influenced by culture and society and that developmental theories should be localized—that is, rather than being universal theories of humankind, they should be considered to be more local, culture-bound theories. Thus, human development is now seen as having a much more diverse framework than ever before. Psychologists cannot define developmental phenomena quantitatively from only a traditional viewpoint to understand them, but rather, they must begin to describe them qualitatively.

Empirical researchers of developmental psychology have also begun to recognize the significance of qualitative research. Endo (2007) stated that there are at least three reasons why developmental researchers have recently become interested in qualitative research. First, they want to attend to the everyday reality of development more now than in the past. Endo (2007) suggested that sophisticated experimental methods sometimes overestimate or underestimate children's ability, and pointed out that qualitative observation in everyday situations could produce more ecologically valid findings. Second, increasingly more researchers are placing importance on the individual and situated nature of development. Data acquired through quantitative research are likely to hide many variations in the developmental phenomena so prevalent in ordinary life. Valsiner (2007) also maintained that qualitative case studies of "outliers" can increase our knowledge of development. Finally, researchers are becoming more interested in the subjective aspects of development, which traditional quantitative methods are not good at investigating. Understanding these aspects, such as the meaning that an individual makes of his or her life, is important for applying the knowledge on human development to clinical practice or counseling.

2. DEVELOPMENT OF QUALITATIVE RESEARCH IN JAPAN

Qualitative research in Japan did not develop only within the discipline of developmental psychology; indeed, it was supported by interest in the qualitative approach in other fields. In many ways, the groundwork for qualitative research was originally laid out in Japan. For example, the pioneering ethnologist Kunio Yanagita (1875–1962) extracted Japanese racial characteristics from the stories collected among local people. His work influenced not just ethnology but also social scientific methodology in general (Kato, 1988). Muto (2013) pointed out that Japan has a tradition of action research, first conducted by teachers in the Meiji period. They repeated an attempt to construct local knowledge based upon descriptive data in the field of education though they did not have a clear methodology. In addition, philosophers who were active in the Taisho and

Showa periods, such as Kitaro Nishida (1870–1945) and Tetsuro Watsuji (1889–1960), argued about agency and humanism, and their arguments pioneered the critical mindset of qualitative studies in practical fields.

Few Japanese psychologists conducted qualitative research until the 1980s, whereas researchers in other fields of social science adopted it as a feasible research option before that time. Two pioneers of Japanese qualitative research, both of whom had studied psychology in Japan, acquired their methods abroad while studying other disciplines. Yasuko Minoura studied at the department of cultural anthropology at the University of California, Los Angeles, while Ikuya Sato studied at the department of sociology at the University of Chicago. They published results of their empirical work in Japanese in the 1980s and began to teach qualitative methods for psychology at Japanese universities (Minoura, 1984; I. Sato, 1984). They later wrote textbooks on qualitative methodology, specifically on micro-ethnography and fieldwork, and had an impact on research conducted by subsequent psychologists (Minoura, 1999; I. Sato, 1992).

Qualitative research was not just brought to Japanese developmental psychology from other disciplines and other countries—indeed, developmental psychologists in Japan initiated the trend toward qualitative research in the 1980s. Yoko Yamada, Takeshi Asao, and others organized a diary research circle, in which they analyzed their own diaries; these diaries contained descriptions of their children's behaviors along with their interactions with their children (Yamada, 2013). Without relying on concrete procedures for qualitative analysis, these researchers tried to inductively construct empirical models of early child development. These models suggested what was missing from previous quantitative research on parent-child interactions. The fruits of this circle's activity were published later (Yamada, 1987; Asao, 1992).

In the 1990s, more attention began to be paid to qualitative research. Many sessions were carried out in the domestic conferences of the Japan Society of Developmental Psychology. Hirofumi Minami, who had learned qualitative methodology at Clark University, was one of the active organizers of these academic sessions. He advocated field research as an alternative, promising methodology for the psychological sciences (Suzuki, 2000). In the mid-1990s, Tatsuya Sato and several other psychologists played a key role in organizing a series of presentations at the annual conferences of the Japanese Psychological Association. In this series, named "Field Research in Action," recent qualitative studies conducted by Japanese psychologists were introduced, besides presenting new investigations. The series, which continued for 10 years, provided a place for psychologists who were interested in qualitative methodology to meet and exchange information.

The 2000s saw the creation of an academic journal and the organization of an academic society for qualitative research. In 2002, T. Muto, Y. Yamada, T. Asao, H. Minami, and T. Sato, all of whom worked in the field of developmental psychology, launched an annual journal titled the *Japanese Journal of Qualitative Psychology*. At first, this journal was similar to a private magazine, but it also openly invited original manuscripts and reviewed them for publication, thereby providing an outlet for the qualitative studies that were beginning to be conducted in Japan at the time. In 2004, the Japanese Society of Qualitative Psychology was founded in response to the popularity of the journal, and it adopted the journal as its official publication. In addition to the journal, annual conventions of the society have provided opportunities for qualitative researchers in several fields of study to interact with and inspire each other.

Stimulated by this trend, empirical studies using a qualitative method are being published more often in other academic journals. Saiki-Craighill (2013) investigated the number of articles that used a qualitative method in medicine and nursing. The result showed approximately 10 articles in 1999, around 100 in 2003, and a rapid increase to approximately 300 in 2007. The same trend can be observed in the discipline of developmental psychology and related fields. This suggests that researchers have come to recognize the significance of the qualitative approach in psychology, not to mention in social science in general.

3. SIGNIFICANT OUTCOMES OF QUALITATIVE RESEARCH IN DEVELOPMENTAL PSYCHOLOGY

This section presents several empirical studies that used the qualitative method to demonstrate how it can be used to further developmental psychology and related disciplines. Although there is a wide variety of qualitative research, a recent theoretical work classified four forms of knowledge revealed by qualitative research: local, systemic, process-oriented, and interactive (Nochi, 2011a). These forms of knowledge contrast with the knowledge that traditional quantitative research mainly attempts to develop. By and large, the latter is universal, lacks consideration of temporal or unique contexts, and likely ignores the influence of the researcher on the subjects. Each of these four forms of knowledge will be examined here to show aspects of qualitative research at the frontier of developmental psychology in Japan.

Local knowledge refers to knowledge that is valid among people in a specific area or group who share unique values and rules. The number of people is different for each research study, and if the number is low, then knowledge of an individual person can become "local." In developmental psychology research, qualitative researchers have been interested in the characteristics of developmental phenomena specific to a certain culture or group of individuals. They have also focused on how these characteristics are generated or transformed by interactions with other people in a local context, thus building their reality or "life-world." Some studies have tried to clarify unique features of the experiences that certain groups of people share. For instance, Imao (2009) studied the process of mourning that chronically ill patients are likely to go through after their diagnosis. Matsumoto (2009) interviewed individuals with cleft lips and palates to clarify their self-images and life stories. These studies not only focused on groups of people so far unexplored by researchers, but also tried to understand their experiences within their local environments in present-day Japanese society. In addition, qualitative researchers may discover locality in everyday interactions, while others may identify commonality in apparently local characteristics. For example, Fujie (1999) found original utterance styles in the classroom conversations of primary school children. Additionally, Nochi (2006) analyzed the adaptation process of an aphasic person to local welfare facilities, and pointed out the changed meaning of the facility, which was found to be similar to the environmental transition among non-aphasic people.

Systemic knowledge is a form of knowledge based on system theory. According to the theory, a certain phenomenon is constructed through a relationship or a system, which is composed of regularly interacting groups of activities. The whole system is more than the sum of the components. In fact, a recent viewpoint in ethnography regards an individual as similar to a node in a relational network. An action or a statement does not come from his or her hypothetical inner entity alone, but is always influenced by the configuration of many factors. This is an essential characteristic of a "field," which is distinctive from a laboratory in which most factors are controlled, except for the dependent variable. One example of empirical research on this type of knowledge is a study by Taniguchi (2004), who conducted fieldwork at a class in a hospital school. She described the educational practices not only as the teacher's actions toward the child patients, but rather, as an act of forging connections among multiple parties, including children, family members, medical professionals, and teachers from the children's original schools. Sakagami (2002) carried out longitudinal participant observations of a child's self-adjustment behavior. The results clearly showed that behavioral development was part of the changing interactions between the mother and the child, not just a result of the child's development. These studies represent one of the directions of qualitative research, in which an attempt is made to understand a behavior or an action that seemingly belongs to an individual as an expression of an interactive system among several people.

Process-oriented knowledge is constructed when the researcher tries to understand a phenomenon in the context of a relatively long period. An event experienced in life does not stand alone, but is influenced by preceding events and then influences subsequent events in turn. Due to the uniqueness of this sequence, people do not experience a given event as something replicative but as something that happens only once. Understanding the event in these contexts allows the researcher to see how the meanings in these events can change over time. For example, Shoji (2009) presented a variation on the meaning of conflicts between couples while investigating conflict narratives longitudinally. The results suggested that although conflicts were generally considered to have a negative effect, relationship conflicts had widely disparate influences on the relationship, depending on the meaning of the conflict. Tokuda (2004) also examined the meanings that mothers assigned to childrearing in their life stories, discovering five patterns. Thus, the meaning of child-rearing that the mothers had constructed interacts with the way they understand their own lives, and because these both change over time, they can result in widely different patterns of behavior and meaning.

Interactive knowledge refers to the knowledge based on, or in consideration of, the interaction between the research subject and people around him or her in the setting of the investigation. Gubrium & Holstein (2009) maintained that a person's statements, as well as behaviors in general, are not expressions of his or her internal "truth," but are affected by various levels of the "narrative environment." It goes without saying that professional practices, including therapy or research, are part of that environment, and so we should therefore consider that narrative or behavioral data might vary according to interactions with the professionals. For instance, Matsushima (2002) suggested that juvenile delinquents do not necessarily have a "problem," and to explore this, conducted a fieldwork study in a juvenile group home. The author demonstrated how the "problem" could be constructed in conversations between the staff and the delinquents during social skills training sessions. Furthermore, some qualitative studies have begun to incorporate the researcher into the data. Shojima (2010), for example, conducted continuous interviews with the mother of a child with gender identity disorder. In the analysis of the narrative data, the author examined how she, as the interviewer, had affected the mother's narrative reconstruction of her experiences. Developmental psychology has already begun an attempt to explore interactive knowledge.

4. Educational needs and development of
   qualitative methods

Qualitative studies like these are producing new hypothetical models for use in developmental psychology and its related fields. They seemed to have contributed towards improving the status of qualitative research in the field of psychology. In the United States, for instance, the American Psychological Association (APA) recently published a three-volume handbook on research methodologies in psychology (Cooper, 2012). This handbook starts with a chapter on the qualitative approach, followed by several chapters on qualitative methods. In Japan, too, many textbooks on psychological research methods have begun to refer to qualitative inquiry. In 2011, the Japanese Society of Developmental Psychology published a series of handbooks on developmental science, one of which (*Research Methodology and Measurement*) has chapters that emphasized the significance of qualitative research for understanding human development.

Meanwhile, qualitative research has come to be recognized as a part of the undergraduate psychology curriculum. This is shown in a document issued by the Science Council of Japan (2008). It is an official proposal for improvement of the quality of undergraduate psychology education, and included qualitative analysis as a part of "the standard curriculum of undergraduate psychology." It is natural in this context that increasing numbers of students want to learn qualitative methods now. In fact, the membership of the Japanese Society of Qualitative Psychology has grown from 200 to 1000 members over the past ten years, and about one-fourth of current members have the status of student membership. They may wish to master a qualitative method as a tool that, like a statistical technique, can be applied to various kinds of data without needing to know the nature of the data. In this situation, more universities and colleges have begun to teach qualitative methods and its concrete procedures in graduate and undergraduate courses.

The KJ method and Grounded Theory (GT) answer the desire to use qualitative methods as a research tool. Both appear more approachable because they are formalized in comparison with other qualitative methods. "KJ" comes from the initials of the Japanese geographer J. Kawakita, who invented this method to sort out diverse kinds of data obtained in fieldwork (Kawakita, 1967). Its main goal is to provide insight into the research topic, not just to analyze data. The procedures partially resemble those of GT. The first phase is card making, in which data are divided into meaning units and written on cards. The second phase is grouping and naming, in which cards are grouped by contents and a name is given to each group. The group is called basic data for abduction, which means "idea creation". In the next phase, connections among groups are examined, depicted with a chart, and described. Kawakita Institute Co., Ltd., has registered the trademark of the KJ method and provides strict oversight of the process. Without formal education from this institute, the method cannot be used formally. However, the procedure has frequently been used in the teaching of qualitative research in Japan.

GT is a bottom-up method for building a theory grounded on data that was originally proposed by the sociologists Glaser & Strauss (1967). Strauss & Corbin (1990) modified this method (now popularly called the Strauss version of GT), which now consists of three phases: open coding, axial coding, and selective coding. In comparison with the KJ method, GT is unique in that it moves continuously between data collection and analysis. In Japan, the nursing researcher Saiki-Craighill, who had learned qualitative methods under Strauss, presented a modified Strauss version (now called the Saiki-Craighill version) in some Japanese textbooks (e.g., 2013). She placed importance on the concepts of "property" and "dimension," and used them as "auxiliary tools" from the beginning of the analysis. Property is a type of viewpoint to analytically recognize an object, whereas dimension is an attribute that appears depending on the viewpoint. For example, the property of "color" has dimensions such as "black," "red," and so on. By using these tools, Saiki-Craighill attempted to make the analytic procedure more accessible to other researchers, and to produce more valid knowledge that has falsifiability.

Recently, the Modified GT approach (M-GTA), which was devised by the sociologist Kinoshita, has become popular among Japanese students who are interested in qualitative research. It is an analytical procedure that he simplified and made easier to use because he had found the Strauss version of GT too complicated (e.g.; Kinoshita, 1999). According to Kinoshita, M-GTA is an empirical analysis method grounded on data, integrating the spirit of Glaser & Strauss' original version with Glaser's later version. He created several analytical concepts, such as "the focus person" to guide analysis of the data from that person's viewpoint. Not relying on conceptual tools such as coding or properties, M-GTA thus limits the scope of interpretation and generates concepts from the data in more direct ways. The analyst finds meaning units based on his or her research questions without slicing data, and advances from the generation of concepts and discovery of categories to model construction. This apparently simple procedure has attracted many students in various fields of social science and contributed to the spread of qualitative research in Japan. However, M-GTA is not a magic wand that makes every aspect of GT "user-friendly"; indeed, one should not forget that it has its own difficulties and requires time and energy to master.

5. A NEW FRONTIER OF QUALITATIVE RESEARCH IN JAPAN

With such methodological developments in Japan, education in qualitative research seems to be expanding by degrees; however, we cannot be satisfied with just the direction of this expansion. The KJ method and GT are only part of the available qualitative methods. In the APA handbook on psychological methods for instance, it is possible to find "sequence analyses," such as narrative analysis, discourse analysis, and conversation analysis, as well as other methods that share characteristics with GT, such as interpretive hermeneutic analysis (Cooper, 2012). It is certain that GT, and possibly the KJ method as well, has easily become accepted in the discipline of psychology because it has formal analytical steps that appear similar to those in statistical procedures. Certainly, these methods contribute to the expansion of qualitative research in psychology. However, I am concerned that psychology researchers do not have many options when they seek to learn qualitative methods.

The currently limited selection of qualitative research methods may lead to limited views by researchers. Endo (2007) suggested that the quantitative method might restrain the direction of knowledge production in the field of human development, but the same criticism can be directed toward the qualitative methodology. As Nochi (2011b) pointed out, "category analyses," including the KJ method and GT, assume the existence of a stable "reality" behind the data, overlooking the construction of data through interactions at the level of data collection. The strength of qualitative research is that it can go beyond traditional views of the world or people and build a new hypothesis from a renewed viewpoint. Without an understanding of the qualitative methodology other than the KJ method or GT, such as narrative analysis and discourse analysis, the formation of new hypotheses by researchers may become compromised.

For qualitative research, it is essential to select an appropriate method for the research question from a wide variety of options and then develop it to meet the characteristics of the data and other conditions under which the research is conducted.

In keeping with Willig's (2012) comparison of qualitative research to an adventure, it is essentially a movement to find uncultivated ground and push its way through, rather than to conserve already cultivated territory. In order to keep standing on the frontier of developmental psychology, qualitative research should not forget its "frontier spirit," which was necessary for qualitative psychologist to have a few decades ago when academia did not demonstrate much acceptance. This is true not just for constructing a hypothesis on reality, but also for devising new research methods. The illustrations of good qualitative research mentioned above, in fact, did not just follow the standard procedures of a brand-name method. Concerning methodology, T. Sato (2009), a Japanese theorist of qualitative research, proposed TEM (Trajectory Equifinality Model) to analyze a life story by breaking it into various trajectories. He does not present it as a standard tool, but one that evolves constantly. These examples maintain the original spirit of qualitative research. Hopefully, qualitative researchers will continue to explore this new frontier of knowledge on the reality of human life and continue to devise methods with which to begin such inquiries.

REFERENCES

Asao, T. (1992). *Miburi kara kotoba e* [From gestures to speech]. Tokyo: Shin'yosha.

Asao, T. (2013). *Firudo ni okeru hattatsuteki kenkyu* [Developmental research in the field]. In Y. Yamada, T. Asao, T. Sato, M. Nochi, K. Akita, K. Yamori (Eds.) *Shitsuteki shinrigaku handobukku* [Handbook of qualitative psychology]. (pp. 223–238). Tokyo: Shin'yosha.

Bogdan, R. C., & Biklen, S. K. (2006). *Qualitative research for education: An introduction to theory and methods* (5th ed.). Boston: Allyn and Bacon.

Cooper, H. (Ed.). (2012). *APA handbook of research methods in psychology.* Volumes 1, 2, 3. Washington, DC: American Psychological Association.

Endo, T. (2007). Intorodakushon: Shitsuteki kenkyu to iu shikoho ni shitashimo [Introduction: Let's become familiar with "the way of thinking" in qualitative research]. In T. Endo & Y. Sakagami (Eds.), *Hajimete no shitsuteki kenkyuho: Shogai hattatsu hen* [Qualitative research methods for beginners: Life-long developmental psychology]. Tokyo: Tokyo-Tosho.

Fujie, Y. (1999). Issei jugyo ni okeru kodomo no hatsuwa sutairu [A qualitative analysis of children's classroom communication styles]. *Hattatsu Shinrigaku Kenkyu* [Japanese Journal of Developmental Psychology], 10, 125–135.

Giorgi, A. (2009). *The descriptive phenomenological method in psychology: A modified Husserlian approach.* Pittsburgh, PA: Duquesne University Press.

Glaser, B. G., & Strauss, A. L. (1967). *The discovery of grounded theory: Strategies for qualitative research.* Chicago: Aldine Publishing Company.

Gubrium, J., & Holstein, J. (2009). *Analyzing narrative reality.* Los Angeles: Sage.

Imao, M. (2009). Shishunki/seinenki kara seijinki ni okeru mansei-shikkan kanja no moningu waku no purosesu [The process of mourning in chronic illnesses between early adolescence to early adulthood]. *Hattatsu Shinrigaku Kenkyu* [Japanese Journal of Developmental Psychology], 20, 211–223.

Japanese Society of Developmental Psychology (Ed.) (2011). *Hattatsu kagaku handobukku 2: Kenkyuho to shakudo* [Handbook of developmental science 2: Research methods and scales]. Tokyo: Shin'yosha.

Kato, H. (1988). Qualitative sociology in Japan. *Qualitative Sociology*, 11 (1-2), 55–62.

Kawakita, J. (1967). *Hasso-ho* [A method of idea creation]. Tokyo: Chuo-koron-sha

Kinoshita, Y. (1999). *Guraundeddo seori apurochi* [Grounded theory approach]. Tokyo: Kobundo.

Matsumoto, M. (2009). Koshinretsu kogairetsu-sha no jiko no imizuke no tokucho [Characteristics of meaning of self among people with cleft lip and/or palate]. *Hattatsu Shinrigaku Kenkyu* [Japanese Journal of Developmental Psychology], 20, 234–242.

Matsushima, H. (2002). Ikani hiko-shohnen wa mondai no aru jinbutsu to naru no ka?: Aru kosei-hogo-shisetsu de no sosharu-sukiru-toreningu ni okeru gengoteki sogo koi [How delinquent youths in a juvenile group home come to be seen as troublesome people: A study on the verbal interactions between the staff and delinquents in social skills training sessions. *Shitsuteki Shinrigaku Kenkyu* [Qualitative Research in Psychology], 1, 17-35.

Minoura, Y. (1984). *Kodomo no ibunka-taiken* [Cross-cultural experience among children]. Tokyo: Shisaku sha.

Minoura, Y. (1999). *Firudowaku no giho to jissai* [Techniques and practices of fieldwork]. Kyoto: Minerva shobo.

Muto, T, (2013). *Jissen shiko no shitsuteki kenkyu no naritachi* [Origin of qualitative research oriented to the practice]. In Y. Yamada, T. Asao, T. Sato, M. Nochi, K. Akita,

K. Yamori (Eds.) *Shitsuteki shinrigaku handobukku* [Handbook of qualitative psychology]. (pp. 239–258). Tokyo: Shin'yosha.

Nochi, M. (2006). Aru shitsugo-sho kanja ni okeru "ba no imi" no hensen [Changing interpretations of place by an individual with aphasia]. *Shitsuteki Shinrigaku Kenkyu* [Qualitative Research in Psychology], 5, 48-69.

Nochi, M. (2011a). *Hattatsu no shitsuteki kenkyuho to jitsurei* [Qualitative research on human development and demonstrations]. In Japanese Society of Developmental Psychology (Ed.), *Hattatsu kagaku handobukku 2: Kenkyuho to shakudo* [Handbook of developmental science 2: Research methods and scales]. (pp. 73–83). Tokyo: Shin'yosha.

Nochi, M. (2011b). *Shitsuteki kenkyuho* [Qualitative research methods]. Tokyo: Tokyo Daigaku Shuppan kai.

Nochi, M. (2013). *Rinsho shinrigaku ni okeru shitsuteki-kenkyu no imi to kanosei* [Significance and potentials of qualitative research in clinical psychology]. *Rinsho Shinrigaku* [Japanese Journal of Clinical Psychology], 13, 352-355.

Rogoff, B. (2003). *The cultural nature of human development*. Oxford: Oxford University Press.

Saiki-Craighill, S. (2013). *Shitsuteki kenkyuho zeminaru* [Seminar on the qualitative research method], second edition. Tokyo: Igaku Shoin.

Sakagami, Y. (2002). Hoko-kaishiki ni okeru boshi no kattoteki yaritori no hattatsuteki henka [Developmental changes in conflicts between a mother and a toddler]. *Hattatsu Shinrigaku Kenkyu* [Japanese Journal of Developmental Psychology], 13, 3, 261-273.

Sato, I. (1984). *Bosozoku no esunogurafi* [Ethnography on motorcycle gangs]. Tokyo: Shin'yosha.

Sato, I. (1992). *Firudo-waku* [Fieldwork]. Tokyo: Shin'yosha.

Sato, T. (2009). *TEM de hajimeru shitsuteki kenkyu* [Qualitative research that starts with TEM]. Tokyo: Seishin Shobo.

Science Council of Japan. (2008). *Gakushi-katei ni okeru shinrigaku kyoiku no shitsuteki kojo to kyaria pasu no kakuritsu ni mukete* [A proposal for the quality improvement of the undergraduate psychology education and for the establishment of career paths]. Retrieved from http://www.scj.go.jp/ja/info/kohyo/pdf/kohyo-20-t55-2.pdf

Shoji, R. (2009). *Jizokuteki kankei ni okeru katto e no imizuke no henka* [The meaning-making process in repeated marital conflicts among newlywed couples]. *Hattatsu Shinrigaku Kenkyu* [Japanese Journal of Developmental Psychology], 20, 299–310.

Shojima, S. (2010). Seibetsu no henko o nozomu wagako kara kamingu-auto o uketa hahaoya ni yoru keiken no katarinaoshi [A mother's retelling of experiences about her child's desire to live as another gender]. *Hattatsu Shinrigaku Kenkyu* [Japanese Journal of Developmental Psychology], 21, 83–94.

Sigelman, C. K. (1999). *Life-span human development* (3rd ed.). Pacific Grove, CA: Brooks/Cole.

Strauss, A. & Corbin, J. (1990). *Basics of qualitative research: Techniques and procedures for developing grounded theory.* Thousand Oaks, CA: Sage.

Suzuki, K. (2000). Qualitative research in Japan. *Forum: Qualitative Social Research* [On-line serial], 1(1). Article 5. Retrieved from http://www.qualitative-research. net/index.php/fqs/article/view/1115

Taniguchi, A. (2004). *Byoin nai gakkyu ni okeru kyoiku jissen ni kansuru esunogurafikku risachi* [The meaning of teacher practices: An ethnographic study at an in-hospital school). *Hattatsu Shinrigaku Kenkyu* [Japanese Journal of Developmental Psychology] 15, 172–182.

Tokuda, H. (2004). Narachivu kara toraeru kosodate-ki josei no imizuke [A narrative analysis of the meaning of childcare for women raising young children]. *Hattatsu Shinrigaku Kenkyu* [Japanese Journal of Developmental Psychology], 15, 13–26.

Valsiner, J. (2007). *Culture in minds and societies: Foundations of cultural psychology.* New Delhi: Sage.

Willig, C. (2012). *Introducing qualitative research in psychology* (3rd ed.). Berkshire, UK: Open University Press.

Yamada, Y. (1987). *Kotoba no mae no kotoba* [The Language before language]. Tokyo: Shin'yosha.

Yamada, Y. (2013). *Shitsuteki shinrigaku no rekishi* [A history of qualitative psychology]. In Y. Yamada, T. Asao, T. Sato, M. Nochi, K. Akita, K. Yamori (Eds.) *Shitsuteki shinrigaku handobukku* [Handbook of qualitative psychology]. (pp. 24–53). Tokyo: Shin'yosha.

Developmental Psychology in Japan:
Developmental Follow-up Studies

—

Masumi Sugawara, Satoko Matsumoto,
and Atsushi Sakai

Since the 1920s, several pioneering longitudinal studies on human development have been started overseas, mainly in the United States (e.g., Terman, 1925; Beyley, 1956; Kagan & Moss, 1962; Block, 1971; Werner & Smith, 1982). Today, many developed countries are conducting large-scale national longitudinal surveys. In Japan, birth-cohort studies in the field of developmental psychology began in the 1960s. In this chapter, we will describe the longitudinal studies that have been carried out in Japan, mainly focusing on those starting from infancy.

1. LONGITUDINAL STUDIES IN JAPAN: THE BEGINNING (1960–1980)

The first full-fledged developmental follow-up study in Japan was launched in 1966 by a group led by Kazuo Miyake (Miyake, 1991; Miyake & Takahashi,2009) at Hokkaido University. Miyake studied at Harvard University in the early 1960s where he was exposed to Kagan's longitudinal study (Kagan & Moss, 1962). After returning to Japan, Miyake started several birth cohort studies Table 1). In all of these, the main methodology used was natural observation of mother-child interactions. In the first study, 50 newborns were followed up to third grade to examine the relationship between temporal changes in mother-child interactions and the children's temperament and intellectual development. They found that maternal caregiving, infant temperament manageability, and intellectual development during infancy and childhood affected each other. In 1981, a second cohort study that followed children up to five years old was launched to examine the antecedents of attachment development and its effects on subsequent development. The results of these studies have been reported in several articles as cross-cultural comparative studies (Miyake, Chen & Campos, 1985; Rothbaum, Weisz, Pott, Miyake & Morelli, 2000).

A group led by Kosawa (1979; 1981) conducted a developmental follow-up study on mother-child interaction in the early 1970s. In this study, 100 pairs of mothers and their children were followed from birth to three years old (TableX-1), and the relationship between newborn behavioral characteristics and subsequent mother-child interaction was examined. Although not a birth cohort study, a United States–Japan comparative study was conducted in the 1970s to examine the cross-cultural validity of the Bernstein hypothesis (Bernstein, 1960), which posited a relationship between a disparity in the social class of the home language and a child's intellectual development (Azuma, Kashiwagi, & Hess, 1981). The results of three measurements prior to elementary school entry generally supported the Bernstein hypothesis in both countries. In addition, follow-up studies during childhood were conducted (Kashiwagi et al., 1984). Among those that followed subjects for three years before school entry, intellectual development of 44 of 58 children from Japan and 47 of 66 children from the U.S. was measured again at 11 years of age. Only Japanese samples, but not U.S. samples, showed long-term effects of the home environment during infancy, indicating a difference in results between Japan and the United States.

As mentioned above, full-scale developmental follow-up studies began in the 1960s in Japan. Conducting these kinds of longitudinal studies is relatively costly as it involves recruiting and maintaining longitudinal samples and measuring various developmental variables of mothers and children by intensive natural observation. In Japan, the scale of grants for psychological research is relatively small compared to that of the natural sciences. In addition, because the funding period is quite short (three–five years maximum), it is not suitable for conducting longitudinal developmental studies, which require maintaining a research organization for long periods of time. Therefore, it was difficult for Japanese researchers to follow children over long periods of time and/or use large samples as researchers conducting longitudinal studies in other countries do.

2. VARIOUS LONG-TERM LONGITUDINAL STUDIES (1980S TO PRESENT)

The research interests of early longitudinal studies were centered on mother-infant interactions. In the 1980s, the topic of study and age bracket chosen diversified; early studies focused on infancy, but in the 1980s, many longitudinal studies were started when subjects were older in order to investigate adolescence and adulthood. We will summarize these studies by decade.

1980s. In the 1980s, two longitudinal birth cohort studies (starting from pregnancy) were begun, and these were ongoing in 2014. In 1984, a group led by Kitamura and Sugawara (Kitamura et al., 1996; Sugawara et al., 1999a, 1999b, 1999c; Sugawara, 2005) started a longitudinal study at Kawasaki City, Kanagawa Prefecture, by registering 1,320 expectant mothers as a cohort-sample. This project focuses on maternal depression during pregnancy and post-partum and examines the long-term effects on children (Table 1). Until now, 16 assessments have been implemented: three in pregnancy and 13 after childbirth. At the assessment conducted in 2014, the age of the target child was 27. In the early stages of this study, the main focus was on mother/child mental health, but after 1996 fathers were also included in this study as developmental psychologists began to study family relationships. Since then, this study has continued examining the relationship between the mental health of family members and child development from a developmental, psychopathological perspective (Cummings et al., 2002).

In 1998, a still-ongoing multi-cohort study was initiated by a group led by Yamagata (Table 1). All expectant mothers (and eventually their babies) living in the city of Enzan (now Koshu) in Yamanashi prefecture were registered as participants in this study (on average, 200–250 babies are born annually in this city). The focus of this study was physical development, and assessments were conducted during public health checkups, when the target child was 18 months, three, and five years old. By making use of elementary and middle school health records, follow-up assessments have been performed, and an investigation into childhood obesity has been published (Suzuki et al., 2009). In 1986, a nationwide panel study of more than 2,000 people over 60 years of age was begun (Tokyo Metropolitan Institute of Gerontology). In this study, assessments have been conducted every three years, and eight assessments were completed by 2012.

1990s. In late 1990s, a developmental behavioral genetic study focusing on the relative effect of genetics and environmental factors was undertaken. Ando and colleagues started a longitudinal study of adolescent and adult twins (aged 15 through 30; Ando et al., 2013). During 1998 to 2011, they registered a total of 2,246 twin pairs, examining various aspects of development (including biology, cognition, social attitude, personality, mental health, and parenting) and have published many journal articles. In 1999, Sugawara and colleagues began a longitudinal study of families raising twins (0 to 15 years old; Table 1). Since then, assessments administered every two years have investigated the relationships between personality, problem behaviors, mental health, socio-emotional development, and the child-rearing environment using a developmental behavioral genetic approach.

2000s. Inspired by studies conducted in Western countries in the late twentieth century, such as the Dunedin Multidisciplinary Health & Development Study (New Zealand) and the NICHD Study of Early Child Care (United States), many longitudinal studies on child development were started in Japan during the 2000s. In 2003, the above-mentioned Ando group (Keio University), launched a birth cohort study of twins living in the Tokyo metropolitan area. The follow-up assessments from birth to first grade are now completed (Table 1). Also in 2003, NHK (Japan Broadcasting Corporation) and university researchers started a longitudinal follow-up study on media usage (television, video/DVD, videogames) and child development. This project was designed to follow children from 0 to 12 years old. Over 1,000 households living in the city of Kawasaki, Kanagawa prefecture, were registered in this study, and they participated in various types of research. For example, at the same time each year, they are asked to fill out a one-week media diary to measure the target child's media usage. Questionnaires and experiments of target children and parents are also administered to measure language development, academic achievement and socio-emotional development (Sugawara et al., 2015). A summary of the findings during the preschool period has been published as an interim report (NHK, 2011) and the twelfth assessment was completed in March 2014. In 2003, a group at Ochanomizu University started a longitudinal study to follow 700 children from 0 years old to sixth grade. This is an ongoing study and examines how aspects of the child-rearing environment, such as the family's socio-economic status, parenting, and quality of out-of-home childcare, affect child development through the parent/child quality of life (Table 1). A research group at Hamamatsu University School of Medicine is also conducting a longitudinal birth cohort study to investigate the physical and mental development of children (Table 1). This project enrolled a sample from children born in the city of Hamamatsu, Shizuoka prefecture, between 2007 and 2011. A total of 1,200 children are participating this project from 0 years old.

2010. In 2010, Sakai and colleagues started a longitudinal study examining the effects of the human capital network (the network among siblings, friends, families, neighborhoods, and schools) on children's social development by expanding the traditional home-caring model (Table 1). To date, 580 (including twins) one- to three-year-olds have been registered and registration is ongoing. In 2012, a large-scale longitudinal study of adolescence was undertaken by Hasegawa (Tokyo Teen Cohort Study). The study aims to register as many as 4,500 mothers and their nine- to 10-year-old children living in three areas of Tokyo. Follow-up assessments are planned through adulthood, investigating health and development during and after the period of secondary sexual development. This project is a collaborative project with the Millennium Cohort (United Kingdom), and comparative studies between the two countries are also planned.

The above-mentioned studies are all multi-disciplinary, developmental, follow-up studies, incorporating multiple fields related to human development, such as developmental psychology, medicine, and behavioral genetics. Some of the projects incorporate biological assessments

Table 1 Longitudinal birth-cohort studies from infancy in Japan

Researcher / Project	Implementation	Area	Sample: N (age*)	Topic	Main measurement / methods / Web-site
			Pioneering		
Miyake, K. (1991)	1966–1977	Hokkaido	50 (0–9)	mother-child interaction	RITQ, WISC / natural observation
Miyake, K. (1991)	1980–1982	Hokkaido	66 (0–5)	mother-child interaction	SSP / natural & lab observation
Kosawa, Y. (1981)	1976–1982	Tokyo	100 (0–3)	mother-child interaction	NBAS / natural observation
			Ongoing		
Yamagata, Z. (1999) / "Project Koshu"	1988–	Yamanashi	200–250/year (pregnancy – 5)	maternal and child health	physical growth / questionnaire / http://www.med.yamanashi.ac.jp/medicine/birthcohort/study/summary/koshuProject.html.
Sugawara. M., et al. (1999a, b) / "Kawasaki Longitudinal Study"	1984–	Kanagawa	1,320 (pregnancy–)	family mental health	CBCL, CAS / questionnaire, diagnostic interview
Sugawara. M. (2000, 2008) / "Twin Multi-cohort Project"	1999–	Nationwide (Twin Mothers Club)	2,135 pairs (registration age range = 0–15)	twin study (personality & psychopathological development)	Ps-TCI & JTCI, CBCL, CSDS / questionnaire
Sugawara. M. (2014) / "Better Environment for Children Project"	2003–	Kanagawa	918 (0–)	influence of the home and child-care/school environment	KINDL, SDQ, CHAOS,ORCE/ questionnaire, observation
NHK Broadcasting Culture Research Institute (2011) / "Better Broadcasting for Children Project"	2003–	Kanagawa	1,360 (0–11)	influence of screen media	media-use diary, MCDI SDQ / questionnaire, on-site assessment / http://www.nhk.or.jp/bunken/english/reports/pdf/report_11040102.pdf

				National Survey	
Ando, J., et al. (2013) / "Tokyo Twin Cohort Project"	2004–	Tokyo metropolitan area	1,760 pairs (0–)	twin study (physical and mental development)	IBQ-R, CBQ, BIS/BAS, SDQ, PSI / questionnaire, lab & home observation http://kotrec.keio.ac.jp/.
Hamamatsu University School of Medicine Research Center for Child Mental Development / "Hamamatsu Birth Cohort for Mothers and Children"	2007–	Shizuoka	1,200 (0–4)	physical and neurological development	screening for ASD, postpartum depression / questionnaire, biological assessment / http://rccmd.org/
Sakai, A., et al. (2012)	2008–	Tokyo, Kumamoto, Nagano, Yamanashi and other prefectures	580 (registration age range = 1–3)	sibling relation (incl. twin pairs)	SCBE, SIDE, Social Capital Scale / questionnaire, lab & home observation
Neuroscience and Education (Ministry of Education, Culture, Sports, Science and Technology)	2004–2008	Osaka, Tottori, Shimane	393 (registration age range 0–8)	Brain science and socio-emotional development	/questionnaire, lab observation, neurological assessment / http://childstudy.jp/studies/studies2.html
The Japan Environment and Children's Study (JECS) Ministry of the Environment	2010–	Nationwide	103,104 (pregnancy–)	Evaluation the impact of various environmental factors on children's health and development	/questionnaire, biological assessment/ http://www.env.go.jp/en/chemi/hs/jecs/
The Longitudinal Survey of Babies in the 21st Century The Ministry of Health, Labour and Welfare	2001–	Nationwide	23,423 (2001-birth, 0–), 38,554 (2010-birth, 0–)	Demographic feature and child development (parental labor, child-care use, attitude toward child-rearing, health, child/family life)	/questionnaire / http://www.mhlw.go.jp/english/database/db-hw/vs03.html (English Page)

Note   RITQ = Revised Infant Temperament Questionnaire, WISC = Wechsler Intelligence Scale for Children, SSP=Strange Situation Procedure, NBAS=Neonatal Behavioral Assessment Scale, CBCL= Child Behavior Checklist, CAS= Child Assessment Scale, psTCI = Preschool Temperament and Character Inventory, JTCI = Junior Temperament and Character Inventory, CSDS = Child Self-rating depression Scale, KINDL=Questionnaire for assessing Health-Related Quality of Life in children and adolescents, SDQ = Strengths and Difficulties Questionnaire, ORCE = Observational Record of the Caregiving Environment, MCDI = MacArthur Communicative Development Inventories, IBQ-R = Infant Behavior Questionnaire-Revised, CBQ = Children's Behavior Questionnaire, BIS/BAS = Behavioral Inhibition and Activation Systems Scales, PSI = Parenting Stress Inventory, SCBE = Social Competence and Behavior Evaluation, SIDE = Sibling Inventory of Differential Experience such as genetic analysis and examine brain functioning. Most of the studies are currently limited to a specific geographical area, but with the advancement of longitudinal data analysis methodology, it will be possible to conduct multivariate causal analyses, and more multi-dimensional research result regarding human development is expected.

3. LAUNCHING A LARGE-SCALE NATIONAL PROJECT (2000–)

Moving into the twenty-first century, the Ministry of Health, Labour and Welfare (MHLW), the Ministry of Education, Culture, Sports, Science and Technology (MEXT), and the Ministry of the Environment (MOE) have independently announced the launch of a national large-scale, developmental, follow-up research project (Table 1). In 2001, MHLW started a big project called the "Longitudinal Survey in the Twenty-first Century." This project comprises three ongoing panel studies: the "Longitudinal Survey of Newborns in the Twenty-first Century," "Longitudinal Survey of Adults in the 21st Century," and "Longitudinal Survey of Middle-aged and Elderly Persons." The aim of this project is to obtain the information needed for policy making in view of the falling birth rate and aging population in Japan. To achieve this goal, the project is designed to measure basic information on demographics relevant to the life course. For the "Longitudinal Survey of Newborns in the Twenty-first Century," the sample consists of a birth cohort of 23,423 children born throughout Japan in 2001. Annual assessments have been conducted, the most recent at age 11. Another birth cohort has also been launched with a participant pool of 38,554 children born in 2010.

In 2011, the MOE launched a national epidemiological birth cohort study, the "Japan Environment and Children's Study" (JECS), which involves 100,000 children throughout Japan. This study, which was initiated following the "Miami Declaration on Children's Environmental Health" and adopted at the G8 Environment Ministers' Meeting in 1997, is a part of an international cooperative study (e.g., National Children's Study (United States) and ELFE cohort (France) and aims to evaluate the effects of toxic chemicals in the environment including water and soil.

Children will be followed from 0 to 13 years old, and during the first registration, which closed in March, 2014, 103,104 children were registered. The National Center for this project was established in the National Institute for Environmental Studies (NIES), and data collection will be conducted at 15 regional centers throughout Japan, most of them in medical universities. Six Physical health indices are measured: physical development, congenital abnormalities, sexual differentiation disorders, developmental disorders, immune system deficiencies, and metabolism/endocrine system disorders. Questionnaires on the child's environment; collection of blood, urine, and hair samples from mother and child; children's medical records (including height, weight); medical check-ups; and psychiatric interviews are all scheduled.

Since 2001, MEXT has been preparing for the launch of a large-scale longitudinal cohort study on children's social development. As a part of this preparation, an exploratory cohort study was carried out from 2004 through 2005 to develop the research methodology. This project, titled "Investigation of factors influencing children's cognitive and behavioral development in Japan," conducted an exploratory cohort study with a sample of 0- to 8-year-old children in three prefectures (Osaka, Mie, and Tottori). The aim of the large-scale project is to investigate the processes and factors that influence language and socio-emotional development using neuroscientific methodology. More than ten years have been spent on the preparatory study, but the long-term main survey has not yet been scheduled.

We summarized three national follow-up studies launched in the twenty-first century. Projects led by MHLW and MOE are building large-scale longitudinal databases, and thus progress towards academically and politically-informative analyses is expected. However, each project is based on a different discipline: demography (MHLW), medicine (MOE), and neuroscience (MEXT), and none fully incorporate developmental psychology theories, hypotheses, and methodology, which are necessary to scientifically clarify the developmental process and the effective mechanism(s) of environmental factors. The challenge for the future is to enhance the contribution of developmental psychology to each project.

4. FUTURE DIRECTIONS

In this chapter, we summarized Japanese developmental cohort studies from the 1960s to the present. We would like to close by pointing out some future challenges of longitudinal studies. As we mentioned in section 3, registration on a very large scale (more than 100,000 children) for longitudinal studies has already been completed in Japan, and this has necessitated the construction of a national database on human development. However, these projects do not fully address topics such as attachment, personality development, development of self-consciousness, cognitive development, socio-emotional development, and psychopathological development. Additionally, the number of studies addressing the effects of childcare and school education (early childcare and education, primary/secondary/higher education) on human development is very limited. In order to develop an effective educational system, efforts to encourage longitudinal studies of educational psychology are also necessary. Starting a new large-scale cohort project to study aspects of developmental psychology using appropriate methodologies may be another big challenge.

Generally, cohort studies are very costly, and long-term studies are not easy to replicate. Setting appropriate study topics is as important as thoughtful planning before implementation (sophisticated measurement scales, statistical methodologies, and valid sampling). The influence of out-of-home childcare, intergenerational transmission of poverty, problem behaviors such as delinquency, onset of psychopathology, the effects of parental divorce, abuse, social adjustment of children with mental disorders, adulthood difficulties in entering the workforce (e.g., individuals classified as Not in Education, Employment or Training (NEET), non-regular employment), and successful aging, are some examples of major problems in Japan's society today. We expect more longitudinal projects to be launched to examine the causal relations between the above-mentioned problems and an effective implementation of findings within society.

References

Ando, J., Fujisawa, K.K., Shikishima, C., Hiraishi, K., Nozaki, M., Yamagata, S., et al. (2013). Two cohort and three independent anonymous twin projects at the Keio Twin Research Center (KoTReC). *Twin Research and Human Genetics*, 16(1), 202–216.

Ando, J. (n.d.). Citing Websites. In *Keio Twin Research Center (KoTReC)*. Retrieved August 31, 2014, from http://kotrec.keio.ac.jp/.

Azuma, H., Kashiwagi, K., & Hess, R.D. (1981). *Hahaoya no taido kodo to kodomo no chiteki hattatsu: Nichibei hikaku kenkyu* [The effects of mother's attitude and behavior on the cognitive development of the child: A U.S.-Japan comparison]. Tokyo: Tokyodaigaku Shuppankai.

Bernstein, B. (1960). Language and social class. *British Journal of Sociology*, 11, 271–276.

Beyley, N. (1956). Individual patterns of development. *Child Development*, 27, 45–74.

Block, J. (1971). *Lives through time*. Berkeley: Bancroft Books.

Cummings, E. M., Davies, P. T., & Campbell, S. B. (2002). *Developmental Psychopathology and Family Process: Theory, Research, and Clinical Implications*. New York: Guilford Press

Hamamatsu Birth Cohort for Mothers and Children. (n.d.). Citing Websites. In *Research Center for Child Mental Development (RCCMD)*. Retrieved August 31, 2014, from http://rccmd.org/.

Kagan, J., & Moss, H. A. (1962) *Birth to maturity: A study in psychological development*. New York: Wiley.

Kashiwagi, K., Azuma, H., Miyake, K., Nagano, S., Hess, R. D., & Holloway, S. D. (1984). Japan-US comparative study on early maternal influence upon cognitive development: A follow-up study. *Japanese Psychological Research*, 26, 82–92.

Kitamura, T., Sugawara, M., Sugawara, K. Toda, M.A., & Shima, S. (1996). A Psychosocial study of depression on early pregnancy. *British Journal of Psychiatry*, 168, 732–738.

Kosawa, Y. (1979). *Shinseiji no kotaiteki hannosei* [Individual responsiveness of human neonates]. *Japanese Psychological Review*, 22, 5–27.

Kosawa, Y. (1981). *Hattatsu shoki ni okeru boshi sogosei ni kansuru judanteki kenkyu* [Longitudinal study of early mother-infant interaction]. (Grants-in-Aid for Scientific Research Final research report, Research Project Number: 241005).

Ministry of the Environment. (n.d.). Citing Websites. In *Japan Environment and Children's Study (JECS)*. Retrieved August 31, 2014, from http://www.env.go.jp/en/chemi/hs/jecs/.

Ministry of Education, Culture, Sports, Science and Technology. (n.d.). Citing websites. In *Center for the Study of Child Development*. Retrieved August 31, 2014, from http://childstudy.jp/studies/studies2.html.

Ministry of Health, Labour, and Welfare. (n.d.). Citing Websites. In *Longitudinal survey of newborns in the 21st century*. Retrieved August 31, 2014, from http://www.mhlw.go.jp/english/database/db-hw/vso3.html.

Miyake, K., & Takahashi, K. (2009). *Judan kenkyu no chosen: Hattatsu wo rikai suru tame ni* [Challenge of longitudinal studies: Towards an understanding of development]. Tokyo. Kaneko Shobo.

Miyake, K. (Ed.). (1991). *Nyuyoji no jinkaku keisei to boshi kankei* [Early temperament development and mother-infant interaction]. Tokyo: Todai Shuppanai.

Miyake, K., Chen, S.J., & Campos, J.J. (1985). Infant temperament, mother's mode of interaction, and attachment in Japan: an interim report. *Monographs of the Society for Research in Child Development*, 50 (No. 1/2), 276–297.

NHK Broadcasting Culture Research Institute, Better Broadcasting for Children Project. (2011). Television and Japanese Children: a longitudinal study from zero to twelve: Interim report from zero to five. Retrieved from http://www.nhk.or.jp/bunken/english/reports/pdf/report_11040102.pdf

Project Koshu. (n.d.). Citing Websites. In *Center for Birth Cohort Studies* (*CBCS*). Retrieved August 31, 2014, from http://www.med.yamanashi.ac.jp/medicine/birthcohort/study/summary/koshuProject.html.

Rothbaum. F., Weisz, J., Pott, M., Miyake, K., & Morelli, G. (2000). Attachment and culture. Security in the United States and Japan. *American Psychologist*, 55, 1093–1104.

Sakai, A., Maeshiro, K., Maekawa, H., Norisada, Y., Kaminaga, M., Umezaki, T., Tanaka, Y., & Takahashi, E. (2012, November). *The longitudinal study of social development from infancy to early adolescence (1): The relations among mother's social network for childrearing, parenting behavior, and children's problem behavior.* Poster presented at the meeting of the Japanese association of educational psychology, Okinawa, Japan.

Sugawara, M. (2000, July). *Developmental psychopathology: A behavioral genetic approach.* Poster presented at the meeting of the 10th International Congress of Twin Studies, London, UK.

Sugawara, M. (2005). Maternal employment and child development in Japan: A twelve-year longitudinal study. In D. W. Shwalb, J. Nakazawa & B. J. Schwalb (Eds.), *Applied Developmental Psychology: Theory, Practice, and Research from Japan* (pp. 225–240). Charlotte, NC: Information Age Publishing.

Sugawara, M. (2008, July). *Development of problem behaviors among Japanese children: A behavioral genetic approach.* Poster presented at the meeting of the XXIX International Congress Psychology, Berlin, Germany.

Sugawara, M. (2014). Hinkon to kodomo no QOL [Poverty and Children's QOL]. In N. Hiraki, K. Inagaki, M. Kawai, K. Saito, K. Takahashi & Y. Yama (Eds.), Jido shinrigaku no shinpo (pp. 222-241). Tokyo, Kaneko shobo.

Sugawara, M., Kitamura, T., Toda, M.A., & Shima, S. (1999a). Longitudinal relationship between maternal depression and infant temperament in a Japanese population. *Journal of Clinical Psychology*, 55, 869–880.

Sugawara, M., Kitamura, T., Toda, M.A., Shima, S., Sato, T., & Mukai, T. (1999b). *Kodomo no mondai kodo no hattatsu: Externalizing-na mondai keiko ni Kansuru seigo 11-nenkan no judan kenkyu kara* [Development of problem behavior: A longitudinal study of externalizing problems from infancy to middle-childhood]. *The Japanese Journal of Developmental Psychology*, 10, 32–45.

Sugawara, M., Mukai, T., Kitamura, T., Toda., M.A., Shima, S., Tomoda, A., et al. (1999c). Psychiatric disorders among Japanese children. *Journal of American Academy of Child and Adolescent Psychiatry*, 38, 444–452.

Sugawara, M., Matsumoto, S., Murohashi, H., Sakai, A., Isshiki, N. (2015). Trajectories of early television contact in Japan: Relationship with preschoolers' externalizing problems. *Journal of Children and Media*, 9, 453–471. DOI:10.1080/17482798.2015.1089298.

Suzuki, K., Ando, D., Sato, M., Tanaka, T., Kondo, N., & Yamagata, Z. (2009). Association between maternal smoking during pregnancy and childhood obesity persists up to 9–10 years of age. *Journal of Epidemiology*, 19(3); 136–142.

Terman, L.M. (1925). *Genetic studies of genius. Mental and physical traits of a thousand gifted children*. Palo Alto: Stanford University Press.

Tokyo Metropolitan Institute of Gerontology. (n.d.). Citing Websites. In *Zenkoku Koureisha Panel Chousa (JAHEAD)* [Panel study on national sample of Japanese older adults]. Retrieved August 31, 2014, from http://www2.tmig.or.jp/jahead/researcher/member.html.

Werner, E., & Smith, R. S. (1982) *Vulnerable but invincible: A longitudinal study of resilient children and youth*. New York: McGraw Hill.

Yamagata, Z. (1999) Shoni no hoken ikuji ni kansuru joho no shushu to sono riyo 1: Hoken senta de no joho shushu to sono riyo: Enzan-shi Boshi Hoken Chosa 10-nen no ayumi kara [Collection of information on health and childcare of infants and utilization 1. Collection of information in health centers and utilization: From 10 years of progress in the maternal and child health study in the city of Enzan]. *Japanese Journal of Pediatric Medicine*, 31(2), 242–244.

2 Frontiers of
Developmental Psychology in Japan

Cerebral Lateralization of Speech Processing Assessed with Near Infrared Spectroscopy: Typical and Atypical Development

Yasuyo Minagawa and Sho Tsuji

Cognitive neuroscience techniques are increasingly popular in the field of developmental psychology. They now bridge different levels of evidence between infants' and children's brains and their behavior. One of the driving forces behind this trend is innovation in neuro-imaging methodologies including functional magnetic resonance imaging (fMRI), diffusion tensor imaging (DTI), and near-infrared spectroscopy (NIRS). Among these, NIRS provides a unique method for examining the infant brain by measuring changes in the concentrations of oxygenated and deoxygenated hemoglobin (Minagawa-Kawai, Mori, Hedben, & Dupoux, 2008; Minagawa-Kawai, Naoi, & Kojima, 2009b for the general principles of NIRS and its technical advantages and limitations). Some advantages of NIRS for assessing infants include its resistance to motion artifacts, innocuousness, and noise-free instrumentation, not to mention its non-invasiveness. These advantages make NIRS an ideal tool for performing various types of experiments, including auditory experiments as well as "live" experiments examining such topics as social interaction or motor tasks. The introduction of multi-channel NIRS in the early 1990s led to the development of the technique for measuring human cognitive functions sometimes referred to as functional NIRS (fNIRS) (e.g., Villringer, Planck, Hock, Schleinkofer, & Dirnagl, 1993). Since then, more than 80 papers have been published on the neurocognitive functions of the infant brain (cf. online database of infant fNIRS studies (DBIfNIRS, https://sites.google.com/site/dbifnirs/); Cristià et al., 2013). Among those papers, about 70 percent (based on DBIfNIRS as of January 2014) are from Japanese institutions, suggesting Japanese researchers play a leading role in this field of study. By presenting part of this work by Japanese researchers, the present chapter reviews some of the discoveries made so far in this expanding field. We highlight in particular the study of cerebral lateralization during speech processing. Based on previous studies of cerebral responses to speech in infants, we propose a model of functional cerebral lateralization in speech processing. We further review two NIRS studies on atypical development and attempt to integrate them into the framework of this model.

---

1. ACQUISITION OF SPOKEN LANGUAGE IN THE INFANT BRAIN:
   FUNCTIONAL CEREBRAL LATERALIZATION

Typically, adult brain activation during language processing is lateralized to the left hemisphere. The perception of phonemes (vowels and consonants), which are the basic units of the sound system of a language, is lateralized to the left auditory areas, while the processing of prosodic functions like intonation is mostly lateralized to the right auditory areas (e.g., Zatorre, Evans, Meyer, & Gjedde, 1992; Furuya & Mori, 2003). A special case where prosody is processed in a left-dominant way is lexical prosody, which serves the function of distinguishing between word meanings (i.e., lexical tone in Mandarin Chinese or lexical pitch accent in Japanese). In the following, we will look at the development of hemispheric specialization for language processing in infancy.

Half a century ago, Lenneberg (1967) suggested that both brain hemispheres possess the same potential to process language early after birth, based on research on children with brain injury. Since then, many researchers have investigated the development of hemispheric lateralization with methods like dichotic listening or electroencephalography (EEG). However, probably due to the low sensitivity of the former and the restricted spatial resolution of the latter method, to date no consistent evidence regarding the development of left- and right-dominance has been obtained (Novak, Kurtzberg, Kreuzer, & Vaughan, 1989; Simos & Molfese, 1997). The development of near-infrared spectroscopy (NIRS), a neuroimaging method with relatively high spatial resolution, provides a novel opportunity to investigate functional differences between left and right hemisphere processing and its development. Indeed, recent NIRS research has demonstrated the lateralization of infants' responses to different kinds of stimuli involving phonemes and continuous speech.

An early NIRS experiment on language development showed that newborn infants' brain responses to a continuous speech sample in their native language elicited significant left-dominant activation, while no such strong activation was obtained when the speech sample was played backwards (Peña et al., 2003). This early left-hemisphere advantage seemed consistent with the assumption of an innate system for language processing. However, later research put forward an alternative interpretation, namely that left-dominance could originate from the acoustic characteristics of speech sounds rather than from their linguistic characteristics. In adults, left-dominant or bilateral responses are elicited when they listen to quickly changing sounds (sounds with sudden spectral changes like consonants), while a right-dominant response is elicited when they listen to slowly changing sounds (i.e., prosody or music) (Boemio, Fromm, Braun, & Poeppel, 2005; Zatorre & Belin, 2001). These different acoustic properties present in the speech signal could thus have an impact on infants' lateralization patterns. Infants' left-dominant responses to speech sounds could also be hypothesized to derive from the comparatively fast spectral changes characteristic of vowels and consonants. This suggestion that the physical acoustic signal is the principle cause for functional lateralization is called the signal-driven hypothesis.

Evidence for such signal-driven lateralization has been obtained in neonate NIRS research (Telkemeyer et al., 2009; Minagawa-Kawai et al., 2011b). Infants' responses to continuous speech have also been reported to lead to a bilateral rather than a left-lateralized response (e.g., May, Byers-Heinlein, Gervain, & Werker, 2011; Sato et al., 2012; see Minagawa-Kawai, Cristià, & Dupoux, 2011a for a detailed discussion). These findings provide evidence that the acoustic characteristics of speech sounds influence lateralization, rather than supporting the notion of a specialized, left-lateralized language system that is in place immediately after birth.

However, because continuous speech like that contained in sentences not only includes fast-changing elements like vowels and consonants but also slow-changing prosodic elements, it is difficult to determine from these results which characteristics of the complex speech signal actually lead to left or right dominance. We will therefore review the following infant NIRS research focused on the processing of phoneme contrasts. The acoustic characteristics of these contrasts are well controlled. Thus, the research presented in the following paragraphs potentially provides clearer insights into developing lateralization.

A common method to investigate listeners' responses to sound changes in EEG experiments is the oddball paradigm, in which listeners' responses to deviant sounds in a succession of baseline sounds are detected. A similar method to measure brain responses to phonemic changes has been applied to NIRS. An experiment could, for instance, consist of alternations between 15-second baseline blocks with tokens of /itta/ and 15-second target blocks with random alternations of /itta/, /itte/. If the change in the target blocks is detected, it should lead to an increase in oxygenated hemoglobin and a decrease in deoxygenated hemoglobin concentrations around the auditory cortex in the temporal lobe (Furuya & Mori, 2003). Note that this is a typical hemoglobin response pattern for adults, while infants tend to show various hemodynamic response patterns such as synchronous increases of oxygenated and deoxygenated hemoglobin. As illustrated in Figure 1, adults' temporal lobe responses are indeed left-lateralized in response to the phonemic (vowel) contrast in /itta/,/itte/, but right-lateralized in response to the prosodic (intonational) contrast between /itta/,/itta?/. This result is consistent with previous studies using fMRI and EEG, where left-lateralized responses to native phoneme contrasts have been reported (e.g., Näätänen et al., 1997; Zevin & McCandliss, 2005).

By applying the same method to infants, the developmental lateralization of their responses to phonemic and prosodic contrasts can be investigated. To date, experimental work has assessed infants' brain responses to contrasts involving native and non-native phonemes, lexical pitch accent, and prosody. Figure 2 illustrates the results of a meta-analysis of developmental changes in the lateralization of responses to different types of speech sound contrasts that is based on these previous studies

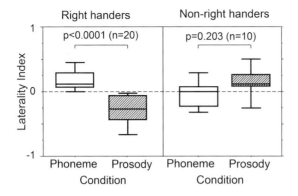

Figure 1 Laterality indices in phonemic and prosodic conditions for right handers and non-right handers
Laterality index (LI) was calculated by the formula LI = (L−R)/(L+R), where L and R are the maximum values of total hemoglobin changes in the left and right auditory area. Data were adopted from Furuya and Mori (2003).

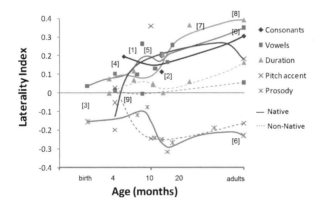

Figure 2 Developmental changes of laterality index in various phonological contrasts
Original data are from [1] Furuya, Mori, Minagawa-Kawai, & Hayashi (2001) and [2] Sato, Sogabe, & Mazuka (2007) for consonants, [3] Arimitsu et al. (2011), [4] Minagawa-Kawai et al. (2009b), [5] Sato et al. (2003), and [6] Furuya & Mori (2003) for vowels, [7] Minagawa-Kawai, Mori, Naoi, & Kojima (2007), and [8] Minagawa-Kawai, Mori, & Sato, (2005) for durational contrast, [1,2] and [9] Sato, Sogabe, & Mazuka (2010) for pitch accent and [3,5,6] for prosody. All studies use the same change-detection paradigm to examine cerebral responses around the auditory area. The laterality index is above zero for left dominance and below zero for right dominance. This is adopted from Minagawa-Kawai et al. (2011a).

(Minagawa-Kawai et al., 2011a). The degree of lateralization is expressed by the laterality index (LI; cf. caption of Figure 1 for a detail). As described in the following, the developmental trajectories differ between different types of speech sound contrasts. First, Figure 2 shows different trajectories for vowels and consonants in the processing of phonemic changes. For native vowel contrasts, brain responses move from a bilateral response to a left-dominant response from six months of age (cf. solid line with square points in Figure 2). Unlike the response to native vowels, non-native vowel contrasts continue to be processed bilaterally (broken line with square points in Figure 2), suggesting that a specialized circuit in the left auditory language area develops only for those (native) vowel contrasts that infants are continuously exposed to. Studies of infants' processing of consonants are less numerous, and extant studies suggest that left-lateralization is already observable at four to five months of age for native consonant contrasts (solid line with diamond-shaped points in Figure 2).

Secondly, focusing on prosodic changes, Figure 2 illustrates that a right-dominant response is observed from birth onwards and continues to be elicited until adulthood (cf. solid and broken lines with star-shaped points in the figure). A different trajectory can be observed for Japanese infants listening to pitch accent contrasts, local prosodic contrasts that can distinguish meaning in their native language. These Japanese lexical pitch accent contrasts, which are characterized by the same slow transitions as prosodic changes (for instance, *ame* (rain) follows the high-low pitch pattern, and *ame* (candy) follows the low-high pitch pattern), elicit a rather right-dominant response early in development. Interestingly, however, this response becomes left-dominant over the course of development (solid line with cross-shaped points in the figure). Such a developmental change is not observed for non-native pitch changes (in this case, non-linguistic pitch changes), the processing of which remains right-lateralized.

What do the results summarized in Figure 2 tell us about the development of brain functions for processing speech sounds? Based on the developmental changes illustrated in the figure and previous brain research, Minagawa-Kawai et al. (2011a) proposed a model of developmental hemispheric lateralization in speech sound processing. This model is explained by the following hypothesis, shown in the schematic illustration in Figure 3. The horizontal and vertical axes resemble those of Figure 2, representing how lateralization changes with age. The model assumes that the acoustic characteristics of speech sounds determine the degree and directionality of lateralization in the early stages of development (signal-driven lateralization). The hemispheric lateralization of different speech sound contrasts in these early stages is assumed to differ depending on their acoustic characteristics. The processing of global prosodic functions, like intonation, with their slow sound changes is right-dominant, while dynamic spectral contrasts like consonants are processed in a left-dominant way. Steady-state spectral contrasts like vowels, which contain less rapid changes than consonants, elicit a bilateral response. The model assumes that infants process speech sounds according to such acoustic characteristics until the age of around five to six months. After infants are exposed to their native language input for more than six months, they acquire native phoneme categories by extracting native rules and categories based on learning biases. These linguistically relevant categories are assumed to be processed increasingly efficiently in the left hemisphere, leading to functionally specialized lateralization for language processing (domain-driven lateralization). Therefore, functional lateralization of non-native phoneme categories does not follow this developmental trajectory.

The hemispheric lateralization model is well suited to illustrate developing lateralization in response to Japanese lexical pitch accent contrasts. Initially and consistent with the signal-driven hypothesis, the acoustic characteristics of pitch accent lead to right-lateralized processing. Since the functional lateralization of pitch accent differs from that of prosody, its processing becomes left-dominant during development (cf. Figure 3). This is probably related to the fact that lexical access requires rapid language processing in the left language area. The same left-dominant response to pitch changes is observed in tone languages, for instance in adult native speakers of Mandarin Chinese or Thai (Gandour et al., 2002). On the other hand, no left-dominance develops in response to intonational contrasts, which do not involve core linguistic characteristics to the same extent as phoneme contrasts, and which do not require rapid processing. (Note, however, that depending on their content and

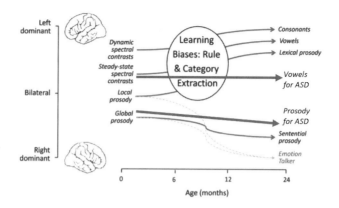

Figure 3 A schematic model of development of hemispheric lateralization
Bold lines indicate the developmental process of ASD children. This figure is a modified version of Figure 2 in Minagawa-Kawai et al. (2011a).

linguistic function, aspects of intonation such as grammatical prosody can elicit left-dominant responses as well.)

Previous research (McNealy, Mazziotta, & Dapretto, 2006) suggests that the above-described rule and category extraction mechanisms are related to left hemispheric language networks in the Broca area, basal ganglia, and areas surrounding the Sylvian fissure. Indeed, NIRS has revealed left-dominant brain responses in neonates' frontal lobes during speech segmentation (the mechanism by which infants are thought to extract phonotactic rules). However, the fact that this response pattern is observed only when newborn infants are presented with examples that follow an ABB pattern, but not when the examples follow an ABA pattern, suggests that their learning mechanisms might not yet be fully developed. By seven months of age, left-dominant responses are elicited during word segmentation and the extraction of phonotactic rules (Minagawa et al., submitted), implying that infants' learning mechanisms might develop together with their brains and be dependent on language input. Future research should investigate when and how these learning mechanisms fall into place.

2. ATYPICAL PATTERN OF FUNCTIONAL CEREBRAL LATERALIZATION: AUTISM SPECTRUM DISORDERS

This section first summarizes two previous NIRS studies that examined speech perception in children with autism spectrum disorder (ASD). We will then explain the results in light of the lateralization model introduced in the previous section. In these two studies, we investigated functional lateralization by presenting phonemic and prosodic contrasts in a change detection paradigm. We used /itta/ vs. /itte/ and /itta/ vs. /itta?/, which have been successfully employed in previous adult and infant studies, as stimuli (cf. Section 1). Because a language deficit including impaired processing of phonemes and prosody is one of the major characteristics of ASD (McCann & Peppe, 2003), we investigated the hemispheric specialization of children's language function at the level of phonetic processing.

The first study compared the brain responses of ASD children and typically developing children (TDC) to the phoneme and prosodic contrasts, particularly focusing on the temporal cortex (see Minagawa-Kawai, Naoi, Kikuchi, Yamamoto, & Kojima, 2009a for details). Auditory evoked responses for thirteen children with ASD (mean age 9.2 years, range 6–11 years) and nine TDC (7.3 years, 5–9 years) were measured by NIRS. As indicated in Figure 4, the laterality index (LI) obtained from the temporal response of ASD children and TDC showed a different tendency. While TDC clearly demonstrated asymmetrical LI for the two conditions, indicating leftward dominance for the phonemic contrast and rightward dominance for the prosodic one, such asymmetry was relatively weak in the ASD group. Although the ASD group showed a similar rightward dominance for the prosodic condition, lateralization for the phonemic contrast was particularly weak, with no leftward tendency. ANOVA supported these tendencies (Minagawa-Kawai et al., 2009a). Behavioral tests were also performed by asking three questions related to phonetic discrimination and awareness of the stimuli just presented after each NIRS session. Behavioral results revealed significantly lower scores in the ASD group for both conditions. These results suggest a weaker or different functional specialization in the temporal areas in children with ASD.

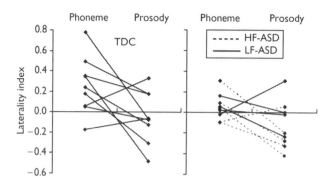

Figure 4 Laterality index (LI) in response to phoneme and prosodic contrasts of TDC and ASD children
ASD children are divided into subgroups of low-functioning ASD and high-functioning ASD. Adopted from Minagawa-Kawai et al. (2009a).

The second study by Naoi et al. (in Minagawa-Kawai et al., 2009b, chapter 3) aimed to examine how behavioral intervention impacts brain plasticity, specifically functional cerebral lateralization in children with ASD. To this end, they performed longitudinal NIRS recordings of five ASD children (mean age 4.2 years, range 2.3–5.4 years). Among them, three children received a regular behavioral intervention based on applied behavior analysis (ABA) by their parent at home. The remaining two children as the control group received non-behavioral treatments through public special education services. NIRS recordings using the phonemic and prosodic contrasts were performed once before the intervention, and three to five times during the one-year intervention period. In general, one-year gains in language and social skills showed larger increases in the ABA group than in the control group, suggesting the effectiveness of ABA treatment. In the NIRS results, we observed longitudinal changes of LI (3 to 5 data points per child) in the five children during one year. These results showed weak lateralization in all five children, particularly for the phonemic contrasts. In the ABA group, right-dominant responses to the prosodic condition started to appear over the course of the intervention (strongly for two children and moderately for one), while LI values for the phonemic contrast remained around zero. The control group didn't exhibit dramatic changes for either the phonemic or prosodic contrast. These results suggest that the behavioral intervention contributed to changing the cerebral basis of speech processing, which is also supported by the improvement of language and social skills. The results further suggest that the cerebral system for prosody processing might be more plastic and easier to reorganize than the phonemic one.

Having reviewed these two studies, we can point out some characteristics of cerebral lateralization in ASD children. First of all, ASD children between six and 11 years of age showed atypical patterns of asymmetry, with no hemispheric specialization for processing phonemic contrasts. This contrasts with the leftward lateralization observed in typically developing children just before one year of age (cf. Section 2). As for the prosodic contrast, ASD children older than six years exhibited rightward lateralization, while those younger than five years did not. However, as a result of behavioral intervention in younger ASD children, functional cerebral lateralization shifted to the typical pattern exclusively for prosodic processing. This suggests that the right-dominant cerebral network for prosody processing is easier to build. It also raises the question of whether the observed right-dominant cerebral activation in ASD children indicates effective processing of linguistic prosody as observed in TDC.

The answer would be "No." This is evident from the behavioral score in the first study, in which the ASD children were not able to properly perceive the prosodic contrast. We assume that ASD children succeed at lower levels of prosodic processing involving perceiving pitch contour, but have difficulties at higher, cognitive processing levels such as extracting the meaning of prosody. Right-dominance in the ASD children may simply reflect the sensory processing of acoustic components, namely slow spectral changes. The reasoning for this assumption is twofold. The first evidence comes from a neonate NIRS study using the same stimuli (Arimitsu et al., 2011). This study revealed that neonates showed rightward functional specialization exclusively for prosodic contrast. This right-dominance was interpreted to reflect the signal-driven mechanism of acoustic processing because it is unlikely that neonates fully understand and process linguistic prosody at this age. We suppose this is also the case for the ASD children. The second reason is based on accumulated literature on auditory perception in ASD children. It is generally pointed out that many ASD children have problems producing and/or perceiving phonemes, as well as the emotional and linguistic aspects of prosody (Cleland, Gibbon, Peppe, O'Hare, & Rutherford, 2010; McCann

& Peppe, 2003). Although detailed results on phonemic and prosodic processing are somewhat divergent due to individual variation, they are at least consistent with the normal or superior ability to process non-verbal acoustic aspects of sounds that ASD children have. For example, they are good at discriminating non-speech pitch contours even in the context of speech. Some ASD children have even better musical or sound discrimination ability than TDC (Peppe, McCann, Gibbon, O'Hare, & Rutherford, 2007; Jarvinen-Pasley, Wallace, Ramus, Happé, & Heaton, 2008), but as soon as linguistically meaningful prosody is involved, their performance diminishes.

Let us consider these data in light of the model of developmental hemispheric lateralization. Overall, ASD children may have different developmental changes compared to TDC, as shown by bold arrows in Figure 3. Although the right-dominance observed in the present paradigm reflects the sensory-perceptual level of prosody, ASD children were revealed to show slower lateralization even for this level of processing, as shown in the bottom part of the figure. ASD children show even less typical lateralization with regard to phoneme processing. Since we have data only on the processing of vowels, which are steady-state spectral contrasts, we discuss them here as representative of phonemes in general. Even in eight-year-old children with ASD, phoneme processing was not functionally lateralized to the left auditory area, and there is no developmental change from birth, as shown by the horizontal arrow in the figure. If we interpret this data in line with the model, we could say that signal-driven processing is still dominant even in older ASD children because the linguistic network that enhances efficient phonemic perception has not been constructed on the left side. According to this model (cf. Section 2; Minagawa-Kawai et al., 2011a), at the initial stage, neural recruitment for speech processing is chiefly influenced by temporal and spectral properties of speech. Subsequently, as infants are exposed to language, newly learned sounds are increasingly processed in the phonetic and lexical circuits around the left temporal areas because of the left hemisphere phonological category learning systems. Children with ASD, who might lack these learning systems for rule and category extraction, may tend to perceive/produce phonemes erroneously due to the lack of an efficient left-dominant network.

124

3. Summary and final remarks

This chapter presented findings on cerebral lateralization in typically and atypically developing brains. We presented a model of developmental hemispheric lateralization in speech perception based on data accumulated over the last decade. This model proposes three developmental steps for the unfolding of lateralization, which combines the signal-driven and learning bias hypotheses, to result in processing that appears to be domain-driven in the adult state. Subsequently, we reviewed several NIRS studies of ASD children's speech processing. The atypical neural recruitment found in these studies was explained in the framework of the model of developmental hemispheric specialization, suggesting that it stemmed from impairment of the children's rule and category extraction mechanism at the second stage of the model. Lack of this learning mechanism may have resulted in failure to construct an efficient linguistic network, as is suggested by the lack of a left-dominant brain response to the phonemic contrast.

Although the model proposed here focuses on the perceptual processing of speech, it could eventually be extended and discussed in the context of the development of speech production, specifically the development of somatosensory processes and motor control. Recent studies provide evidence of a crucial relationship between perception and production. Thus, the left-dominant temporal responses we observe when infants tune their perceptual system to native phonemic patterns may also be related to the infants' developing production of native language phonemes, including the construction of a vocal tract model specific to the native language. This relationship between developing speech perception and production with changes in hemodynamic response patterns should be further investigated in the future, as it may provide some clues to reveal the typical and atypical language development within the framework of embodiment theory.

These findings are uniquely afforded by the use of NIRS, which has a better spatial resolution than EEG. Further advantages of NIRS (e.g., its robustness to movement artifacts and silence) make it possible to measure brain activations in infants and neonates in addition to children with disabilities. At the same time, we have to remark that these NIRS data are chiefly from surface parts of the cerebral cortex (20–30 mm in depth), and we cannot exclude the possibility that critical signals from deeper brain areas have been missed. Although this relatively new technique still has some problems to be solved, the potential of NIRS has been expanded by the application of various analysis and measurement methods. Among them, functional connectivity analysis is a particularly crucial neuronal measure to assess typical and atypical development. Future studies using NIRS should uncover various aspects of neurocognitive development as a functional network system.

References

Arimitsu, T., Uchida-Ota, M., Yagihashi, T., Kojima, S., Watanabe, S., Hokuto, I., & Minagawa-Kawai, Y. (2011). Functional hemispheric specialization in processing phonemic and prosodic auditory changes in neonates. *Frontiers in Psychology*, 2, 202.

Boemio, A., Fromm, S., Braun, A., & Poeppel, D. (2005). Hierarchical and asymmetric temporal sensitivity in human auditory cortices. *Nature Neuroscience*, 8 (3), 389–395.

Cleland, J., Gibbon, F. E., Peppe, S. J., O'Hare, A., & Rutherford, M. (2010). Phonetic and phonological errors in children with high functioning autism and Asperger syndrome. *International Journal of Speech-Language Pathology*, 12(1), 69–76.

Cristià, A., Dupoux, E., Hakuno, Y., Lloyd-Fox, S., Schuetze, M., Kivits, J., & Minagawa-Kawai, Y. (2013). An online database of infant functional near infrared spectroscopy studies: a community-augmented systematic review. *PLoS One*, 8 (3), e58906.

Furuya, I., & Mori, K. (2003). Sayu chokakuya no onsei gengo shori ni okeru kinobunka: tachanneru kinsekigai bunkoho ni yoru kento [Cerebral lateralization in spoken language processing measured by multi-channel near-infrared spectroscopy (NIRS)]. *No to shinkei* [The Brain and Nerves], 55 (3), 226–231.

Furuya, I., Mori, K., Minagawa-Kawai, Y., & Hayashi, R. (2001). Cerebral lateralization of speech processing in infants measured by near-infrared spectroscopy. *IEIC Technical Report* (*Institute of Electronics, Information and Communication Engineers*) 100 (725), 15–20.

Gandour, J., Wong, D., Lowe, M., Dzemidzic, M., Satthamnuwong, N., Tong, Y., & Lurito, J. (2002). Neural circuitry underlying perception of duration depends on language experience. *Brain and Language*, 83 (2), 268–290.

Jarvinen-Pasley, A., Wallace, G. L., Ramus, F., Happé, F., & Heaton, P. (2008). Enhanced perceptual processing of speech in autism. *Developmental Science*, 11 (1), 109–121.

Lenneberg, Eric H. (1967). *Biological Foundations of Language*. New York Wiley.

May, L., Byers-Heinlein, K., Gervain, J., & Werker, J. F. (2011). Language and the newborn brain: does prenatal language experience shape the neonate neural response to speech? *Frontiers in Psychology*, 2, 222.

McCann, J., & Peppe, S. (2003). Prosody in autism spectrum disorders: a critical review. *International Journal of Language & Communication Disorders*, 38 (4), 325–350.

McNealy, K., Mazziotta, J. C., & Dapretto, M. (2006). Cracking the language code: neural mechanisms underlying speech parsing. *Journal of Neuroscience*, 26 (29), 7629–7639.

Minagawa-Kawai, Y., Cristià, A., & Dupoux, E. (2011a). Cerebral lateralization and early speech acquisition: a developmental scenario. *Developmental Cognitive Neuroscience*, 1 (3), 217–232.

Minagawa-Kawai, Y., van der Lely, H., Ramus, F., Sato, Y., Mazuka, R., & Dupoux, E. (2011b). Optical brain imaging reveals general auditory and language-specific processing in early infant development. *Cerebral Cortex*, 21 (2), 254–261.

Minagawa-Kawai, Y., Naoi, N., Kikuchi, N., Yamamoto, J. & Kojima, S. (2009a). Cerebral laterality for phonemic and prosodic cue decoding in children with autism. *Neuroreport*, 20 (13), 1219–1224.

Minagawa-Kawai, Y., Naoi, N., & Kojima, S. (2009b). *New approach to functional neuroimaging: near infrared spectroscopy*. Tokyo: Keio University Press.

Minagawa-Kawai, Y., Mori, K., Hebden, J. C., & Dupoux, E. (2008). Optical imaging of infants' neurocognitive development: Recent advances and perspectives. *Developmental Neurobiology*, 68 (6), 712–728.

Minagawa-Kawai, Y., Mori, K., Naoi, N., & Kojima, S. (2007). Neural attunement processes in infants during the acquisition of a language-specific phonemic contrast. *Journal of Neuroscience*, 27(2), 315–321.

Minagawa-Kawai, Y., Mori, K., & Sato, Y. (2005). Different brain strategies underlie the categorical perception of foreign and native phonemes. *Journal of Cognitive Neuroscience*, 17 (9), 1376–1385.

Minagawa,Y.,Hakuno,Y.,.Kobayashi.A.,Naoi,N.,Kojima,S. (submitted) Infant's word segmentation recruits the cerebral network of short-term memory.

Näätänen, R., Lehtokoski, A., Lennes, M., Cheour, M., Huotilainen, M., Iivonen, A., & Alho, K. (1997). Language-specific phoneme representations revealed by electric and magnetic brain responses. *Nature*, 385 (6615), 432–434.

Novak, G. P., Kurtzberg, D., Kreuzer, J. A., & Vaughan, H. G., Jr. (1989). Cortical responses to speech sounds and their formants in normal infants: Maturational sequence and spatiotemporal analysis. *Electroencephalography and Clinical Neurophysiology*, 73 (4), 295–305.

Peña, M., Maki, A., Kovacic, D., Dehaene-Lambertz, G., Koizumi, H., Bouquet, F., & Mehler, J. (2003). Sounds and silence: An optical topography study of language recognition at birth. *Proceedings of the National Academy of Sciences of the United States of America*, 100 (20), 11702–11705.

Peppe, S., McCann, J., Gibbon, F., O'Hare, A., & Rutherford, M. (2007). Receptive and expressive prosodic ability in children with high-functioning autism. *Journal of Speech Language and Hearing Research*, 50(4), 1015–1028.

Sato, H., Hirabayashi, Y., Tsubokura, H., Kanai, M., Ashida, T., Konishi, I., & Maki, A. (2012). Cerebral hemodynamics in newborn infants exposed to speech sounds: A whole-head optical topography study. *Human Brain Mapping*, 33(9), 2092–2103.

Sato, Y., Mori, K., Furuya, I., Hayashi, R., Minagawa-Kawai, Y., & Koizumi, T. (2003). Developmental changes in cerebral lateralization to spoken language in infants: Measured by near-infrared spectroscopy. *Japan Society of Logopedics and Phoniatrics*, 44 (3), 165–171.

Sato, Y., Sogabe, Y., & Mazuka, R. (2007). Brain responses in the processing of lexical pitch-accent by Japanese speakers. *Neuroreport*, 18 (18), 2001–2004.

Sato, Y., Sogabe, Y., & Mazuka, R. (2010). Development of hemispheric specialization for lexical pitch-accent in Japanese infants. *Journal of Cognitive Neuroscience*, 22 (11), 2503–2513.

Simos, P. G., & Molfese, D. L. (1997). Electrophysiological responses from a temporal order continuum in the newborn infant. *Neuropsychologia*, 35 (1), 89–98.

Telkemeyer, S., Rossi, S., Koch, S. P., Nierhaus, T., Steinbrink, J., Poeppel, D., & Wartenburger, I. (2009). Sensitivity of newborn auditory cortex to the temporal structure of sounds. *Journal of Neuroscience*, 29 (47), 14726–14733.

Villringer, A., Planck, J., Hock, C., Schleinkofer, L., & Dirnagl, U. (1993). Near infrared spectroscopy (NIRS): A new tool to study hemodynamic changes during activation of brain function in human adults. *Neuroscience Letters*, 154 (1-2), 101–104.

Zatorre, R. J., & Belin, P. (2001). Spectral and temporal processing in human auditory cortex. *Cerebral Cortex*, 11 (10), 946–953.

Zatorre, R. J., Evans, A. C., Meyer, E., & Gjedde, A. (1992). Lateralization of phonetic and pitch discrimination in speech processing. *Science*, 256 (5058), 846–849.

Zevin, J. D., & McCandliss, B. D. (2005). Dishabituation of the BOLD response to speech sounds. *Behavioral and Brain Functions*, 1 (1), 4.

Young Children's Cross Mind-Body Awareness
—

Noriko Toyama

In the last three decades, a growing number of researchers have paid attention to young children's biological thought. Piaget (1929) characterized preschoolers' awareness of biological phenomena as animistic, i.e., they do not differentiate between living and non-living things and assign mental states, such as desires and beliefs, to inanimate objects such as the sun and moon. In Piaget's framework, the animistic tendency was taken as a sign of domain-general immaturity of thought.

1. NAÏVE BIOLOGY

In 1985, Susan Carey's pioneering work, *Conceptual Change in Childhood*, re-examined Piaget's claim based on robust experimental data. While Piaget ascribed preschoolers' animistic tendency to domain-general characteristics of the "pre-operational stage," Carey explained this thought as a lack of domain-specific knowledge in biology. However, similar to Piaget, Carey insisted that young children's biological thought was premature and qualitatively different from that of adults, and that preschoolers understand biological concepts by using the framework of intentional causality, and thus, lacked a domain-specific theory of biology.

Since Carey's momentous 1985 publication, there has been a growing debate regarding the nature of children's early awareness of biology. Originally, Carey argued that preschoolers' biological concepts were understood within the earlier-acquired framework of naïve psychology, and thus, an autonomous theory of biology developed in middle childhood. In contrast, numerous subsequent studies have suggested that preschoolers' awareness satisfies the three criteria for recognizing a knowledge system as a naïve theory in the target domain: coherency ontological distinctions, and distinctive causal-explanatory frameworks (Wellman & Inagaki, 1997; Wellman & Gelman, 1997).

A wealth of evidence has suggested that, by preschool-age, young children acquire such knowledge systems for the domains of physics, psychology, and biology (e.g., Coley, 1995; Estes, Wellman, & Woolley, 1989; Hatano & Inagaki, 1994), though some do not agree that young children's grasp of some domains is domain-specific (Carey, 1985; 1995). Concerning naïve biology, previous studies have shown that young children have theoretical insight into growth (Inagaki & Hatano, 1993; 1996; 2002), regrowth (Backscheider, Shatz, & Gelman, 1993), illness (Kalish, 1997; Siegal, 1988; Springer & Ruckel, 1992), inheritance (Keil, 1992; 1994; Springer, 1996), and contamination (Kalish, 1996; Legare, Wellman, & Gelman, 2009; Toyama, 1999; 2000).

2. MIND-BODY RELATIONS

Since Descartes first proposed that the mind and body were separate entities, Western science has made a clear distinction between them. Psychological mechanisms accordingly tended to explain the workings of the mind, whereas biological mechanisms were used to explain bodily processes (Wilkinson, 1988). Along these lines, the complete differentiation of biological phenomena from psychological ones has been an important criterion in the debate over whether preschoolers have a naïve theory of biology (Inagaki & Hatano, 2002). Therefore, previous studies have investigated whether young children differentiate between biological and psychological processes (e.g., Coley, 1995; Estes, Wellman, & Wooley, 1989; Inagaki & Hatano, 1996).

It has been shown that four-year-old preschoolers recognize that organic activities cannot be controlled by one's intentions or desires (Inagaki & Hatano, 1993). They also know that it is more difficult to change physical characteristics than psychological ones (Lockhart, Chang, & Story, 2002), and they can provide distinct explanations for behaviors that were either psychological or biological (Schult & Wellman, 1997). In addition, even preschoolers seem to believe that illness is a bodily condition rather than a psychological one (Springer, 1994), and that illness and contamination are caused by biological rather than psychological factors (Kalish, 1996; Siegal, 1988; Springer & Ruckel, 1992). These results suggest that young children apparently differentiate between mental and bodily processes (Erickson, Keil, & Lockhart, 2010).

However, mind and body cannot be thoroughly differentiated, as typified by psychosomatic illness. As Inagaki and Hatano (1999) pointed out, the issue of the mind-body distinction is more complex. They reported that substantial numbers of Japanese undergraduate students recognized both mental and physical factors as important for physical health. More than one-third of these students responded that mental stress could contribute even to an infectious illness. These results indicate that adults assume that mind and body are mutually interdependent rather than independent. Then, do young children notice the mind-body interdependence, and does this awareness change with development?

3. PSYCHOGENIC BODILY REACTIONS

Psychogenic bodily reactions, defined as bodily reactions that occur because of a mental state, are examples of cross mind-body phenomena. Previously, Bibace and Walsh (1981) reported that until the age of 11 years, children did not acknowledge that mental states can influence bodily functioning. Harris (1989) also reported that less than half of healthy six-year-old children agreed that emotional states would affect healing during an illness.

More recently, Notaro, Gelman, and Zimmerman (2001) directly examined the question of whether young children notice psychogenic bodily reactions. They asked preschool through fifth grade children, as well as adults, whether mental states could cause bodily reactions. Specifically, four-year-old preschoolers, five-year-old kindergarteners, second graders, and fifth graders rated whether several types of psychogenic bodily reactions, such as vomiting caused by feeling nervous and a stomachache due to worrying, would be possible (Study 1). The mean percentage of "yes" responses increased with age (Figure 1). This showed that children were much less likely to accept psychogenic bodily reactions, and were more apt to believe that bodily reactions resulted from physical causes and not from psychological ones.

Toyama (2010) examined the same question using a Japanese sample. Specifically, four- and five-year-old preschoolers, second and fifth graders, and adults responded yes or no to (1) psychogenic items, e.g., "Do you think throwing up [physical health outcomes] could happen because of feeling nervous [psychological events]?" (2) psychological items, e.g., "Do you think trembling legs [behavioral outcomes] could happen because of feeling nervous [psychological events]?" (3) physical items, e.g., "Do you think throwing up [physical health outcomes] could happen because of eating too much candy [physical events]?" and (4) moral items, e.g., "Do you think you would throw up [physical health outcome] because you pulled a cat's tail [moral transgression]?"

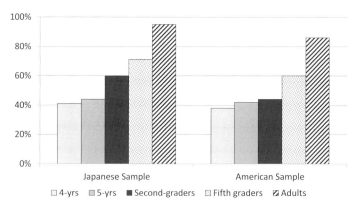

Figure 1 Mean percentages of "yes" responses in Japanese sample (Experiment 1 in Toyama, 2010), and in American sample (Study 1 in Notaro et al., 2001) for Psychogenic tasks.

In the psychogenic tasks, as in the study by Notaro, Gelman, and Zimmerman (2001), the mean percentage of "yes" responses gradually increased with age (Figure 1). Additionally, less than 50 percent of preschoolers responded "yes," suggesting that young children were less likely to agree to the possibility of psychogenic bodily reactions, while adults were more likely to accept that psychological events could cause changes in physical health (more than 90 percent). For the other item types, developmental differences were not observed, in that "no" responses were always frequent for moral tasks, while "yes" responses commonly observed for the psychological and physical tasks across all age groups. Even preschoolers seem to know that psychological events could have behavioral consequences, and that physical events could cause physical health changes. They also noticed that immanent justice was not likely, i.e., moral transgressions did not affect physical health outcomes.

The above results suggest that young children do not have a clear insight into cross mind-body awareness with reference to psychogenic bodily reactions, and that, with development, they become more aware of the mind-body interdependence.

4. TREATMENT OF PSYCHOGENIC ILLNESSES

Difficulties in relating mental states to bodily outcomes among preschoolers were also reported in studies that examined children's awareness of treatment of psychogenic illnesses. Psychogenic illnesses, such as tension headaches, are physical disorders derived from mental causes such as stress. Since both physical and psychological components are involved, both biological and psychological remedies are expected to be effective in treating psychogenic illnesses.

Notaro, Gelman, and Zimmerman (2002) asked four- and five-year-old American preschoolers, second-graders, and adults to judge whether biological treatments (e.g., going to the doctor and taking medicine) and psychological treatments (e.g., going outside to play and thinking about something else) would make a psychogenic illness stop or go away. The four- and five-year-old preschoolers typically responded that only biological treatments are effective. Further, though 87 percent of the four-year-olds acknowledged that biological treatments would be effective, only 13 percent of the children did so for psychological treatments.

This developmental trend was also found in a Japanese sample. In a study by Toyama (2011), four- and five-year-old preschoolers, second-graders, and adults judged the effectiveness of biological and psychological treatments for psychogenic illnesses. The results are shown in Figure 2. Just as with the American preschoolers in the study by Notaro, Gelman, and Zimmerman (2002), the Japanese preschoolers were less likely to agree that psychogenic illnesses could be treated by psychological remedies. Regarding adults, the trends in the Japanese sample were similar to those revealed in the American sample, in that adults seldom agreed that biological treatments would be effective for psychogenic illnesses. Based on this result, Notaro, Gelman, and Zimmerman (2002) argued that even adults have difficulties in appreciating cross mind-body relations. The authors insisted that if respondents understood the dual nature of psychogenic illnesses, they would agree with *both* biological *and* psychological treatments.

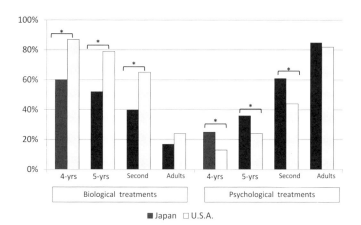

Figure 2 Mean percentages of "yes" responses in Japanese sample (Study 1 in Toyama, 2011), and in American sample (Study 1 in Notaro et al.,2002) for Biological and Psychological treatments for psychogenic tasks.
* $p < .05$

Toyama (2011) questioned this conclusion. The participants in the study by Notaro, Gelman, and Zimmerman (2002) were asked how helpful each cure would be in getting rid of symptoms. The words "get rid of" (*torinozoku* in Japanese) mean eliminating or discarding, and implied that symptoms were induced by a cause. Thus, to get rid of symptoms and prevent their reappearance, causes had to be eliminated. Since psychogenic reactions are assumed to have mental causes, the participants might have supposed that the causes had to be treated before anything else to get rid of the symptoms. Accordingly, they might have rated biological cures as ineffective. In order to examine this point, Toyama (2011) modified the questions by specifically changing the expression "get rid of" to "ease" (*yawarageru* in Japanese). As a result, more than half of the adult participants (57 percent) in Study 2 accepted the efficacy of biological treatments for psychogenic illnesses. Therefore, it is not appropriate to say that even adults are ignorant of the cross mind-body interdependence with reference to psychogenic illnesses.

5. ORIGINS OF AWARENESS

Then, how do children learn about the cross mind-body interdependence in psychogenic bodily reactions? One possibility is that children begin to notice it based on their own experiences. If so, children's awareness would differ according to their prior experiences.

In one study of children's concepts of illness, Harris (1989) found differences between healthy and hospitalized children in terms of their awareness of psychosomatic causality. As compared with healthy children, hospitalized 6- and 10-year-old children were less willing to grant the possibility of psychogenic causation, and more often rejected the idea that emotion could affect the speed of recovery. Based on these data, Harris speculated that the experience of illness was important to children's awareness of the mind-body interdependence. Notaro, Gelman, and Zimmerman (2001) also found that children's self-reported personal experiences with psychogenic bodily reactions were correlated with their performance on corresponding psychogenic tasks. In their study, however, children who reported previous experiences of bodily ailments with psychological origins were more likely to accept the possibility of psychogenic bodily reactions.

Although the relationships between recognition and experience reported by Notaro, Gelman, and Zimmerman (2001) were the opposite of Harris' findings, we can conclude from both studies that experience had some role in children's awareness. However, Notaro, Gelman, and Zimmerman (2001) also found that parental reports of children's psychogenic experiences were not associated with either children's self-reports or with children's performance on items about psychogenic reactions.

In order to examine the effects of previous experiences on children's awareness, Toyama (2007) interviewed mothers of first and second graders about (1) whether their children had had any psychogenic bodily reactions when they entered elementary school; (2) if they did, what kind of bodily reactions their children had; and (3) what were the possible causes of these reactions. In addition, mothers reported their children's medical history. If mothers reported psychogenic bodily reactions, children were asked to explain why they had these reactions. All children were then asked whether mental states could cause bodily reactions.

If previous experiences had a role in children's awareness, then children whose mothers reported that their children had experienced psychogenic bodily reactions would tend to agree with the possibility of psychogenic bodily reactions, as compared to children without such reports. However, the results did not support these assumptions. Even when mothers of these first and second graders reported that their children had psychogenic bodily ailments, the children had some difficulty conceiving their experiences in psychosomatic terms. These results could not be attributed to children's lack of memory regarding such personal experiences, since most children remembered the same events. Although they remembered their experiences, children tended to explain these events in terms of their poor bodily conditions, e.g., "'Cause I had a cold, I got stomachaches." In addition, children's performance did not differ according to their mothers' reports on the children's previous experiences of psychogenic bodily reactions.

These results suggest that experience alone is not sufficient for seven- and eight-year-olds to attribute psychological factors for their bodily ailments, and the same may be true for younger children as well.

6. Causal explanatory frameworks

At every age, children actively work to understand the world around them. In doing so, causal explanatory frameworks guide children to seek adequate explanations of how and why things happen (Carey, 1985; Keil, 2006). Children use these frameworks to explain the evidence they encounter, which enables them to invoke well-suited justifications for why objects behave as they do, and thus, to predict future behaviors (Gottfried & Gelman, 2005). Causal explanatory frameworks play a vital role by guiding predictions and reasoning. As causal notions develop, children come to acquire more elaborate or newly established perspectives about the world.

Then, what changes in their causal explanatory frameworks enable children to become aware of psychogenic bodily reactions? How do children and adults explain why mental factors result in bodily reactions? In a study by Notaro, Gelman, and Zimmerman (2002), children, but not adults, were asked to explain why mental states would lead to bodily reactions. Their explanations were much like restatements of questions, for example, in response to the question, "Why do you blush when you are shy?" they responded, "Sometimes we blush when we are shy." Therefore, it was not clear what led these children to assume psychogenic bodily reactions.

On the other hand, Toyama (2010) sought explanations from both children and adults. In her Experiment 3, five- and six-year-old preschoolers, second and fifth graders, as well as adults, were asked to explain the occurrence of psychogenic bodily reactions (e.g., vomiting caused by worrying) and physically-induced reactions (e.g., vomiting caused by eating rotten apples). Elementary school children and preschoolers often relied on vitalistic causality when explaining physically-induced reactions, whereas adults did so to explain psychogenic bodily reactions. Typical adult explanations indicated that deprivation of "vital force" due to worries or stress causes bodily reactions. This finding suggests that implications of vitalistic causality changes with development and plays a role in the awareness of psychogenic bodily reactions.

As noted above, in the studies by Notaro, Gelman, and Zimmerman (2001) and Toyama (2007), children's awareness of psychogenic bodily reactions were not associated with their mothers' reports of the children's previous experiences. In addition, Harris (1989) and Notaro, Gelman, and Zimmerman (2001) revealed contradicting results. Harris (1989) reported that more than hospitalized children, healthy children agreed with the possibility of psychogenic reactions, whereas Notaro, Gelman, and Zimmerman (2001) reported that children who reported their own previous experiences of psychogenic bodily ailments were more likely to agree that psychological factors cause bodily reactions, than were children without previous experiences. These inconsistent results can be explained if we assume that it is not previous experience but children's causal explanatory frameworks that make children notice psychogenic bodily reactions.

7. Vitalistic causality

Vitalistic causality, as proposed by Inagaki and Hatano (1993, 2002), has been posited as a causal-explanatory framework in the domain of biology, along with Gelman's psychological essentialism (Gelman, 2003; Gelman, Coley, & Gottfried, 1994; Gelman & Wellman, 1991) and Keil's teleology (Keil, 1992; 1994). These causalities are not necessarily domain-specific, but they appear to be applied selectively to biological phenomena.

Vitalistic causality presumes that bodily phenomena result from the workings of a vital force, i.e., "some unspecified substance, energy, or information that is essential for maintaining and enhancing life" (Inagaki & Hatano, 1999). In their study, preschoolers applied this causality to biological phenomena such as digestion and blood circulation, but not to psychological phenomena. According to Inagaki and Hatano (2002), vitalistic causality personifies internal organs by attributing agency to them. Under this view of causation, internal organs themselves are considered to have an inherent willingness to function for biological purposes, and thus people cannot intentionally control their bodily processes. This type of causality involves the transmission of a vital force that is ingested from materials such as food, air, or water, and this force enables people to maintain life.

In past research, adults seldom appeared to rely on vitalistic causality;

however, the adults in Toyama's (2013) study tended to refer to vitalistic concepts for psychogenic bodily reactions. They relied on this causality to explain why nervousness, worrying, shyness, and frustration would cause poor physical conditions. According to their explanations, unhealthy mental conditions can deprive people of the vital force and cause sickness. Here, the vital force was assumed to have psychological implications, and vitalistic causality implies the possibility that mental factors influence bodily conditions. That is, in adult explanations, the vital force was conceptualized as having both physical and mental power.

Inagaki and Hatano (2002) stated that under this causality "the mind and body are always interdependent to some degree," and the vital force "can be lost quickly if a person experiences stress, either physical or psychological." They also claimed that the "obvious sources for ingesting vital force are food and water, but in more elaborate forms of vitalism, some additional sources like air (taken in through breathing) and other peoples' power (taken through sympathy) are also included." Toyama's (2013) results suggest that in the adult form of vitalism, the mind and body are interdependent, and the vital force has both material and mental sources. Adult conceptions of the vital force seem to have cross mind-body implications, whereas children's conceptions appear to be analogous to an authentic bodily force. This contrast suggests that vitalistic causality obtains cross mind-body implications with age.

However, adult participants did not apply this causality to psychological phenomena. In Experiment 2 of Toyama's (2013) study, both adults and children almost never referred to vitalistic concepts to explain psychological behavior such as "becoming quiet due to worries" and "trembling legs due to nervousness." Inagaki and Hatano (1993) reported that 6-year-olds applied vitalistic causality to biological, but not psychological phenomena. Similarly, the adults in Toyama's (2013) study applied vitalistic causality in a limited way. Thus, vitalistic causality would be a conceptual framework that is organized around biological processes that maintain life and health, and therefore, may be irrelevant to psychological behavior that lacks health implications.

8. CULTURAL DIFFERENCES

Concerning psychogenic bodily reactions, Japanese children and adults were more likely to accept the impacts of psychological states on bodily outcomes than those from the United States were. In Toyama's (2010) study, the Japanese respondents were more likely to agree with the possibility of psychogenic bodily reactions than the Americans in the study of Notaro, Zimmerman, and Gelman (2001). Additionally, in the study by Toyama (2011), the Japanese children and adults more easily recognized psychological components in treatments for psychogenic bodily reactions than did the Americans in the 2002 study of Notaro, Zimmerman, and Gelman. It was evident that, in both studies, cross mind-body awareness was more clearly exhibited in the Japan rather than the U.S. sample.

These differences could be related to the cultural notion of vitalism. In research across three cultures, not only Japanese (Inagaki & Hatano, 1993; 2002) but also Australian (Morris, Taplin, & Gelman, 2000; see also Miller & Bartsch, 1997) and American preschoolers (Jaakkola & Slaughter, 2002; Slaughter & Lyons, 2003) have been reported to rely on vitalistic causality when making inferences about biological processes such as growth and illness. In these studies, it was shown that several ideas of vitalistic causality, such as "organ intentionality," "transmission of vital force," and "maintenance of life" transcended culture (Jaakkola & Slaughter, 2002; Miller & Bartsch, 1997; Morris, Taplin, & Gelman, 2000; Slaughter & Lyons, 2003). However, as stated above, in Japan, vitalism includes one other key idea, i.e., mind-body interdependence. Currently, it is not certain if Western cultures also subscribe to this idea. As Slaughter and Lyons (2003) suggested, Western cultures do not necessarily have a concept equivalent to the Japanese concept of "vital force." For better understanding of cultural differences in the awareness of psychogenic bodily reactions, it would be helpful to examine the extent to which Japanese and Western cultures share vitalistic conceptions.

One other important question remains unsettled. In Toyama's (2010) study, which examined children's awareness of the causes of psychogenic bodily reactions, cultural differences were not observed among preschoolers, but they became gradually prominent with age. This result supports the idea of the theory-theory. If children worldwide share a framework theory for a biological domain and gradually obtain culturally specific notions, their inferences about biological phenomena would be initially similar across several cultures, and would gradually diverge later on. However, the results reported by Toyama (2011), on children's awareness of the treatment of psychogenic illnesses did not support this idea. The Japanese preschoolers more readily evaluated psychological cures but underestimated biological cures for psychogenic bodily reactions as compared with the American children in the study of Notaro, Zimmerman, and Gelman (2002), but such cultural differences were not observed in the adults' performance. Bloch, Solomon, and Carey (2001) reported the same pattern of cultural group differences. In their study, American and Zafimaniry adults shared the same beliefs regarding the biological inheritance of bodily features, but the children in both the groups did not respond the way the adults did.

What, then, is the explanation for the increase in cultural differences with age, and the fact that fewer differences were observed among adults than in young children? As Waxman, Medin, and Ross (2007) reported, discourse within a community seems to supplement a basic universal mode of biological notions, which may result in the cultural differences even among preschoolers. Within each culture, some information may be easily accessed by young children, while other information is deliberately hidden from them (Rogoff, 2003). Concerning causes of psychogenic bodily reactions, Japanese mothers sometimes hesitate to explain that their children's sickness may have resulted from anxiety or worry. Toyama (2007) reported that some mothers apparently responded, "I guessed my son's tummy-ache was psychogenic. However, I did not tell him anything about it. Instead, I told him that he might have eaten too much candy. If I had told him my guess, it would make the situation worse." Evidently, young Japanese children might be purposefully distanced from information about the causes of psychogenic bodily reactions in their society. On the contrary, Japanese mothers and nursery teachers often explained the biological importance of hygiene, health maintenance, and food intake to young children (Toyama, 2000; 2016). Indeed, future research needs to clarify the role of social information on developing children's biological awareness within each culture.

9. PROCESS-DEPENDENT AWARENESS

Previous studies on cross mind-body phenomena have primarily focused on illness (Notaro, Zimmerman, & Gelman, 2001; Raman, 2009; Raman & Gelman, 2008; Schulz, Bonawitz, & Griffiths, 2007; Toyama, 2010, 2013), or more specifically, on foodborne illness (Fallon, Rozin, & Pliner, 1984; Toyama, 1999). More recently, Raman (2011) extended this area of research by focusing on other biological processes. She presented children with two characters who consumed the same amount of the same food but had different taste sensations, i.e., tasty vs. not tasty. She then asked the children which character would grow taller, gain more weight, and more easily catch a cold. Raman examined the cross mind-body awareness of growth and illness by using these tasks. She reported that the four-year-old preschoolers and second-graders tended to answer that the character who thought the food was "yummy" would grow taller and gain more weight than the other character who thought the food was "yucky." However, even preschoolers did not assume that the tastiness of food would have an impact on catching a cold. In contrast, adults seldom assumed that the tastiness of food would affect growth or illness.

These findings are important because they suggest that cross mind-body assumptions are specific and not generalized across all processes. Depending on the biological process, children may assume either distinctions between domains or cross-domain interactions. They seemed to easily assume that psychological factors have an impact on growth processes but not on contagious illness.

Toyama (2015) examined this issue more precisely and found that process-dependent awareness is not limited to young children. Japanese five-year-old preschoolers, second-graders, fifth-graders, and adults judged the impact of psychological and biological factors on psychological states and on biological processes such as growth, contracting and recovering from illness, and injury. These results suggest that young children's and adults' awareness tended to be process-specific. Both children and adults were less likely to assume the effects of psychological factors on the tendency to catch a contagious illness. According to their thinking, it was biological factors, i.e., the nutritive value of food, that determined the likelihood of getting a cold, and thus, psychological factors, i.e., taste

142

experiences, were not related to contagion. In contrast, with reference to fatigue, participants from all age groups more often admitted the effects of psychological factors. Concerning this experiment, however, one important question remains to be addressed. Gustatory sensibility and physical condition are often correlated and confounded, and thus, cannot be clearly differentiated. For example, we often lose the sense of taste when we have a cold. In addition, foods' tastes and nutritive values are usually highly correlated. Therefore, detailed interviews are necessary to clarify participants' reasoning as to why they assumed the impact of psychological factors on biological processes.

As shown in these results, depending on the biological process, the thinking of children, and even adults, appears to be based on either domain distinctions or cross-domain interactions. Five-year-old pre-schoolers already know that psychological factors would have little relation to catching a contagious illness, while for other biological processes, such as growth, psychological factors were assumed to play a role. Then, in what other contexts do young children show cross-domain awareness? For example, do children understand the impact of psychological factors on digestion, the immune system, or the aging process? Are there any age differences involved in the cross mind-body awareness? As we examine these questions, we may find that there are principles that explain when children will, appropriately or inappropriately, believe in the impact of psychological factors.

10. SUMMARY AND CONCLUSION

The mind and body are not totally independent, as typified by psychogenic bodily reactions. Concerning this type of cross mind-body phenomena, young children seem to have difficulties in appreciating mind-body interdependence. With development, from around the middle of elementary school age, children begin to notice the contributions of mental factors in bodily processes. This cross mind-body awareness does not appear to originate in prior experiences per se. A simple account of knowledge acquisition, in that children would reach some awareness through direct experiences, does not apply to the awareness of psychogenic bodily reactions. Thus, the point is not previous experiences, but rather, children's causal explanatory framework. As these results suggest, with regard to psychogenic bodily reactions, children demonstrated some difficulties in appreciating mind-body interdependence. However, such difficulties do not generalize across all bodily processes. These are important suggestions in the sense that cross mind-body awareness could be process-dependent. Future research should examine situations when children, and adults, easily assume mind-body interdependence.

Finally, what implications can we derive from these findings for health practices? In Japan, and in other industrialized countries, it is becoming more and more common for children to report recurrent physical symptoms with no physical cause. Some of these physical complaints may be a reflection of stress, i.e., psychosomatic illness. In the field of pediatric care, more importance has been placed on informed consent or assent, i.e., ensuring an individual, having been fully informed about the nature, benefits, and risks of a clinical trial, agrees to their own participation in the care process. However, for psychosomatic illness, as shown in the above studies, children generally lack a full understanding of its causes and treatments. Thus, healthcare professionals, parents, and teachers should be very careful when and how they explain physical symptoms and medical care.

REFERENCES

Backscheider, A. G., Shatz, M., & Gelman, S. A. (1993). Preschoolers' ability to distinguish living kinds as a function of regrowth. *Child Development*, 64, 1242–1257.

Bibace, R., & Walsh, M. E. (1981). Children's conceptions of illness. In R. Biace & M. E. Walsh (Eds.), *Children's conceptions of health, illness, and bodily functions* (pp. 31–48). San Francisco: Jossey Bass.

Bloch, M., Solomon, G., & Carey, S. (2001). Zafimaniry: An understanding of what is passed on from parents to children. A cross-cultural investigation. *Journal of Cognition and Culture*, 1, 43-68.

Carey, S. (1985). *Conceptual change in childhood.* Cambridge, MA: MIT Press.

Carey, S. (1995). On the origin of causal understanding. In D. Sperber, D. Premack, and A. J. Premack (Eds.), *Causal cognition: A multi-disciplinary debate.* New York: Oxford University Press.

Coley, J. D. (1995). Emerging differentiation of folkbiology and folkpsychology: Attributions of biological and psychological properties to living things. *Child Development*, 66, 1856–1874.

Erickson, J. E., Keil, F. C., & Lockhart, K. L. (2010). Sensing the coherence of biology in contrast to psychology: Young children's use of causal relations to distinguish two foundational domains. *Child Development*, 81, 390–409.

Estes, D., Wellman, H. M., & Wooley, J. D. (1989). Children's folk psychology: Attributions of biological and psychological properties to living things. *Child Development*, 66, 1856–1874.

Fallon, A. E., Rozin, P., & Pliner, P. (1984). The child's conception of food: The development of food rejections with special reference to disgust and contamination sensitivity. *Child Development*, 55, 566–575.

Gelman, S. A. (2003). *The essential child: Origins of essentialism in everyday thought.* New York: Oxford University Press.

Gelman, S. A., Coley, J. D., & Gottfried, G. M. (1994). Essentialist beliefs in children: The acquisition of concepts and theories. In L. A. Hirschfeld and S. A. Gelman (Eds.), *Mapping the mind: Domain specificity in cognition and culture* (pp. 341–365). Cambridge University Press.

Gelman, S. A., and Wellman, H. M. (1991). Insides and essences: Early understandings of the nonobvious. *Cognition*, 38, 213–244.

Gottfried, G. M., & Gelman, S. A. (2005). Developing domain-specific causal-explanatory frameworks: The role of insides and immanence. *Cognitive Development*, 20, 137-158.

Harris, P. L. (1989). *Children and emotion: The development of psychological understanding.* New York: Basil Blackwell.

Hatano, G., & Inagaki, K. (1994). Young children's naïve theory of biology. *Cognition*, 50, 171–188.

Inagaki, K., & Hatano, G. (1993). Young children's understanding of the mind-body distinction. *Child Development*, 64, 1534–1549.

Inagaki, K. & Hatano, G. (1996). Young children's recognition of commonalities between animals and plants. *Child Development*, 67, 2823–2840.

Inagaki, K., & Hatano, G. (1999). Children's understanding of mind-body relationships. In M. Siegal and C. C. Peterson (eds.), *Children's understanding of biology and health* (pp. 23–44). New York: Cambridge University Press.

Inagaki, K., & Hatano, G. (2002). *Young children's naïve thinking about the biological world.* New York: Psychology Press.

Jaakkola, R., & Slaughter, V. (2002). Children's body knowledge: Understanding "life" as a biological goal. *British Journal of Developmental Psychology*, 20, 325–342.

Kalish, C. W. (1996). Preschoolers' understanding of germs as invisible mechanisms. *Cognitive Development*, 11, 83–106.

Kalish, C. W. (1997). Preschoolers' understanding of mental and bodily reactions to contamination: What you don't know can hurt you, but cannot sadden you. *Developmental Psychology*, 33, 79–91.

Keil, F. C. (1992). The origins of an autonomous biology. In M. R. Gunnar, & M. Maratsos, *Modularity and constraints in language and cognition. Minnesota symposium on child psychology* (Vol. 25) (pp. 103–138). Hillsdale, NJ: Erlbaum.

Keil, F. C. (1994). The birth and nurturance concepts by domains: The origins of concepts of living things. In L. A. Hirschfeld, & S. Gelman (Eds.), *Mapping the mind: Domain specificity in cognition and culture* (pp. 234–254). Cambridge, England: Cambridge University Press.

Keil, F. (2006). Explanation and understanding. *Annual Review of Psychology*, 57, 227–254.

Legare, C. H., Wellman, H. M., & Gelman, S. A. (2009). Evidence for an explanation advantage in naïve biological reasoning. *Cognitive Psychology*, 58, 177–194.

Lockhart, K. L., Chang, B., & Story, T. (2002). Young children's beliefs about the stability of traits: Protective optimism? *Child Development*, 73, 1408–1430.

Miller, J. L., & Bartsch, K. (1997). The development of biological explanation: Are children vitalists? *Developmental Psychology*, 33, 156–164.

Morris, S. C., Taplin, J. E., & Gelman, S. A. (2000). Vitalism in naïve biological thinking. *Developmental Psychology*, 36, 582–595.

Notaro, P. C., Gelman, S. A., & Zimmerman, M. A. (2001). Children's understanding of psychogenic bodily reactions. *Child Development*, 72, 444–459.

Notaro, P. C., Gelman, S. A., & Zimmerman, M. A. (2002). Biases in reasoning about the consequences of psychogenic bodily reactions: Domain boundaries in cognitive development. *Merrill-Palmer Quarterly*, 48, 427–449.

Piaget, J. (1929). *The child's conception of the world.* London: Routledge & Kagan Paul.

Raman, L. (2009). Can we get sick if we want to?: Children's and adults' recognition of intentionality in the origins of illness and injuries. *British Journal of Psychology*, 100, 721–751.

Raman, L. (2011). Does "yummy" food help you grow and avoid illness?: Children's and adults' understanding of the effect of psychobiological labels on growth and illness. *Child Development Research, Volume 2011*, Article ID 638239, 10 pages.

Raman, L. & Gelman, S. A. (2008). Do children endorse psychosocial factors in the transmission of illness and disgust? *Developmental Psychology*, 44, 801–813.

Rogoff, B. (2003). *The cultural nature of human development.* New York: Oxford University Press.

Schult, C. A., & Wellman, H. M. (1997). Explaining human movements and actions: Children's understanding of the limits of psychological explanation. *Cognition*, 62, 291–324.

Schulz, L. E., Bonawitz, E. B., & Griffiths, T. L. (2007). Can being scared cause tummy aches? Naïve theories, ambiguous evidence, and preschoolers' causal inferences. *Developmental Psychology*, 43, 1124–139.

Siegal, M. (1988). Children's knowledge of contagion and contamination as causes of illness. *Child Development*, 59, 1353–1359.

Slaughter, V., & Lyons, M. (2003). Learning about life and death in early childhood. *Cognitive Psychology*, 46, 1–30.

Springer, K. (1994). Beliefs about illness causality among preschoolers with cancer: Evidence against immanent justice. *Journal of Pediatric Psychology*, 19, 91–101.

Springer, K. (1996). Young children's understanding of a biological basis for parent-offspring relations. *Child Development*, 67, 2841–2856.

Springer, K., & Ruckel, J. (1992). Early beliefs about the cause of illness: Evidence against immanent justice. *Cognitive Development*, 7, 429–443.

Toyama, N. (1999). Developmental changes in the basis of associational contamination thinking. *Cognitive Development*, 14, 343–361.

Toyama, N. (2000). Young children's awareness of socially mediated rejection of food: Why is food dropped at the table "dirty"? *Cognitive Development*, 15, 523–541.

Toyama, N. (2007). The role of previous experience on children's awareness of psychogenic bodily reactions. *Japanese Journal of Cognitive Psychology*, 5, 11–21. (in Japanese with English abstract)

Toyama, N. (2010). Japanese children's and adults' awareness of psychogenic bodily reactions. *International Journal of Behavioral Development*, 34, 1–9.

Toyama, N. (2011). Japanese children's and adults' reasoning about the consequences of psychogenic bodily reactions. *Merrill-Palmer Quarterly*, 57, 129–157.

Toyama, N. (2013). Children's causal explanations of psychogenic bodily reactions. *Infant and Child Development*, 22, 216–234.

Toyama, N. (2015). Japanese children's awareness of the effect of psychological taste experiences. *International Journal of Behavioral Development*, 0165025415597548, first published on July 30.

Toyama, N. (2016). Preschool teachers' explanations on hygiene habits and young children's biological awareness of contamination. *Early Education and Development*, 27, 38–53.

Waxman, S., Medin, D., & Ross, N. (2007). Folkbiological reasoning from a cross-cultural developmental perspective: Early essentialist notions are shaped by cultural beliefs. *Developmental Psychology*, 43, 294–308.

Wellman, H. M., & Gelman, S. (1997). Knowledge acquisition in foundational domains. *Handbook of Child Psychology* (5th ed.), Vol. 2 (D. Kuhn and R. Segler, eds.): *Cognition,*

Perception and Language. New York: Wiley.

Wellman, H. M., & Inagaki, K. (1997). *The emergence of core domains of thought: Children's reasoning about physical, psychological, and biological thought,* New Directions for Child Development, no. 75.

Wilkinson, S. R. (1988). *The child's world of illness: The development of health and illness behavior.* New York: Cambridge University Press.

Conceptual Understanding in Childhood

—

Nobuyuki Fujimura

International studies assessing students' literacy or academic achievement in mathematics, science, and reading have revealed that students of many Asian countries or economies such as Singapore, Korea, Chinese Taipei, and Japan scored higher than those of other countries (Martin, Mullis, Foy, & Stanco, 2012; Mullis, Martin, Foy, & Arora, 2012; OECD, 2014; Stigler, Lee, & Stevenson, 1990). Careful analyses of their achievement on the international tests such as PISA or TIMSS, however, reveal that East Asian students are good at applying procedural knowledge, but that Japanese students' level of conceptual understanding is relatively low compared to their level of procedural skills (Fujimura, 2012). Students in countries which are well-known for their high levels of academic achievement, including Finland and China, seldom have attained high levels of conceptual understanding, including detailed verbal explanations of their solutions on non-routine problems that require deeper and essential conceptual understanding to solve (Fujimura, 2004; Fujimura, 2014).

---

1. CONCEPTUAL UNDERSTANDING AND CHILDREN'S NAIVE THEORIES

Conceptual understanding requires relating new information in an area to students' related prior knowledge, so that the various kinds of knowledge are integrated as a new framework. It may be that many students have not attained high levels of conceptual understanding, in part because attention has not been fully paid to the developmental processes of students' prior knowledge in childhood. For example, through everyday experiences, somewhat elaborated multiplicative understanding such as "halving", "doubling," or "dividing equally" (Fujimura, 1997), or basic qualitative understanding of the relationship among time, distance, and speed (Matsuda, 2001) has developed in childhood. On the other hand, junior high school students often have difficulties in understanding mathematical concepts such as ratio and proportion or intensive quantities including velocity, density, or concentration (Fujimura, 2011). This latter tendency may be due to teachers' lack of appreciation for the richness of students' prior knowledge related to the subject matter they have been studying and for connecting the development of the students' knowledge through childhood and subject-matter learning.

In order to facilitate students' conceptual understanding, it may be promising to organize classroom lessons based on students' ideas or conceptions that they have developed through their everyday activities and previous learning experiences in childhood. Recent studies in the realm of learning sciences have also pointed out that deeper conceptual understanding could be attained through instruction based on learners' various prior knowledge (e.g., Sawyer, 2014).

Therefore, it is important, for both developmental psychology and learning sciences regarding learning of school subjects, to clarify 1) processes of conceptual development in childhood and 2) effects of utilizing children's various ideas or conceptions developed during the processes in classroom learning on improving their conceptual understanding.

As processes of conceptual development, children's naive theories have been intensively studied since "conceptual change" in children was proposed (Carey, 1985). Compared to the large number of studies on naive physics or naive mathematics in infancy and those on naive biology and theory of mind in preschoolers, research on such naive understanding in childhood has been limited (e.g., naive astronomy by Vosniadou and Brewer, 1992) and has room for further developmental research.

Although children's knowledge increases through childhood, their growth during childhood has mainly been studied in the area of psychology of learning and instruction, and has often been judged according to whether children answer problems correctly or not. As Wellman and Gelman have pointed out, one of the essential factors of children's naive theories is causality (Wellman & Gelman, 1998). Therefore, children's causal reasoning could be a key to understanding the processes of conceptual development in childhood. Not only whether children's explanations are scientifically appropriate or not but also how children integrate various bits of information to explain causal relationships in each domain or to justify decisions should be studied as the development of children's naive theories.

This chapter focuses on elementary school children's understanding of economics (naive economics) and mathematics (naive mathematics), both of which have not been intensively studied in developmental psychology regarding childhood. Because various social factors are related to their understanding of economics, research on the former may help clarify the variability of children's conceptual understanding in childhood. On the other hand, because children often have difficulties in learning some kinds of mathematical concepts, research on the latter may contribute to development of effective learning processes or methods for facilitating children's understanding of those difficult concepts from the viewpoint of children's conceptual development.

2. CHILDREN'S UNDERSTANDING OF ECONOMICS AND SOCIETY

Within the area of children's development of understanding of society, the development of economic understanding has been investigated from the viewpoint of developmental psychology (e.g., Furth, 1980; Tamaru, 1993). More recent studies have focused on children's naive understanding of economics (e.g., Siegler & Thompson, 1998; Thompson & Siegler, 2000). Although studies dealing with children's "naive economics" have revealed their understanding of the relationship between sales and other economic factors, children's understanding of price, which is an economically important factor, as well as one familiar to children as consumers,

151

has not been fully addressed. Fujimura (2002) examined children's thinking about causal relationships between prices and factors such as supply and demand. Fourth to sixth graders (N = 82) in a public elementary school in Japan participated in the study. They individually answered questions about why one type of good was priced differently (e.g., berries sold in December vs. those sold in May). Children were also asked to indicate the mediating factors that related their explanations to price differences. Analysis of children's explanations revealed that older children more often used causal reasoning between prices and production factors (supply, cost, and profit) than younger ones (Figure 1). In addition, variability in children's reasoning and the causal links in their reasoning increased with age. Even fourth graders were able to choose some appropriate economic factors, depending on the characteristics of the goods.

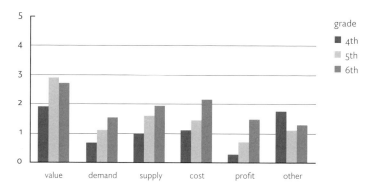

Figure 1   Mean number of problems in which each rule (max: 5) was used by grade school students.
Source Fujimura, 2002

In order to understand economic society and to solve social problems collaboratively with others, children should consider producer viewpoints as well as those of the consumer and should relate such viewpoints. Although children, as daily buyers, can easily understand consumer views, it is difficult for them to infer producer views and understand economic factors such as cost or profit. An interview study (Fujimura, 2010) examined whether imagining a producer's life and her/his beliefs in an everyday problem setting facilitates children's understanding of producer viewpoints and their thinking about economic factors that mediate a commodity distribution system. Fourth graders (N = 60) in a public elementary school in Japan participated in this study. They individually answered questions about why a kind of good was priced differently (e.g., a watermelon sold in summer vs. that sold in winter). Children were also asked to indicate the mediating factors that related their explanations to price differences. After answering these questions, they were asked to imagine the life of an imaginary baker, to price a new type of bread from the viewpoint of the baker, and to justify their decision. Finally, they answered again the same questions that they had been asked at the beginning. Analysis of children's explanations revealed that 1) an activity which included imagining a baker's life and pricing by the imaginary baker facilitated the children's reasoning between prices and production factors (supply, cost, and profit), and 2) variability in children's causal reasoning was increased through the activity. For example, the percentage of children who referred to a production factor, cost, increased from 29 percent on the pretest to 60 percent on the posttest. Consideration of other people's lives or beliefs in daily situations and discussion of these ideas may develop in children the deeper societal understanding that is required in sustainable societies.

The studies mentioned above revealed that children enlarge the variability of their economic understanding during childhood and that knowledge integration between various everyday knowledge and problem situations may contribute to the children's conceptual development. In the next section, developmental processes of understanding mathematical concepts, in which children integrate several kinds of intuitive understanding through inquiries by themselves and through social interactions with peers in a classroom so that they can understand difficult concepts, are examined.

3. DEVELOPMENT AND FACILITATION OF CHILDREN'S MATHEMATICAL UNDERSTANDING

Proportional reasoning requires mathematical understanding, which is especially difficult for children and adolescents. The Piagetian approach regards metrical proportion as one of the indicators of formal operational thought that emerges around the age of eleven (Inhelder & Piaget, 1955; Piaget & Inhelder 1966). Other studies have shown that even adolescents have difficulty in understanding proportions in many cases where quantitative understanding is necessary (Karplus, Pulos, & Stage, 1983; Noelting, 1980; Siegler, 1981).

Proportional reasoning involves both qualitative and quantitative methods of thought. Fujimura (1995) examined the relationship between qualitative and quantitative proportional reasoning of elementary school children. Two ratio types, velocity and concentration, were chosen. In the qualitative reasoning task, children were asked to determine the direction in which the numerator of the ratio would change (decrease, stay the same, or increase in value), when the denominator of the ratio changed and when the ratio was constant (direction task). In the quantitative reasoning task, children were given three components of two equal ratios and were asked to solve for the fourth component (missing-value task). These tasks were individually administered to 30 third-grade, 29 fourth-grade, and 30 fifth-grade students. The results revealed that qualitative reasoning preceded quantitative reasoning for each ratio type, while the success rate on quantitative reasoning tasks increased with age (Figure 2).

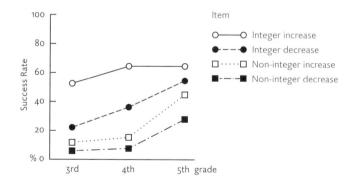

Figure 2 Success rates of each item on quantitative reasoning task (velocity)
Source Fujimura, 1995

As shown in Figure 2, even in the third grade, more than half the children were able to solve integer-increase type problems (such as, "A toy car runs 6 meters in 2 seconds. How far will the car run in 4 seconds, if it runs at the same speed?") based on their intuitive knowledge of multiplication such as "doubling" or "halving." In the fifth grade, about half of the children were able to solve non-integer-increase type problems (such as, "A toy car runs 6 meters in 3 seconds. How far will the car run in 7 seconds, if it runs at the same speed?"), although they had not formally learned ratios or proportions yet at school. They often use a generative "building-up" strategy. For example, they infer as follows: "The car runs 6 meters in 3 seconds. It runs another 6 meters in 3 seconds. The distance the car runs in 1 second is 2 meters, because 3 seconds are needed for the car to run 6 meters. Then, the answer is 6 + 6 + 2 = 14 meters." This self-generative strategy used by children who had not experienced formal instruction in ratios and proportions seemed to resemble strategies shown in peddling situations by street children or fishermen who had experienced a few years of formal schooling in Brazil (Carraher, Carraher, & Schliemann et al., 1985; Schliemann & Nunes, 1990) in that those strategies rely on building-up addition instead of numerically simple multiplication.

The difference in ratio types, velocity and concentration, affected qualitative reasoning tasks only in third graders. Children's ability to reason qualitatively appeared to have a strong impact on their performance of quantitative reasoning tasks, as a kind of background knowledge that constrained directions of quantitative reasoning.

Among proportion problems, comparison problems were used in some studies (e.g., Noelting, 1980), which require the solver to compare magnitudes of an intensive quantity (e.g., velocity) based on two sets of two numbers denoting the magnitudes of two kinds of extensive quantities (e.g., distance and time). These are relatively difficult for children and appeared to be correctly solved at a later age than the "missing-value" problems that were used in other studies (Dean & Frankhouser 1988; Tourniaire, 1986), which require the solver to apply a proportional relationship to calculate a number.

In the study by Fujimura (2001), 140 fourth graders were asked to solve proportion comparison problems about juice-mixing situations both before and after an intervention that used a manipulative model or other materials in three experiments. Figure 3 shows the manipulative model used in this study.

155

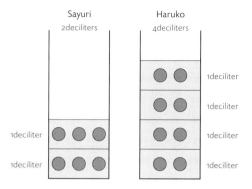

Figure 3 Manipulative model for comparing concentration. This figure shows the anticipated appropriate distribution of magnets.
Source Fujimura, 2001

Using a manipulative model based on children's prior knowledge about crowdedness and equal distribution was effective in letting children discover a unit strategy during the intervention phase and at the posttest. Using a unit strategy, children integrate information about the amount of concentrate and that of water, calculate unit values (amount of concentrate per amount of water), and judge the concentration according to the magnitudes of unit values. This unit strategy is a general strategy and useful for solving proportion problems. Using a unit strategy with appropriate verbal justification is thought to demonstrate a high level of conceptual understanding of proportions.

The model was more effective for those who had an appropriate unit representation but could not correctly compare the concentration of juice than it was for those who didn't have the representation. Based on this study, different approaches appear to be necessary to facilitate children's proportional reasoning, depending on the reasoning process (representation or comparison) with which children have difficulties. Interventions based on the process model and learning that builds on partially appropriate intuitive knowledge (such as a unit representation in this study) seem to be promising for facilitating children's mathematical understanding.

4. Processes and effects of concept-based learning (collaborative inquiry learning) on children's mathematical understanding

From the viewpoint of cognitive developmental psychology, it has been proposed that building on children's intuitive knowledge may be a useful way to introduce difficult mathematical concepts (English & Halford, 1995; Nunes, Schliemann, & Carraher, 1993). As ways of building on children's intuitive knowledge, choosing examples from everyday contexts and encouraging students to find their own ways of solving problems have been illustrated. Therefore, mathematics instruction that always builds on students' various prior knowledge, which I call here "concept-based learning" or "collaborative inquiry learning," may be promising for facilitating students' conceptual understanding.

Children's strategy discovery has been studied in areas of mathematical thinking such as number conservation and basic addition (Siegler & Jenkins, 1989; Siegler, 1995). In order to clarify the processes of strategy change regarding more challenging concepts such as ratio and proportion, it may be useful to examine how children get new information from the ideas of others and come to change their own strategies through comparing and relating different types of strategies in classroom discussion. Fujimura & Ohta (2002) examined the processes of children's strategy change in the domain of proportional reasoning through social interaction and inquiry in the mathematics classroom.

4.1 *Methods*

A teacher organized mathematics lessons on intensive quantity (e.g., density or velocity) for two fifth-grade classes by either a method based on children's various intuitive strategies (collaborative inquiry learning) or a method mainly oriented toward the use of a new strategy (conventional problem-solving learning). In the former method, children engaged with an introductory problem that could be solved using their existing strategies, compared their strategies with a new, more sophisticated strategy (i.e., a unit strategy; see 3 of this chapter) during the classroom discussion, and then individually solved a problem that could be solved by using the new strategy. In the latter method, children engaged with a problem that was rather difficult to solve by their intuitive strategies, and the teacher mainly led the discussion toward the use of a new strategy; then the children individually solved a similar problem. Table 1 shows the differences between the two learning methods.

Children in both classes (27 children each: M = 11 years 3 months) were asked to solve proportion problems before and after the lesson. Both the pretest and the posttest consisted of six items, three concerning walking speed and three about juice concentration (far-transfer task). In addition, the posttest included a problem about crowdedness, which was similar to the tasks used in the lesson (near-transfer task).

Table 1 Differences between two learning methods.

Experimental Lesson (concept-based: Collaborative Inquiry Learning)			Conventional Lesson (procedure-based: Problem-Solving Learning)		
"Some children are playing in two different playgrounds. Which of the following two playgrounds is more crowded?"			"Some children are playing in two different playgrounds. Which of the following two playgrounds is more crowded?"		
	East Playground	West Playground		North Playground	South Playground
Area	200 square meters	400 square meters	Area	300 square meters	500 square meters
Number of Children	15 children	45 children	Number of Children	30 children	40 children
This problem can be solved by using a multiplication strategy (e.g., doubling or halving of area: *intuitive strategies*), as well as by using a unit strategy (e.g., calculating the number of children for each square meter: *new strategy*).			This problem can *only* be solved by using a unit strategy (e.g., calculating the number of children for each square meter: *new strategy*)		
Experimental Lesson (concept-based: Collaborative Inquiry Learning)			Conventional Lesson (procedure-based: Problem-Solving Learning)		
Children compared their *intuitive strategies* with a *new strategy* that a few children had presented in the class.			The teacher focused children's attention to a *new strategy* that a few children had presented in the class, and added information to it.		

Source Fujimura and Ohta, 2002.

4.2 Results

An analysis was made of 1) children's performance on the pre- and post-tests, 2) a video recording of the overall lesson, and 3) the worksheets used by the children during the lesson.

Three points were summarized. First, the learning method based on children's intuitive thought (collaborative inquiry learning) was more useful when children were solving near-transfer tasks on the posttest than through conventional problem-solving learning (Figure 4-1). Second, children who had not said anything during the discussion (silent participants) and those who had made comments (vocal participants) both benefited from this collaborative inquiry learning (Figure 4-2). Third, those who understood other children's ideas presented in the classroom and incorporated those ideas into their own strategies during the collaborative inquiry learning (the incorporation group) significantly increased their use of a sophisticated strategy, that is, a unit strategy based on calculations and comparisons of unit values, from the pretest to the posttest. On the other hand, those who superficially imitated other children's ideas during the experimental lesson (the imitation group) didn't increase their use of the sophisticated strategy from the pretest to the posttest (Figure 4-3).

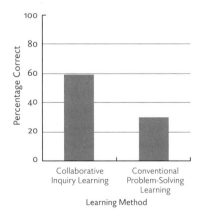

Figure 4-1 Percentage correct on the near-transfer task: Comparison between the two learning methods (posttest)

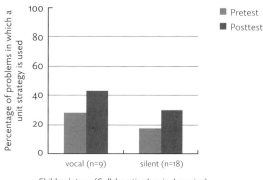

Figure 4-2 Average percentage of use of a unit strategy between vocal and silent participants (far-transfer task)

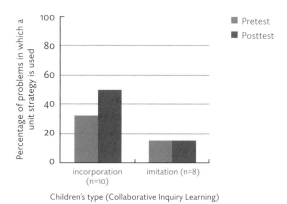

Figure 4-3 Average percentage of use of a unit strategy between the categories of incorporation and imitation (far-transfer task)

Moreover, children who had used varied strategies including a somewhat elaborated strategy (a multiplication strategy) before the instruction tended to incorporate the ideas of others presented during the discussion.

4.3 Discussion

Overall, children who had used varied strategies on the pretest tended to fully understand other children's ideas during the classroom discussion and then often used the sophisticated strategy on the posttest. On the other hand, those who had used limited strategies on the pretest tended to imitate other children's ideas during the lesson and then seldom used the sophisticated strategy on the posttest (Figure 4-4). These features seem to be common to some of the general characteristics of strategy change (Siegler, 2000); that is, 1) a correlation between variability in children's ideas and the rate of change, and 2) gradual change of strategy use. Analyzing children's classroom behaviors (vocal or silent) and their expressions on worksheets (incorporation or imitation) may contribute to clarifying the processes of strategy change (i.e., deepening processes of conceptual development) through social interaction.

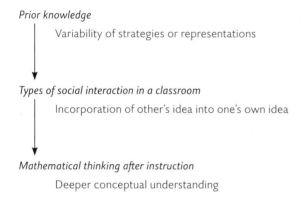

Figure 4-4 Path of conceptual development through classroom interactions

5. Conclusion

As for conceptual understanding in childhood, the studies mentioned above revealed that elementary school children develop variable and flexible knowledge structures in each domain by incorporating everyday knowledge and previously acquired knowledge through subject-matter learning. Social interactions with peers as well as individual inquiries may be promising factors for facilitating children's conceptual understanding. However, it should be noted that relating new information to existing knowledge structures by themselves through the social interaction or individual inquiry may be a key to elaborate their conceptual frameworks.

References

Carey, S. (1985). *Conceptual change in childhood.* Cambridge, MA: MIT Press.

Carraher, T. N., Carraher, D. W., & Schliemann, A. D. (1985). Mathematics in the streets and in schools. *British Journal of Developmental Psychology*, 3, 21–29.

Dean, A. L., & Frankhouser, J. R. (1988). Way-stations in the development of children's proportionality concepts: The stage issue revisited. *Journal of Experimental Child Psychology*, 46, 129–149.

English, L. D., & Halford, G. S. (1995). *Mathematics education: Models and processes.* Mahwah, NJ: Lawrence Erlbaum Associates.

Fujimura, N. (1995). A developmental study on the proportional reasoning in school age children (II): Qualitative reasoning and quantitative reasoning. *Japanese Journal of Educational Psychology*, 43, 315–325. (in Japanese)

Fujimura, N. (1997). *A developmental study on children's understanding of mathematical concepts: Proportions, intensive quantities, and multiplicative structures.* Tokyo: Kazama Shobo. (in Japanese)

Fujimura, N. (2001). Facilitating children's proportional reasoning: A model of reasoning processes and effects of intervention on strategy change. *Journal of Educational Psychology*, 93, 589–603.

Fujimura, N. (2002). Causal reasoning and the development of children's economic thinking. *The Japanese Journal of Developmental Psychology*, 13, 20–29. (in Japanese)

Fujimura, N. (2004). Japanese and Chinese children's mathematical thinking: A comparative study. *Japanese Journal of Educational Psychology*, 52, 370–381. (in Japanese)

Fujimura, N. (2010). Facilitating children's economic understanding. Paper presented at the 26th World Congress of World Organization for Early Childhood Education.

Fujimura, N. (2011). Change processes of students' mathematical concepts through teaching-learning activities. *Japanese Psychological Review*, 54, 296–311. (in Japanese)

Fujimura, N. (2012). Psychology of mathematical and scientific literacy: How do children improve their learning. Tokyo: Yuhikaku (in Japanese).

Fujimura, N. (2014). Characteristics of Finnish children's thinking and related environmental factors: From the analyses of processes of mathematics lessons in elementary schools. *Bulletin of the Graduate School of Education, the University of Tokyo*, 53, 273–283. (in Japanese)

Fujimura, N. & Ohta, K. (2002). How children change their strategies through mathematics instruction: Mathematical problem solving. *Japanese Journal of Educational Psychology*, 50, 33–42. (in Japanese)

Furth, H. G. (1980). *The world of grown-ups: Children's conceptions of society.* New York: Elsevier.

Inhelder, B., & Piaget, J. (1955). *De la Logique de l'enfant à la logique de l'adolescent* [The growth of logical thinking from childhood to adolescence]. Paris: Presses Universitaires de France.

Karplus, R., Pulos, S., & Stage, E. K. (1983). Proportional reasoning of early adolescents. In R. Lesh & M. Landau (Eds.), *Acquisition of mathematics concepts and processes.* (pp.45–90). Orlando, FL: Academic Press.

Martin, M.O., Mullis, I.V.S., Foy, P., & Stanco, G.M. (2012). *TIMSS 2011 international results in science.* Chestnut Hill, MA: TIMSS & PIRLS International Study Center, Boston College.

Matsuda, F. (2001). Development of concepts of interrelationship among duration, distance, and speed. *International Journal of Behavioral Development,* 25, 466–480.

Mullis, I.V.S., Martin, M.O., Foy, P., & Arora, A. (2012). *TIMSS 2011 International results in mathematics.* Chestnut Hill, MA: TIMSS & PIRLS International Study Center, Boston College.

Noelting, G. (1980). The development of proportional reasoning and the ratio concept: Part 1. Differentiation of stages. *Educational Studies in Mathematics,* 11, 217–253.

Nunes, T., Schliemann, A. D., & Carraher, D. W. (1993). *Street mathematics and school mathematics.* Cambridge: Cambridge University Press.

OECD (2014). *PISA2012 results:What students know and can do. Student performance in mathematics, reading, and science* (vol.1) (revised edition). OECD.

Piaget, J., & Inhelder, B. (1966). *La Psychologie de l'enfant* [The psychology of the child]. Paris: Presses Universitaires de France.

Sawyer, R. K. (ed.) (2014). *The Cambridge handbook of the learning sciences.* (2nd ed.) (Cambridge handbooks in psychology). New York: Cambridge University Press.

Schliemann, A. D., & Nunes, T. (1990). A situated schema of proportionality. *British Journal of Developmental Psychology,* 8, 259–268.

Siegler, R. S. (1981). Developmental sequence within and between concepts. *Monographs of the Society for Research in Child Development,* 46, Serial No. 189.

Siegler, R. S. (1995). How does change occur: A microgenetic study of number conservation. *Cognitive Psychology,* 28, 225–273.

Siegler, R. S. (2000). The rebirth of children's learning. *Child Development,* 71, 26–35.

Siegler, R. S., & Jenkins, E. (1989). *How children discover new strategies.* Hillsdale, NJ: Lawrence Erlbaum Associates

Siegler, R. S., & Thompson, D. R. (1998). "Hey, would you like a nice cold cup of lemonade on this hot day?": Children's understanding of economic causation. *Developmental Psychology,* 34, 146–160.

Stigler, J. W., Lee, S., & Stevenson, H. W. (1990). *Mathematical knowledge of Japanese, Chinese, and American elementary school children.* Reston, VA: National Council of Teachers of Mathematics.

Tamaru, T. (1993). *Children's development and social cognition.* Kyoto: Hosei Shuppan. (in Japanese)

Thompson, D. R., & Siegler, R. S. (2000). Buy low, sell high: The development of an informal theory of economics. *Child Development*, 71, 660–677.

Tourniaire, F. (1986). Proportions in elementary school. *Educational Studies in Mathematics*, 17, 401–412.

Vosniadou, S., & Brewer, W. F. (1992). Mental models of the earth: A study of conceptual change in childhood. *Cognitive Psychology*, 24, 535–585.

Wellman, H. M., & Gelman, S. A. (1998). Knowledge acquisition in foundational domains. In D. Kuhn, & R. S. Siegler (Eds.), *Handbook of child psychology* (5th ed.): vol. 2 *Cognition, perception, and language.* (pp. 523–573). New York: Wiley.

Getting Older, Getting Happier?
Self-regulation and Age Trends in Well-being in Japan
—

Hideki Okabayashi

Are people getting happier or unhappier with age? This is an old question in the psychology of aging literature. Although a deterioration of physical functioning with age would be expected to make people unhappier, systematic reviews of the literature on subjective well-being suggest the existence of a phenomenon known as the paradox of aging (Diener, 1984; Diener, Suh, Lucas, & Smith, 1999). This means that subjective well-being increases with age, or at least is maintained, even as one's physical health declines. Recently, in the field of economics, Blanchflower and Oswald (2008) showed that after adjusting for the cohort effects of 10 successive birth cohorts over 100 years, each of which was divided into a 10-year range, subjective well-being changed in a U-shaped pattern throughout adulthood in the United States and Western European countries. That is, life satisfaction, or happiness, decreased from young into middle adulthood and then increased into late adulthood. They also found a similar U-shaped pattern across the life span in other parts of the world; for example, in Eastern European, Latin American, and Asian nations, although these cohort effects were not controlled for, due to data limitations. The authors inferred the following reasons for this age trend: (1) people curb their aspirations that are not feasible by middle age, (2) cheerful people live longer than miserable ones, which is also known as the selection effect, and (3) older people are more likely to compare themselves with those who they believe are less fortunate. However, the authors also suggest the need for future investigations to clarify the roots of the U-shaped pattern (Blanchflower & Oswald, 2008).

As implied in reasons (1) and (3), proposed by these economists, a personal factor, specifically, "self-regulation" may account for this age trend, as suggested in the psychological literature. There are three well-known models of self-regulation strategies. The Selective Optimization with Compensation (SOC) model posits that assuming that one's resources, such as time and energy dwindle over the course of life, it is important for people to allocate their resources more efficiently with age (Baltes, 1997). The Optimization of Primary and Secondary Control (OPS) model (Heckhausen, 1997, 2010) and the dual-process model (Brandtstädter & Renner, 1990) posit that people first try to change their environment according to their preference (primary control: Heckhausen, 1997, 2010; assimilative strategy: Brandtstädter & Renner, 1990). Then, when they find it too difficult to do so, they try to control their motivation to protect or strengthen the self (secondary control: Heckhausen, 1997, 2010; accommodative strategy: Brandtstädter & Renner, 1990). However, the effects of these self-regulation strategies on age-related trends in well-being have not been examined.

The current study explores the mechanisms underlying age trends in well-being in Japan. Specifically, I address three issues concerning adult development and aging: (1) age trends in subjective well-being; (2) the factor structure of self-regulation strategies; and (3) the effects of self-regulation strategies on age trends in subjective well-being.

The first aim was to identify age trends in subjective well-being in Japan. Based on the findings reported by Blanchflower and Oswald (2008), I hypothesize that there is a U-shaped change in subjective well-being throughout adulthood. That is, life satisfaction falls from young to middle adulthood and then rises in late adulthood. On the other hand, the depressive tendency should rise from young to middle adulthood and fall in late adulthood.

Second, I examined the factor structure of a questionnaire measuring self-regulation strategies. Brandtstädter and Renner (1990) presented a dual-process model that consists of two modes of coping: assimilative and accommodative strategies. The assimilative strategy refers to the transformation of developmental circumstances in accordance with personal preferences. The accommodative strategy entails the adjustment of personal preferences to situational constraints. These strategies have been measured by a questionnaire consisting of two independent scales: the Tenacious Goal Pursuit (TGP) and Flexible Goal Adjustment (FGA) scales, the "TenFlex" scales. Brandtstädter and Renner (1990) found that both scales were positively correlated with subjective well-being, and that there was a gradual shift from an assimilative mode to an accommodative mode of coping as people aged in Germany. Although the dual-process model is easily understood in terms of the relationship between goal-related motivation and adaptation, some researchers have noted a problem with the factor structure of this questionnaire (Mueller & Kim, 2004). In particular, Heckhausen (1997) from Germany and Matsuoka (2006) from Japan suggested that items on the TGP scale should be divided into two different factors, one consisting of positive items and the other consisting of negative items. Matsuoka (2006) also found that all three self-regulation strategies (as measured by the FGA, the positive items of the TGP, and the negative items of the TGP scales) increased through young to late adulthood in her Japanese sample. I attempt to confirm whether the two-factor model or the three-factor model is more appropriate. Then I create a new framework to reorganize the factors found in this study, referring to these three models of self-regulation strategies (Baltes, 1997; Brandtstädter & Greve, 1994; Heckhausen, 2010).

Third, I aimed to clarify the effects of self-regulation strategies on age trends in subjective well-being. I examine the role of the underlying mechanisms when subjective well-being changes with age, that is, whether self-regulation strategies mediate the relationship between age and subjective well-being. Based on their finding that the use of an assimilative strategy decreased and the use of an accommodative strategy increased from young into late adulthood, Brandtstädter and Renner (1990) suggested that the accommodative strategy mediated the age trend in well-being, although the researchers did not examine this directly. To my knowledge, no studies have investigated the mediation effects of self-regulation strategies on age trends in subjective well-being. I hypothesize that all of the self-regulation strategies, especially the accommodative strategies (e.g., FGA), increase with age, have beneficial effects on subjective well-being, and mediate the relationship between age and subjective well-being.

1. METHOD

Participants
Using a systematic sampling method, potential recruits were randomly selected from a list of 123,420 people aged 25 to 79 years on the basic resident register of Hino City, a suburban area of Tokyo. A survey questionnaire was mailed to 3,000 community residents aged 25 to 79 years in October 2011, and 1,205 valid responses were returned (response rate = 40.2%).

Measurements
Subjective Well-being. Subjective well-being consists of two components: satisfaction with life and positive affect (Diener, 1984). I used two aspects of well-being (life satisfaction and depressive tendency) to measure these constructs. Life satisfaction was measured using one item: "How much are you satisfied with your life as a whole?" Participants were instructed to choose one of seven alternatives, ranging from 1 to 7: (very unsatisfied = 1, neutral = 4, to very satisfied = 7). Depressive tendency is one of many aspects of mental health and it is considered an affective component of subjective well-being, in opposition to positive affect. Depressive tendency was measured using 20 items from the Japanese version of the Center for Epidemiologic Studies Depression Scale (CES-D) (Radloff, 1977), which was standardized by Shima (1998). Each item asks participants how often they have experienced different types of depressive symptoms during the past week. Participants rate the frequency of their experiences of depressive symptoms using a scale ranging from 0 to 3 (none = 0, 2 days a week = 1, 3 or 4 days a week = 2, more than 5 days a week = 3); a higher score indicates greater psychological distress. Cronbach's alpha coefficient in the current study was .861.

Self-regulation Strategies. The Japanese version (Matsuoka, 2006) of the TenFlex, developed by Brandtstädter and Renner (1990), was used to measure self-regulation strategies. This measure consists of 17 items selected from the instruments' original 30 items (Matsuoka, 2006). The 17 items, of which eight belong to FGA and nine to TGP, are rated on a scale ranging from 1 (disagree with the statement) to 5 (agree with the statement). Cronbach's alpha coefficients in the current study were .843 for the FGA and .663 for the TGP scales. The internal consistency of the TGP scale was relatively low. The results of an examination of the factor structure of this questionnaire will be described later.

Demographic Variables. Gender was used as a dummy variable, where male = 1 and female = 0; age was measured in years, and subjective health was measured using four response options, ranging from 1 to 4 (poor = 1, somewhat poor = 2, fair = 3, and good = 4). Subjective financial status was measured using four options ranging from 1 to 4 (marginal = 1, somewhat marginal = 2, somewhat affluent = 3, and affluent = 4). Educational attainment was measured using five alternatives ranging from 1 to 5 (no education = 1, junior high school graduate = 2, high school graduate = 3, junior college graduate = 4, and university graduate or finished graduate school = 5). Marital status was used as a dummy variable, with married = 1 and unmarried = 0. Job status was used as a dummy variable, with working = 1 and not working = 0. Friendship was used as a dummy variable, where having friends =1 and no friends = 0. Living alone was used as a dummy variable, where living alone = 1 and living with someone = 0. The number of children was measured by using the actual number of children.

2. RESULTS

Descriptive statistics
The means and standard deviations for quantitative variables are presented in Table 1 and the percentages for categorical variables are presented in Table 2. The mean age of the participants was 57.09 (SD = 14.87) years and the percentage of male participants was 45.1 percent. I compared the percentage distribution of the respondents with that of the population in 22 cells crossed by 2 genders and 11 age categories by

dividing 25 to 79 years by 5 years. The distribution by gender and age of the respondents was significantly different from that of the population $[\chi^2 (10, N = 1,204) = 328.333, p < .001]$. The proportions of the young and middle-aged males aged 25 to 49 years and young females aged 25 to 29 years were lower than those found in the population, and the proportions of the older males and females aged 60 to 79 years were higher than those found in the population. The mean of the participants' health status scores (3.07) was higher than its midpoint (2.5); therefore, most of the respondents apparently judged themselves to be relatively healthy. The mean of the participants' life satisfaction scores (4.83) was higher than the neutral (4) rating on the scale; therefore, most of the respondents were relatively satisfied with their own life as a whole. Approximately 80 percent of the respondents were married, 55 percent were working, 11 percent were living alone, and 70 percent had some friends. Correlations among all the variables in this study are shown in the Appendix.

Age trends in subjective well-being

The age trends in subjective well-being were examined using regression analysis. When life satisfaction was regressed on age and the square of age, a linear trend for age was significant (β =.167, p < .001), but a quadratic trend was not (β = -.002, ns). The square of age was calculated by centered values, which were obtained by subtracting the mean age from each participant's actual age, as suggested by Aiken and West (1991). Life satisfaction was found to increase throughout adulthood. In subsequent analyses, I excluded the non-significant quadratic term for age from the equation (Table 3, Figure 1). After adjusting for the demographic and social-relation variables, this age trend was still significant (β = .098, p < .001).

When depressive tendency was regressed on age and the square of age, only a quadratic trend was significant (β = .135, p < .001) (Table 4, Figure 2). Depressive tendency decreased from young to middle adulthood (until 58.4 years old), and then increased into late adulthood. After adjusting for the demographic and social relation variables, this trend was still significant (β = .083, p < .05), and the turning point in the upward trend moved to 62.6 years old.

Table 1 Means and standard deviations of the study variables

Variables	N	Range	M	SD
Age	1,205	25–79	57.09	14.87
Health status[a]	1,197	1–4	3.07	.71
Financial status[b]	1,194	1–4	2.55	.92
Educational attainment[c]	1,197	2–5	3.79	1.01
Number of children	1,199	0–5	1.55	1.05
Flexible goal adjustment	1,122	8–40	28.34	6.09
Tenacious goal pursuit	1,134	10–45	26.26	5.10
Positive items of TGP	1,152	4–20	14.03	3.51
Negative items of TGP	1,145	5–25	17.79	3.93
Life satisfaction	1,192	1–7	4.83	1.30
Depressive tendency	1,177	0–57	11.47	8.58

a Subjective health status was measured on a 4-point scale, with 1 indicating "poor health" and 4 indicating "good health."
b Subjective financial status was measured on a 4-point scale, with 1 indicating "marginal" and 4 indicating "affluent."
c Educational attainment was measured on a 5-point scale, with 1 indicating "no experience with public education" and 5 indicating "university graduate or finishing graduate school."

Table 2 Percentage distribution of the study variables

Variables	N	%
Gender (male = 1, female = 0)	1,204	45.1
Marriage (married = 1, unmarried = 0)	1,194	79.0
Job (working = 1, not working = 0)	1,198	55.4
Friend (have some friends = 1, have no friends = 0)	1,186	69.8
Living arrangement (living alone = 1, living with someone = 0)	1,205	10.8

Table 3 Effects of age, demographic characteristics, and self-regulation strategies on life satisfaction (N = 1,060)

	b	β	b	β	b	β
Intercept	4.843		1.461		.338	
Age	.015	.168***	.009	.098**	.001	.007
Gender (male = 1, female = 0)			.061	.023	.064	.025
Health status (poor = 1 to good = 4)			.392	.212***	.240	.130***
Financial status (marginal = 1 to affluent = 4)			.490	.353***	.446	.322***

(continued)

Table 3 (continued)

	b	β	b	β	b	β
Educational attainment (no experience = 1 to university graduate= 5)			.058	.045	.060	.046
Marriage (married = 1, unmarried = 0)			.317	.100**	.314	.099**
Job (working = 1, not working = 0)			.061	.024	-.024	-.009
Friend (have some friends = 1, have no friends = 0)			.296	.105***	.184	.065*
Living arrangement (living alone = 1, living with someone = 0)			-.144	-.033	-.137	-.032
Number of children			.121	.099**	.103	.084**
FGA					.058	.273***
Positive items of TGP					.012	.033
Negative items of TGP					.001	.004
R^2	.028***		.334***		.402***	
ΔR^2	.028***		.306***		.067***	

*$p < .05$, **$p < .01$, ***$p < .001$.

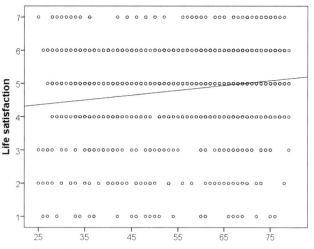

Figure 1 Age trend in life satisfaction (N = 1,192)

Table 4 Effects of age, demographic characteristics, and self-regulation strategies on depressive tendency (N = 1,052)

	b	β	b	β	b	β
Intercept	10.182		33.462		41.972	
Age	-.014	-.024	-.037	-.063	.017	.029
Age²	.005	.135***	.003	.083*	.003	.063*
Gender (male = 1, female = 0)			-1.048	-.060*	-1.083	-.063*
Health status (poor = 1 to good = 4)			-4.778	-.387***	-3.490	-.283***
Financial status (marginal = 1 to affluent = 4)			-1.045	-.112***	-.683	-.073**
Educational attainment (no experience = 1 to university graduate = 5)			-.325	-.037	-.353	-.041
Marriage (married = 1, unmarried = 0)			-1.753	-.083*	-1.699	-.080*
Job (working = 1, not working = 0)			-1.101	-.063*	-.550	-.031
Friend (have some friends = 1, have no friends = 0)			-1.663	-.088**	-.811	-.043
Living arrangement (living alone = 1, living with someone = 0)			1.537	.054	1.487	.052
Number of children			-.413	-.050	-.275	-.034
FGA					-.565	-.398***
Positive items of TGP					.091	.037
Negative items of TGP					.031	.014
R^2		.022***		.278***		.386***
ΔR^2		.022***		.264***		.109***
Age when the depressive tendency is the lowest	58.407		62.595		53.788	

*p < .05, **p < .01, ***p < .001.

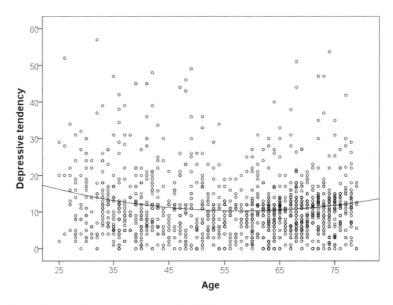

Figure 2 Age trend in depressive tendency (N = 1,177)

Factor structure of self-regulation strategies

To confirm whether the original two-factor model of Brandtstädter and Renner (1990) was appropriate, I conducted confirmatory factor analysis using LISREL 9, in which missing values were treated as multiple imputations using the Monte Carlo Markov Chain (MCMC) method. The overall fit was relatively low [χ^2 (118, N = 1,180) = 3,019.958; RMSEA = .144; GFI = .696; AGFI = .605], suggesting that there could be a more appropriate model. Therefore, I conducted another confirmatory factor analysis with a three-factor model, in which TGP was divided into two factors: four positive items and five negative items. Because the overall fit was better [χ^2(116, N = 1,180) = 1,549.97; RMSEA = .102; GFI = .856; AGFI = .810] but still not sufficiently appropriate, I modified the model to add three error covariances (see Notes below Table 5). The overall fit indices showed a better fit [χ^2(113, N = 1,180) = 1,121.32; RMSEA = .087; GFI = .894; AGFI = .856], and this model showed a significant improvement over the previous one [$\Delta\chi^2(3)$ = 428.650, $p < .001$] (Table 5).

The first factor, which consisted of the eight FGA items (FGA), suggested positive interpretation of negative events and faults to protect the self. The second factor, which consisted of the four positive TGP items

Table 5 Factor loadings of TGP and FGA items

Items	Factor Loadings
Flexible Goal Pursuit (FGA)	
*F1. When I get stuck on something, it's hard for me to find a new approach.	-.499
F2. I find it easy to see something positive even in a serious mishap.	.761
F3. When everything seems to be going wrong, I can usually find a bright side in a situation.	.840
F4. In general, I am not upset very long about a missed opportunity.	.649
F5. I adapt quite easily to changes in plans or circumstances.	.705
F6. I usually find something positive even when giving up something I cherish.	.808
F7. I find that even life's troubles have their bright side.	.841
*F8. It is very difficult for me to accept a setback or defeat.	-.313
Positive items of TGP (P-TGP)	
T1. When faced with obstacles, I usually double my efforts.	.869
T2. Even when things seem hopeless, I keep on fighting to reach my goals.	.876
T8. Even when a situation seems hopeless, I still try to master it.	.711
T9. I stick to my goals and projects even in face of great difficulties.	.678
Negative Items of TGP (N-TGP)	
*T3. I find it easy to give up on a goal if it seems difficult to achieve.	.664
*T4. When I run up against insurmountable obstacles, I prefer to look for a new goal.	.783
*T5. Life is much more pleasurable when I do not expect too much from it.	.620
*T6. I avoid grappling with problems for which I have no solution.	.451
*T7. If I find I cannot reach a goal, I prefer to change my goal than to keep struggling.	.622

Note   Error covariances between T8 and T9, T6 and T7, and F1 and F8 were significant and .24, .25, and .21, respectively. Correlations between FGA and P-TGP, FGA and N-TGP, and P-TGP and N-TGP were significant and .812, .484, and .248, respectively. Indices of goodness of fit were as follows: $\chi 2(113, N = 1{,}180) = 1{,}121.32, p < .001$; RMSEA = .087; GFI = .894; AGFI = .856.
* indicates reverse scoring of items of the original questionnaire of FGA and TGP scales.

(P-TGP), suggested tenaciousness in goal pursuit; that is, keeping up one's motivation to pursue a goal even in difficult situations. The third factor, which consisted of the five negative TGP items (N-TGP), suggested serenity for distancing oneself from an obsolete goal to look for a new goal. All correlations among the three factors were positive and significant (.812 between FGA and P-TGP, .484 between FGA and N-TGP, and .248 between P-TGP and N-TGP; $ps < .001$). For these factors, aggregated scores were used in the following analysis. Cronbach's α's were .843 for FGA, .847 for P-TGP, and .746 for N-TGP.

Mediation effects of self-regulation strategies on age trends in subjective well-being

I examined the mediation effects of the three self-regulation strategies (factors) on the age trends using these criteria. Baron and Kenny (1986) suggested the following criteria for mediation effects:

> A variable functions as a mediator when it meets the following conditions: (a) variations in levels of the independent variable significantly account for variations in the presumed mediator (i.e., Path *a*); (b) variations in the mediator significantly account for variations in the dependent variable (i.e., Path *b*); and (c) when Paths *a* and *b* are controlled, a previously significant relationship between the independent and dependent variables is no longer significant, with the strongest demonstration of mediation occurring when Path *c* is zero (p. 1,176).

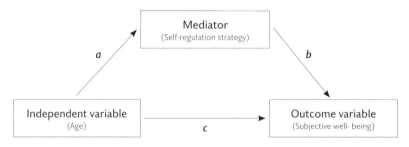

Figure 3 Model of self-regulation as a mediator

Life satisfaction. I analyzed the mediation effects of the three self-regulation strategies on the age trend in life satisfaction separately (Table 6). After adjusting for the demographic and social relation variables, life satisfaction and all the self-regulation strategies increased throughout adulthood (β = .098, p < .01 for life satisfaction; β = .295, p < .001 for FGA; β = .278, p < .001 for P-TGP; and β = .285, p < .001 for N-TGP). All of the self-regulation strategies enhanced life satisfaction (β = .293, p < .001 for FGA; β = .179, p < .001 for P-TGP; and β = .058, p < .05 for N-TGP). After controlling for either the effect of FGA or P-TGP on life satisfaction, the age trend in life satisfaction disappeared (β = .012, *ns* for FGA; β = .049, *ns* for P-TGP). These two self-regulation strategies, FGA and P-TGP, were considered strong mediators that met all the three criteria for mediators described above. However, after controlling for the effect of N-TGP on life satisfaction, the age trend in life satisfaction remained significant (β = .082, p < .05).

Table 6 Path coefficients among age, self-regulation (SR),
and life satisfaction (LS) throughout adulthood (*N* = 1,060)

	Path a Age→SR	Path b SR→LS	Path c Age→LS		Mediating effect
			before adding path b	after adding path b	
FGA	.295***	.293***	.098**	.012	Strong
P-TGP	.278***	.179***	.098**	.049	Strong
N-TGP	.285***	.058*	.098**	.082*	No

*p < .05, **p < .01, ***p < .001.

Depressive tendency. The mediation effects of the three self-regulation strategies on the age trend in depressive tendency were examined in two separate age groups split at the turning point of a quadratic age trend in depressive tendency. While the turning point in age was 58.41 years, it changed to 62.60 years after adjusting for the demographic and social relation factors. I decided to assign the cut-off age as 60 years because the compulsory retirement age for most companies and public offices is approximately sixty years old in Japan, and our lifestyles are likely to be transformed around this age.

Among the adults aged 59 years or under, after adjusting for the demographic and social relation variables, depressive tendency decreased (β = -.126, p < .01), and all of the self-regulation strategies increased until

59 years of age (β = .150, p < .001 for FGA; β = .145, p < .01 for P-TGP; and β = .117, p < .05 for N-TGP) (Table 7). FGA and P-TGP alleviated depressive tendency significantly (β = -.409, p < .001 for FGA; β = -.204, p < .001 for P-TGP), but N-TGP was not effective (β = -.068, ns). After controlling for the effect of FGA on depressive tendency, the age trend in depressive tendency disappeared (β = -.036, ns). Hence, FGA was considered a strong mediator that met all the three criteria for a mediator of the decreasing age trend in depressive tendency among the sample aged 59 years or under in Japan. After controlling for the effect of P-TGP on depressive tendency, the age trend in depressive tendency was attenuated but still significant (β = -.096, p < .05). Therefore, P-TGP was considered a weak mediator of the age trend in depressive tendency. However, after controlling for the effect of N-TGP on depressive tendency, the age trend of depressive tendency remained almost the same (β = -.118, p < .05). Thus, N-TGP did not mediate the age trend in depressive tendency.

Table 7 Path coefficients among age, self-regulation (SR), and depression (CESD) during young and middle adulthood under 60 years old (N = 523)

	Path a Age→SR	Path b SR→CESD	Path c Age→CESD		Mediating effect
			before adding path b	after adding path b	
FGA	.150***	-.409***	-.126**	.036	Strong
P-TGP	.145**	-.204***	-.126**	-.096*	Weak
N-TGP	.117*	-.068	-.126**	-.118*	No

$^*p$ < .05, $^{**}p$ < .01, $^{***}p$ < .001.

Among the adults aged 60 years or over, after adjusting for the demographic and social relation variables, depressive tendency, P-TGP, and N-TGP increased from 60 to 79 years of age (β = .090, p < .05 for depressive tendency; β = .108, p < .05 for P-TGP; and β = .158, p < .01 for N-TGP), but FGA did not (β = .024, ns) (Table 8). FGA and P-TGP alleviated depressive tendency (β = -.298, p < .001 for FGA; β = -.134, p < .001 for P-TGP; β = -.070, ns for N-TGP). Even after controlling for each of the self-regulation strategies, the age trend in depressive tendency remained significant (β = .097, p < .05 for FGA; β = .104, p < .05 for P-TGP; β = .101, p < .05 for N-TGP);

there were no self-regulation strategies that mediated the age-related increase in depressive tendency among the older adults.

Table 8 Path coefficients among age, self-regulation (SR), and depressive tendency (CESD) during late adulthood 60 years old and over ($N = 529$).

	Path a Age→SR	Path b SR→CESD	Path c Age→CESD		Mediating effect
			before adding path b	after adding path b	
FGA	.024	-.298***	.090*	.097*	No
P-TGP	.108*	-.134**	.090*	.104*	No
N-TGP	.158**	-.070	.090*	.101*	No

*$p < .05$, **$p < .01$, ***$p < .001$.

Relationships among self-regulation strategies
When all the self-regulation strategies were entered at once into the regression equation predicting emotional well-being, the age trend in life satisfaction disappeared ($\beta = .007$, *ns*; see Table 3) but the quadratic age trend in depressive tendency remained significant ($\beta = .063$, $p < .05$ in Table 4). While FGA still enhanced life satisfaction ($\beta = .273$, $p < .001$; see Table 3) and alleviated depressive tendency ($\beta = -.386$, $p < .001$; see Table 4), the effects of P-TGP disappeared. Considering these results and the high correlation between FGA and P-TGP ($r = .633$; see Appendix), FGA mediated the effects of P-TGP on the age trend in life satisfaction throughout adulthood and on the age trend in depressive tendency until approximately 60 years of age.

3. DISCUSSION

Age trends in well-being
This study found that while life satisfaction increased throughout adulthood, depressive tendency decreased from young to middle adulthood (at approximately age sixty) and then increased into late adulthood (until approximately age eighty). These trends did not change even after

controlling for the demographic and social relation variables. These findings do not support the hypothesis of a U-shaped change in subjective well-being (Blanchflower & Oswald, 2008) but are partially consistent with the paradox of aging (Diener, 1984; Diener et al., 1999), although the increasing trend in depressive tendency beginning at age sixty is inconsistent with this concept. People seem to evaluate their own life more positively with age. The reason for finding the lowest well-being among young adults may be that adaptive self-regulation strategies, such as FGA and P-TGP, which mediate the age trend of well-being, are less mature in young adults, as discussed later. Another possible explanation is that this young adult cohort may have been influenced by the economic depression during the past decade in Japan. In October 2011, when this survey was conducted, the unemployment rate of adults aged 25 to 34 years was 5.4 percent, which was higher than the average rate of 4.6 percent among people aged 15 to 64 years (Statistics Bureau of Japan, 2015). This economic depression may have caused unhappiness in young adults and made it difficult for them to have high aspirations or dreams for their adulthood. The increasing trend in depressive tendency from middle to late adulthood, which was contrary to the study's hypothesis, may be due to the inevitable physical deterioration in late adulthood, which was not fully adjusted for by the single item used to measure self-rated health status.

Factor structure of self-regulation strategies
The three-factor model consisting of FGA, P-TGP, and N-TGP was better fitted to the data than the original two-factor model of FGA and TGP was. I reinterpret the meaning of these factors, referring to an integrated framework of three distinct models proposed by Baltes (1997), Brandtstädter and Greve (1994), and Heckhausen (2010).

Although Brandtstädter and Renner (1990) proposed a dual-process model, they also implied the existence of a third factor of coping, "immunization" (Brandtstädter & Greve, 1994), which was not operationally defined. This coping strategy strengthens self-referential beliefs or promotes the interpretation of some negative events positively to protect the self. Assimilative or accommodative strategies are hypothesized to be activated after a particular goal is set and discrepancies between the ideal goal and real situation are perceived (Brandtstädter, 2009). In other words, these two strategies do not operate unless a particular goal is set. During the phase in which people have not set any goals and their perceived world is not differentiated between goal and means, another coping strategy, such as "immunization" may be needed. I think that this mechanism should receive more attention when considering coping mechanisms regardless of whether goals are set or not. In the OPS model, Heckhausen (2010) used two dimensions (primary control vs. secondary control and selection vs. compensation) and organized them into two action phases (goal engagement vs. disengagement). In the SOC model proposed by Baltes and his colleagues (1997; Freund & Baltes, 2002), four components [Elective selection (ES), Loss-based selection (LBS), Optimization (O), and Compensation (C)] seem to focus only on the primary control of behavior to change the environment. But, the other two models refer to primary control and secondary control of motivation to protect or strengthen the self.

I attempted to build a new framework and incorporate the three self-regulation factors into it. When the same two dimensions (primary control vs. secondary control and selection vs. compensation) as the OPS model are set, I added another phase labeled the "pre-action" phase to the two original phases (goal engagement and goal disengagement). In the pre-action phase, the perceived world is not differentiated between goal and means. I examined the content of the items of the three self-regulation factors with a fresh eye and included them in the framework (Table 9). Although Brandtstädter and Renner (1990) and Heckhausen (1997) considered TGP an assimilative strategy (or primary control) and FGA an accommodative strategy (or secondary control), I consider the FGA and TGP measures as secondary control of one's motivation to protect or strengthen the self. That is, while the positive items of TGP (P-TGP) measure "selective secondary control" that enhances the motivational commitment to a chosen goal, the negative items of TGP (N-TGP) measure "compensatory secondary control" that serenely distances oneself from obsolete goals. FGA seems to be another secondary control or positive interpretation to protect the self. Therefore, I recommend that these three strategies be incorporated into the different action phases. That is, FGA operates in the pre-action phase, while P-TGP operates in the goal engagement phase, and N-TGP operates in the goal disengagement phase. In the pre-action phase, regardless of whether people engage in or disengage from their own goals, FGA controls one's motivation to protect oneself in the face of unexpected adversities. In Japan, an East Asian country, where different control strategies are emphasized in comparison with Western societies (Azuma, 1984), the blurred pre-action phase should receive more attention. People, especially older adults, do not always seem to be aware of their own life goals. In addition, I consider all of the SOC elements to be assimilative strategies (or primary controls) in the goal engagement phase. After a particular goal is set and the perceived world is differentiated into goal and means, ES and LBS focus on the goal, and C and O focus on the means to change the environment efficiently.

Table 9 Reorganization of self-regulation strategies

		Action phases		
		Pre-action	Goal engagement	Goal disengagement
Primary Control for behavior to change the environment	Selection	---	Elective selection Optimization	---
	Compensation	---	Loss-based selection Compensation	---
Secondary Control for motivation to protect or strengthen the self	Selection	FGA Positive interpretation	P-TGP Tenaciousness in goal pursuit	---
	Compensation		---	N-TGP Serenity for distancing from obsolete goal

There have been other theoretical attempts to integrate the three models. Boerner and Jopp (2007) proposed the dimensions of "improvement/maintenance and reorientation" to integrate the three models, and Greve and Wentura (2007) proposed the dimensions of "personal and sub-personal layers" to do so. Although the framework proposed here is tentative, I hope that this attempt will inspire other researchers in related fields to integrate models of self-regulation strategies.

Mediation effects of self-regulation strategies
on age trends in subjective well-being

According to the three criteria suggested by Baron and Kenny (1986), FGA and P-TGP mediated the age trends in life satisfaction from young to late adulthood and in the depressive tendency from young to middle adulthood. With age, people begin to interpret negative events positively and to pursue their own goals tenaciously even in the face of adversity. As a result, these self-regulation strategies enhance older adults' satisfaction with life and alleviate their depressive tendency even if they experience age-related losses. The fact that FGA also mediated the effects of P-TGP on the age trend in well-being means that positive interpretation is more beneficial than tenaciousness in goal pursuit is.

However, from middle to late adulthood, none of the self-regulation strategies curbed the age-related increase in the depressive tendency, although the two of them (FGA and P-TGP) alleviated depressive tendency directly. This finding may be due to the fact that the most beneficial self-regulation strategy, FGA, reached a plateau at middle adulthood and did not increase in late adulthood. Unless such a self-regulation strategy becomes better able to protect the self among older adults, the inevitable physical decline in later life may exacerbate the depressive tendency.

Altogether, I found that FGA is the most adaptive coping strategy throughout adulthood. Life satisfaction increased throughout adulthood because FGA increased with age. The content of the FGA items point to the positive interpretation of negative events or faults. Such an optimistic attitude is effective in coping with various problems throughout adulthood and enhances or maintains one's satisfaction with life. This mechanism operates whenever adverse events happen, unless people set a particular goal and perceive the world as being differentiated into goals and means. Although the dual-process model is very sensible after a particular goal is set, we should pay more attention to coping mechanisms, such as "immunization" (Brandtstädter & Greve, 1994), which operate in a pre-action phase in which goals and means are undifferentiated. Then, tenaciousness in goal pursuit (P-TGP) is also a beneficial mediator of the age trends in well-being, although its effects were mediated by FGA. After people set a goal, "tenaciousness in goal pursuit (P-TGP)" is effective for their well-being, but "serenity for distancing from an obsolete goal (N-TGP)" is not. Maintaining a high level of motivation to overcome adverse events or situations is also important for people to enhance their emotional well-being throughout adulthood. Additionally, this study replicates the findings by Matsuoka (2006) that tenaciousness increased from young to late adulthood in Japan, which is inconsistent with the declining age trend in tenaciousness demonstrated in Germany by Brandtstädter and Renner (1990). It is not certain whether the differences in these findings may be attributed to measurement or cultural differences. The reason should be considered in future studies.

Limitations

One of the limitations of this study was that the collected data were cross-sectional, which can be influenced by cohort effects. Therefore, the age trends may reflect unique features of the cohorts. In particular, the finding of the lowest level of well-being among young adults might be due to the economic depression in recent years. The use of longitudinal data or more systematic data collection methods, such as sequential designs, may help to control for cohort effects (Schaie, 2013).

Second, the distribution of respondents by age and gender was significantly different from that of the general population, although the data were collected from a representative sample of community residents in a suburban city of Tokyo. Specifically, young adults were less likely to respond to the survey, while older adults were more likely to respond. This inclination may be due to young adults' busy schedules with careers or childrearing, which made them less likely to respond to the survey, and older adults' retirement schedules, which allow them enough time to do it. If unemployed young adults were more depressed and more likely to respond to the questionnaire because they had enough time to do so, their average well-being might be lower than that in the case without selection bias. We should take into account this possibility in interpreting the findings in this study.

Third, a further examination is needed for a reorganized framework of self-regulation strategies. The questionnaire used in this study to measure self-regulation strategies was borrowed from one developed by Brandtstädter and Renner (1990). In future studies, we should prepare more suitable items for the new model and confirm the factor structure again. This model should be considered a tentative one until then.

4. CONCLUSION

The finding that life satisfaction increased throughout adulthood and that the depressive tendency decreased from young until middle adulthood is consistent with the phenomenon known as the paradox of aging (Diener, 1984; Diener et al., 1999). A possible reason for this is that "positive interpretation" and "tenaciousness in goal pursuit" mediate the age trends in well-being. Positive interpretation, which also mediates the effect of tenaciousness, is one of the most beneficial coping strategies. The increasing trend in depressive tendency from middle to late adulthood may be due to the inevitable physical decline in late adulthood. The lowest level of emotional well-being found among the young adults may be due to their immature self-regulation mechanisms. These age trends in well-being should be examined in future studies that are adjusted for cohort effects. In an integrated framework of three existing models of self-regulation strategies (SOC, OPS, and the dual-process model), the importance of the pre-action phase is emphasized. In the pre-action phase, positive interpretation operates beneficially whenever adverse events happen regardless of whether particular goals are set or not. Although research on self-regulation has been more likely to focus on goal-related behavior so far, these findings suggest that we should pay more attention to the pre-action phase before particular goals are set.

ACKNOWLEDGEMENTS

The data used in this chapter were obtained from a survey that the Hino City Government in Tokyo, Japan, commissioned to the principal investigator, Professor Yusuke Takatsuka, at Meisei University. The author was also supported by a Grant-in-Aid for Science Research (C 21530700) from the Ministry of Education, Culture, Sports, Science, and Technology in Japan. The author would like to thank the research participants who generously gave their time.

References

Aiken, L. S., & West, S. G. (1991). *Multiple regression: Testing and interpreting interactions.* Newbury Park, CA: Sage.

Azuma, H. (1984). Secondary control as a heterogeneous category. *American Psychologist,* 39, 970-971.

Baltes, P. B. (1997). On the incomplete architecture of human ontogeny: Selection, optimization, and compensation as foundation of developmental theory. *American Psychologist,* 52, 366–380.

Baron, R. M., & Kenny, D. A. (1986). The moderator-mediator variable distinction in social psychological research: Conceptual, strategic, and statistical considerations. *Journal of Personality and Social Psychology,* 51, 1173–1182.

Blanchflower, D. G., & Oswald, A. J. (2008). Is well-being U-shaped over the life cycle? *Social Science & Medicine,* 66, 1733–1749.

Boerner, K., & Jopp, D. (2007). Improvement/maintenance and reorientation as central features of coping with major life change and loss: Contributions of three life-span theories. *Human Development,* 50, 171–195.

Brandtstädter, J. (2009). Goal pursuit and goal adjustment: Self-regulation and intentional self-development in changing developmental contexts. *Advances in Life Course Research,* 14, 52–62.

Brandtstädter, J., & Greve, W. (1994). The aging self: Stabilizing and protective processes. *Developmental Review,* 14, 52–80.

Brandtstädter, J., & Renner, G. (1990). Tenacious goal pursuit and flexible goal adjustment: Explication and age-related analysis of assimilative and accommodative strategies of coping. *Psychology and Aging,* 5, 58–67.

Diener, E. (1984). Subjective well-being. *Psychological Bulletin,* 95, 542–575.

Diener, E. Suh, E. M., Lucas, R. E., & Smith, H. L. (1999). Subjective well-being: Three decades of progress. *Psychological Bulletin,* 125, 276–302.

Freund, A. M., & Baltes, P. B. (2002). Life-management strategies of selection optimization, and compensation: Measurement by self-report and construct validity. *Journal of Personality and Social Psychology,* 82, 642–662.

Greve, W., & Wentura, D. (2007). Personal and subpersonal regulation of human development: Beyond complementary categories. *Human Development,* 50, 201–207.

Heckhausen, J. (1997). Developmental regulation across adulthood: Primary and secondary control of age-related challenges. *Developmental Psychology,* 33, 176–187.

Heckhausen, J. (2010). A motivational theory of life-span development. *Psychological Review,* 117, 32–60.

Matsuoka, M. (2006). Ideal self across the life span: Roles and regulation process. *Japanese Journal of Educational Psychology,* 54, 45–54. (in Japanese)

Mueller, D., & Kim, K. (2004). The tenacious goal pursuit and flexible goal adjustment scales: Examination of their validity. *Educational and Psychological Measurement,* 64, 120-142.

Radloff, L. S. (1977). The CES-D scale: A self-report depression scale for research in the general population. *Applied Psychological Measurement,* 1, 381–401.

Schaie, K. W. (2013). *Developmental influences on adult intelligence: The Seattle longitudinal study* (2nd ed.). New York: Oxford University Press.

Shima, S. (1998). The Japanese version of the CES-D scale. Chiba Test Center. (in Japanese)

Statistics Bureau of Japan. (2015). *Unemployment rate by age.* Retrieved from http://www.stat.go.jp/english/index.htm

Appendix Correlations among all variables used in this study

	1	2	3	4	5	6	7	8	9	10	11	12	13	14	15
1 Age															
2 Age²	-.44***														
3 Gender	.09**	-.04													
4 Health status	-.10***	.02	.01												
5 Financial status	.13***	-.03	-.04	.29***											
6 Educational attainment	-.28***	.09**	.16***	.14***	.16***										
7 Marriage	.21***	-.24***	.02	.11	.13	.00									
8 Job	-.42***	-.02	.18***	.10*	-.07*	.22***	-.05								
9 Friend	-.06*	.06	-.19***	.22***	.17***	.02	.03	.00							
10 Living alone	.02	.05	.03	-.07*	-.07*	-.05	-.56***	-.01	.00						
11 Number of children	.37***	-.32***	-.05	.03	.05	-.12***	.48***	-.11***	.03	-.28***					
12 FGA	.25***	-.18***	.00	.32***	.24***	.01	.14***	.00	.19***	-.04	.18***				
13 P-TGP	.25***	-.11***	.07	.20***	.17***	.01	.08*	.00	.17***	-.02	.15***	.63***			
14 N-TGP	.25***	-.06*	-.06*	.02	.07*	-.13***	.03	-.11***	-.01	-.04	.08*	.27***	.06*		
15 Life satisfaction	.17***	-.07*	.02	.34***	.46***	.12***	.26***	-.03	.20***	-.17***	.21***	.46***	.34***	.10***	
16 Depressive tendency	-.08**	.14***	-.06*	-.45***	-.27***	-.11***	-.22***	-.06*	-.17***	.15***	-.16***	-.51***	-.31***	-.09**	-.50***

Note   Number of paired responses for each correlation varied from 1,107 to 1,205.
*$p < .05$, **$p < .01$, ***$p < .001$.

Atypical Social Cognition
in Autism Spectrum Disorders

—

Atsushi Senju

Autism spectrum disorder (ASD) is a developmental disorder defined by a profound impairment in interpersonal interaction and communication, and the presence of repetitive, restricted, and stereotypical behaviors and interests (American Psychiatric Association, 2000). ASD is a highly heritable disorder, and more and more about the genetic background of the disorder is being reported (Abrahams & Geschwind, 2008). However, ASD is still a behaviorally defined disorder, which is diagnosed by behavioral observations and interviews of caregivers about the life history of the patients. Thus, a better understanding of the mechanisms underlying behavioral symptoms remains one of the most critical areas in ASD research.

Social cognition refers to the cognitive mechanisms underlying social behavior. It is a highly relevant topic in autism research because ASD can be modeled as a case of atypical development of social cognition, which then leads to symptoms such as the impairment in social interaction and communication. Our research group has been investigating social cognition in children with ASD, with a focus on spontaneous attention to, as well as spontaneous response to, socially relevant stimuli such as eye gaze and communicative action. The current paper presents an overview of the outcome of our autism project, which includes attention to the eyes, contagious yawning, and spontaneous attribution of false belief.

1. ATTENTION TO EYES

Atypical mutual gaze behavior is one of the diagnostic features of autism (American Psychiatric Association, 2000). However, in experimental settings, individuals with ASD show apparently intact capacity to discriminate gaze directions. They can easily tell direct gaze from averted gaze (Baron-Cohen, Campbell, Karmiloff-Smith, Grant, & Walker, 1995), and accurately discriminate between subtle differences in gaze direction (Leekam, Baron-Cohen, Perrett, Milders, & Brown, 1997). These results suggest that individuals with ASD do not have general impairment in gaze processing. However, gaze processing in individuals with ASD becomes less accurate than in typically developing individuals when the gaze stimuli are presented only briefly (Wallace, Coleman, Pascalis, & Bailey, 2006), suggesting that the processing of gaze direction may not be as rapid in individuals with ASD as in typically developing individuals. Our research group conducted three lines of studies to test the spontaneous allocation of attention to eye gaze in children with ASD.

Firstly, we demonstrated that individuals with ASD show a gaze cueing effect (Senju, Tojo, Dairoku, & Hasegawa, 2004), the phenomenon in which an observer shifts attention to the direction of the perceived gaze (Frischen, Bayliss, & Tipper, 2007). In this study, children with and without ASD were presented a sequence of stimuli in which a centrally presented photographed face, looking either to the left or to the right, was followed by a target stimulus presented to the left or the right of the display. Children with ASD, as well as typically developing children, detected the target faster when it was presented on the same side as the direction of the gaze cue than when it was in the opposite direction. This cueing effect remains when the gaze cue was nonpredictive or the target appeared at the cued location in 50 percent of the trials, and even when the cue was counter-predictive or the target appeared at the cued location only in 20 percent of the trials. Similar results have been reported consistently from other studies, with the exception of a few studies that used a schematic face rather than photographed face as a cueing stimulus (Nation & Penny, 2008).

Our study also demonstrated that children with ASD do not spontaneously use the gaze direction of a schematic face to learn a novel word-object association (Akechi et al., 2011). In this study, children were presented with a schematic face "looking" at one of two objects and uttering a novel word. Typically developing children were more likely to associate the novel word with the object being looked at by the schematic face than children with ASD. Eye-tracking data also demonstrated that children with ASD were less likely to follow the gaze of this schematic face than typically developing children. It was also demonstrated that children with ASD associate a novel word and the object when the utterance of the novel word coincided with the bouncing motion of the object, which made the object more visually salient at the time of the word presentation.

Secondly, several lines of research, including our own, have demonstrated that individuals with ASD show an atypical response to a perceived direct gaze, which signals a mutual gaze or eye contact. In typically developing individuals, a perceived direct gaze facilitates concurrent or immediately following processing of social information, a phenomenon that we called the "eye contact effect" (Senju & Johnson, 2009b). A direct gaze facilitates a visual search and captures attention. It also facilitates categorization of gender and the encoding and decoding of facial identity. A direct gaze also facilitates behavioral mimicry and enhances prosocial behavior (Senju & Johnson, 2009b).

Individuals with ASD, by contrast, fail to show the eye contact effect (Senju & Johnson, 2009a). For example, our study presented an array of faces with different gaze directions, and asked children to detect faces with direct or averted gaze (Senju, Hasegawa, & Tojo, 2005). Typically developing children were faster to detect faces with a direct gaze than those with an averted gaze, replicating the "stare-in-the-crowd effect" reported in typical adults (von Grünau & Anston, 1995). Children with ASD, however, were as fast to detect faces with a direct gaze as those with an averted gaze, suggesting that their search performance was not affected by the direction of the gaze. Similarly, Pellicano, et al. demonstrated that individuals with ASD, unlike typically developing individuals, do not show better performance in a task of recognizing the gender of faces when the gaze was direct (Pellicano & Macrae, 2009). These results suggest that a perceived direct gaze does not facilitate cognitive or behavioral performance in individuals with ASD.

However, a few other studies have demonstrated that individuals with ASD show enhanced physiological responses to a perceived direct gaze. In one of these studies, Kylliäinen and Hietanen presented looming faces with either a direct or averted eye gaze and asked subjects to maintain fixation on the faces while doing nothing, and found that the direct gaze elicited a larger amplitude of skin conductance response (SCR) than an averted gaze in ASD, but not in controls (Kylliäinen & Hietanen, 2006). Joseph et al. conducted a similar experiment, but used static images of faces with either a direct or averted eye gaze and asked participants to remember the faces (Joseph, Ehrman, McNally, & Keehn, 2008). The results revealed that participants with ASD showed significantly higher amplitudes of SCR than control participants, but their SCR was not affected by the gaze direction of the stimuli. In addition, the latter study found that SCR in response to a direct gaze, but not to an averted gaze, negatively correlated with the performance on a face recognition task. These studies, combined with the other studies reviewed above, suggest that a perceived direct gaze could elicit nonspecific physiological arousal, but it does not facilitate cognitive or behavioral processing in experimental settings.

Thirdly, we investigated whether reduced fixations on the eyes had downstream impacts on social cognition in ASD (Senju & Johnson, 2009a). For example, Dalton et al. reported that activation of the fusiform gyrus, the cortical area specialized for face processing, correlates with the duration of fixations on the eyes in individuals with ASD (Dalton et al., 2005). It is also reported that instruction to fixate on the eyes significantly increased activation of the fusiform gyrus in individuals with ASD (Hadjikhani et al., 2004).

Based on these findings, we tested whether instruction to fixate on the eyes increased attentional engagement to and delayed disengagement from the faces in children with ASD (Kikuchi et al., 2011). In this study, a face or an object is presented as the center of fixation, followed by a target object appearing to the left or the right of the fixation. Children were instructed to fixate on the central face or object, and saccade to the peripheral target as soon as it appeared. When they were simply instructed to fixate on the face/object, typically developing children were slower to saccade to the target when they fixated on a face than on an object. Children with ASD, by contrast, did not show increased saccade latency from faces. In a follow-up experiment, children were instructed to fixate on the eyes of a face (or equivalent area of an object). In this condition, children with ASD showed more delayed saccading from faces than from objects just like typically developing children. In addition, such a delayed saccade latency from faces disappeared in both groups of children when they were instructed to fixate on the mouth. These results suggest that reduced spontaneous fixation on the eyes would at least partly contribute to the reduced attentional engagement with the faces in children with ASD.

2. CONTAGIOUS YAWNING

Early studies reported that children with ASD had impaired capacity for imitation (Smith & Bryson, 1994), but follow-up studies found inconsistent results (Southgate & Hamilton, 2008). In particular, individuals with ASD can imitate a goal-directed action accurately under clear instruction (Hamilton, Brindley, & Frith, 2007). It is inconsistent with the claim that difficulties in imitation in ASD are based on an impaired mirror neuron system, the network of brain structures representing both executed and observed actions, because it is reported that activation of the mirror neuron system is most commonly reported in the execution and observation of goal-directed actions (Rizzolatti & Craighero, 2004).

Other studies focused on spontaneous imitation or mimicry by individuals with ASD. For example, McIntosh et al. reported that children with ASD do not mimic the observed facial expression during passive viewing, but are able to imitate the same facial expressions when they were explicitly instructed to do so (McIntosh, Reichmann-Decker, Winkielman, & Wilbarger, 2006). However, follow-up studies did not always replicate these findings. For example, one study found intact spontaneous mimicry in individuals with ASD when they were discriminating the sex of models of the stimuli (Magnée, de Gelder, van Engeland, & Kemner, 2007). Similarly another study investigated the latency in making facial expressions when observing others presenting facial expressions, and found that both individuals with ASD and typically developing individuals are faster to display a facial expression when they observe the same, rather than different, facial expression of others (Press, Richardson, & Bird, 2010). It is consistent with a study showing that congruency between self and other actions affect the accuracy of action execution in individuals with ASD (Bird, Leighton, Press, & Heyes, 2007).

Our research group focused on another form of spontaneous behavioral contagion, contagious yawning. Our initial study (Senju et al., 2007) found that children with ASD do not show contagious yawning. In this study, we presented video images of yawning adults and non-yawning adults to children with ASD and typically developing children, and found that typically developing children yawn more when they observe yawning adults than non-yawning adults but that the action of the person in the video stimulus did not affect the frequency of yawning in children with ASD. The absence of contagious yawning in ASD is also reported by two other studies (Giganti & Esposito Ziello, 2009; Helt, Eigsti, Snyder, & Fein, 2010). These studies suggest the absence of spontaneous mimicry, or behavioral synchrony, in ASD. However, in a follow-up study on contagious yawning, we did not find group differences in contagious yawning between ASD and typically developing groups when we instructed the participants to attend to the eyes of the stimuli (Senju et al., 2009). Moreover, when we presented yawning stimuli contingent to participants' fixation on the face (Usui et al., 2013), children with ASD showed clearer evidence for contagious yawning by yawning more frequently in response to yawning stimuli than to control stimuli. Taken together, these studies seem to demonstrate that individuals with ASD mimic another person's actions without explicit instruction in some experimental conditions, when their attention was guided to the relevant action.

3. FALSE BELIEF ATTRIBUTION

In a landmark study, Baron-Cohen, Leslie, and Frith reported that children with ASD do not pass the false belief test, which assesses the capacity to understand that the protagonist makes a mistake about an object in the scene because it was manipulated (e.g. moved, swapped, or removed) in his/her absence (Baron-Cohen, Leslie, & Frith, 1985). The follow-up studies consistently found that before the verbal mental age of 11 years, children with ASD do not pass various versions of the false belief test. Whereas typical four-year-olds correctly anticipate others' behavior based on the attribution of false belief, children with ASD, at the same mental age or even higher, incorrectly predict behavior based on reality without taking the other person's epistemic states (e.g., knowledge and belief) into account (Happé, 1995). This result suggests that children with ASD (with verbal skills equivalent to typically developing children of under 11 years old) fail to infer others' epistemic mental states, or at least fail to do so when others' mental states are different from the child's own. Individuals with ASD with higher verbal skills, by contrast, do pass the standard false belief test. However, qualitative difficulties in social interaction and communication persist even in these "high-functioning" individuals with ASD (Baron-Cohen, O'Riordan, Stone, Jones, & Plaisted, 1999; Castelli, Frith, Happé, & Frith, 2002; Happé, 1994).

We assessed whether individuals with high-functioning ASD fail the spontaneous false belief test, even though they can easily pass standard false belief tests. To test this hypothesis, we used a version of the sponta-neous false belief test that had been used to assess the anticipatory looking based on false belief attribution in two-year-old infants (Southgate, Senju, & Csibra, 2007). In this task, children observed a video presentation in which an object was moved when an actor was looking away. The subject's anticipatory look was then recorded with an eye-tracker, which revealed that infants anticipated the actor's behavior based on his/her false belief and predicted that the actor will look for the location where she last saw the object being hidden.

This task was administered to adults with Asperger Syndrome. Asperger Syndrome is a sub-category of ASD, with similar symptoms but no devel-opmental delay in verbal skills (American Psychiatric Association, 2000). In our experiment (Senju, Southgate, White, & Frith, 2009), 19 adults with Asperger Syndrome watched the video stimuli we used in Southgate and others (Southgate et al., 2007), and their eye movements were recorded with an eye-tracker. No instruction was given to the participants. For comparison with typical development, we also recruited 17 neurotypical adults of similar age, gender ratio, and general cognitive skills. All participants in both groups passed standard false belief tests. As a result, the Asperger group showed significantly less anticipatory looking based on the protagonist's false belief than the neurotypical controls did. A follow-up analysis revealed that the anticipatory looking of neurotypical controls was significantly biased to the correct location. This is not the case for Asperger group, whose anticipatory looking behavior was not biased to either side. A similar group difference was observed in younger children aged 6 to 9 years old with ASD (Senju et al., 2010).

Our study demonstrates that adults with Asperger syndrome do not spontaneously anticipate others' actions in a nonverbal task, although it is closely modelled on the standard false belief test which they pass with ease. In particular, the contrast with neurotypical two-year-olds who spontaneously looked at the correct location on the same task (Southgate et al., 2007) is quite notable. It is unlikely that a general lack of motivation is to blame, as all the participants in the Asperger group showed correct anticipatory looking in the familiarization trials, in which false belief attribution is not necessary.

The results of this study are consistent with the clinical profile of high-functioning individuals with ASD, who show difficulties in social communication in real life despite performing fairly well in a well-controlled experimental or training context. It is also consistent with the findings that training for false belief tests does not necessarily improve social adaptation in ASD (Ozonoff & Miller, 1995): the capacity for false belief attribution may not be sufficient to deal with its spontaneous use in a fluid and rapidly changing "real" social world.

---

4. CONCLUSIONS

The current paper summarized the results of research by our group, as well as other international research groups, investigating the characteristics of atypical social cognition in individuals with ASD.

Firstly, individuals with ASD show a mixed profile in eye gaze processing. They are capable of discriminating gaze direction, and show a typical attention shift to the direction of others' gaze in some experimental conditions. However, they also showed atypical gaze-following behavior when they see schematic faces, which suggests that individuals with ASD might be using different visual features to process gaze direction. In addition, individuals with ASD do not show the eye contact effect, the phenomenon that perceived eye contact facilitates cognitive or behavioral processing of concurrent or immediately following events. This finding contrasts with the physiological studies which demonstrated that perceived direct gaze could elicit non-specific physiological arousal in individuals with ASD. Moreover, unlike typically developing individuals, individuals with ASD are less likely to show the bias to attend to others' eyes, especially when they are observing dynamic, social, and communicative actions. Such a weaker attention to the eyes might partly explain the atypical face processing of, and attentional engagement with, faces, because when they were instructed to attend to the eyes, individuals with ASD show more similarities with typically developing individuals in the behavioral and neural response to the perceived faces.

Secondly, individuals with ASD do not spontaneously mimic others' actions such as facial expression and yawning, even though they can imitate the same actions under explicit instructions. Follow-up studies demonstrated that individuals with ASD could produce spontaneous mimicry, including contagious yawning, when their attention is directed to the relevant action. These studies suggest that the absence of spontaneous mimicry in ASD could, at least partly, result from the weaker spontaneous attention to others' actions in the absence of relevant task demands.

Thirdly, individuals with ASD do not spontaneously attribute false belief to others, even those with high verbal and cognitive skills who can easily do so when explicitly instructed to. Thus the absence of spontaneous theory of mind would cause difficulty in social interaction and communication, even in adults with high verbal and cognitive skills beause we have to process socially relevant information rapidly, spontaneously, and on-line in order to achieve day-to-day social interaction. Further studies will be required to specify the mechanism underlying the absence of spontaneous theory of mind in ASD.

These studies seem to suggest that atypical social cognition in ASD could be, at least partly, characterized by the weaker tendency to spontaneously attend to socially relevant information. Individuals with ASD have less difficulty in processing social information when their attention is directed to the relevant features by explicit task instruction, or the design of the task such as the stimulus presentation and the task demands. Further studies will be required to identify the mechanisms underlying spontaneous attention to socially relevant information in a naturalistic environment by typically developing individuals, and its atypical development in individuals with ASD.

Many of our research findings have been replicated in European and American populations, suggesting that this atypical profile of social cognition in ASD is universal and not specific to a Japanese population. However, it is also important to study the effect of cultural environment on the development of individuals with ASD (Freeth, Sheppard, Ramachandran, & Milne, 2013; Koh & Milne, 2012). Further studies will be required to identify both the universal and culture-dependent features of autistic symptoms, which would show how the social environment modulates the development of individuals with ASD.

ACKNOWLEDGEMENT

I thank Musashino Higashi School for continuous collaborations in autism research, which lead to the research outcomes summarized in this paper. The author was supported by a UK Medical Research Council Career Development Award (G1100252) during the preparation of this chapter.

REFERENCES

Abrahams, B. S., & Geschwind, D. H. (2008). Advances in autism genetics: on the threshold of a new neurobiology. *Nature Reviews Genetitcs*, 9(5), 341–355.

Akechi, H., Senju, A., Kikuchi, Y., Tojo, Y., Osanai, H., & Hasegawa, T. (2011). Do children with ASD use referential gaze to learn the name of an object? An eye-tracking study. *Research in Autism Spectrum Disorders*, 5(3), 1230–1242.

American Psychiatric Association. (2000). *Diagnostic and statistical manual of mental* disorders (4th ed., text revision), *DSM-IV-TR*. Washington, DC: APA.

Baron-Cohen, S., Campbell, R., Karmiloff-Smith, A., Grant, J., & Walker, J. (1995). Are children with ASD blind to the mentalistic significance of the eyes? *British Journal of Developmental Psychology*, 13(4), 379–398.

Baron-Cohen, S., Leslie, A. M., & Frith, U. (1985). Does the autistic child have a "theory of mind"? *Cognition*, 21(1), 37–46.

Baron-Cohen, S., O'Riordan, M., Stone, V., Jones, R., & Plaisted, K. (1999). Recognition of faux pas by normally developing children and children with Asperger syndrome or high-functioning autism. *Journal of Autism and Developmental Disorders*, 29(5), 407–418.

Bird, G., Leighton, J., Press, C., & Heyes, C. (2007). Intact automatic imitation of human and robot actions in autism spectrum disorders. *Proceedings of the Royal Society B: Biological Sciences*, 274(1628), 3027–3031.

Castelli, F., Frith, C., Happé, F., & Frith, U. (2002). Autism, Asperger syndrome and brain mechanisms for the attribution of mental states to animated shapes. *Brain*, 125, 1839–1849.

Dalton, K. M., Nacewicz, B. M., Johnstone, T., Schaefer, H. S., Gernsbacher, M. A., Goldsmith, H. H., et al. (2005). Gaze fixation and the neural circuitry of face processing in autism. *Nature Neuroscience*, 8(4), 519-526.

Freeth, M., Sheppard, E., Ramachandran, R., & Milne, E. (2013). A Cross-Cultural Comparison of Autistic Traits in the UK, India and Malaysia. *Journal of Autism and Developmental Disorders*, 43(11), 1–15.

Frischen, A., Bayliss, A. P., & Tipper, S. P. (2007). Gaze cueing of attention: visual attention, social cognition, and individual differences. *Psychological Bulletin*, 133(4), 694–724.

Giganti, F., & Esposito Ziello, M. (2009). Contagious and spontaneous yawning in autistic and typically developing children. *Current Psychology Letters*, 25(1).

Hadjikhani, N., Joseph, R. M., Snyder, J., Chabris, C. F., Clark, J., Steele, S., . . . Tager-Flusberg, H. (2004). Activation of the fusiform gyrus when individuals with autism spectrum disorder view faces. *Neuroimage*, 22(3), 1141–1150. S1053811904001636 [pii]

Hamilton, A. F., Brindley, R. M., & Frith, U. (2007). Imitation and action understanding in autistic spectrum disorders: How valid is the hypothesis of a deficit in the mirror neuron system? *Neuropsychologia*, 45(8), 1859-1868.

Happé, F. G. (1994). An advanced test of theory of mind: Understanding of story characters' thoughts and feelings by able autistic, mentally handicapped, and normal children and adults. *Journal of Autism and Developmental Disorders*, 24(2), 129–154.

Happé, F. G. (1995). The role of age and verbal ability in the theory of mind task performance of subjects with autism. *Child Development*, 66(3), 843–855.

Helt, M. S., Eigsti, I. M., Snyder, P. J., & Fein, D. A. (2010). Contagious yawning in autistic and typical development. *Child Development*, 81(5), 1620–1631.

Joseph, R. M., Ehrman, K., McNally, R., & Keehn, B. (2008). Affective response to eye contact and face recognition ability in children with ASD. *Journal of International Neuropsychological Society*, 14(6), 947–955.

Kikuchi, Y., Senju, A., Akechi, H., Tojo, Y., Osanai, H., & Hasegawa, T. (2011). Atypical disengagement from faces and Its modulation by the control of eye fixation in children with ASD spectrum disorder. *Journal of Autism and Developmental Disorders*, 41, 629–645.

Koh, H., & Milne, E. (2012). Evidence for a cultural influence on field-independence in autism spectrum disorder. *Journal of Autism and Developmental Disorders*, 42(2), 181–190.

Kylliäinen, A., & Hietanen, J. K. (2006). Skin conductance responses to another person's gaze in children with ASD. *Journal of Autism and Developmental Disorders*, 36(4), 517–525.

Leekam, S., Baron-Cohen, S., Perrett, D., Milders, M., & Brown, S. D. (1997). Eye-direction detection: A dissociation between geometric and joint attention skills in autism. *Brititsh Journal of Developmental Psychology*, 15(1), 77–95.

Magnée, M. J., de Gelder, B., van Engeland, H., & Kemner, C. (2007). Facial electromyographic responses to emotional information from faces and voices in individuals with pervasive developmental disorder. *Journal of Child Psychology and Psychiatry*, 48(11), 1122-1130.

McIntosh, D. N., Reichmann-Decker, A., Winkielman, P., & Wilbarger, J. L. (2006). When the social mirror breaks: Deficits in automatic, but not voluntary, mimicry of emotional facial expressions in autism. *Developmental Science*, 9(3), 295-302.

Nation, K., & Penny, S. (2008). Sensitivity to eye gaze in autism: Is it normal? Is it automatic? Is it social? *Development and Psychopathogy*, 20(01), 79–97.

Ozonoff, S., & Miller, J. N. (1995). Teaching theory of mind: A new approach to social skills training for individuals with autism. *Journal of Autism and Developmental Disorders*, 25(4), 415–433.

Pellicano, E., & Macrae, C. N. (2009). Mutual eye gaze facilitates person categorization for typically developing children, but not for children with ASD. *Psychonomic Bulletin & Review*, 16(6), 1094-1099.

Press, C., Richardson, D., & Bird, G. (2010). Intact imitation of emotional facial actions in autism spectrum conditions. *Neuropsychologia*, 48(11), 3291–3297.

Rizzolatti, G., & Craighero, L. (2004). The Mirror-neuron system. *Annual Review of Neuroscience*, 27(1), 169-192. doi: doi:10.1146/annurev.neuro.27.070203.144230

Senju, A., Hasegawa, T., & Tojo, Y. (2005). Does perceived direct gaze boost detection in adults and children with and without autism? The stare-in-the-crowd effect revisited. *Visual Cognition*, 12(8), 1474–1496.

Senju, A., & Johnson, M. H. (2009a). Atypical eye contact in autism: Models, mechanisms and development. *Neuroscience & Biobehavoral Review*, 33(8), 1204–1214.

Senju, A., & Johnson, M. H. (2009b). The eye contact effect: Mechanisms and development. *Trends in Cognitive Sciences*, 13(3), 127–134.

Senju, A., Kikuchi, Y., Akechi, H., Hasegawa, T., Tojo, Y., & Osanai, H. (2009). Brief Report: Does Eye Contact Induce Contagious Yawning in Children with ASD Spectrum Disorder? *Journal of Autism and Developmental Disorders*, 39(11), 1598–1602.

Senju, A., Maeda, M., Kikuchi, Y., Hasegawa, T., Tojo, Y., & Osanai, H. (2007). Absence of contagious yawning in children with ASD spectrum disorder. *Biological Letters*, 3(6), 706-708.

Senju, A., Southgate, V., Miura, Y., Matsui, T., Hasegawa, T., Tojo, Y., et al. (2010). Absence of spontaneous action anticipation by false belief attribution in children with ASD spectrum disorder. *Development and Psychopathology*, 22, 353–360.

Senju, A., Southgate, V., White, S., & Frith, U. (2009). Mindblind eyes: An absence of spontaneous theory of mind in Asperger Syndrome. *Science*, 325(5942), 883–885.

Senju, A., Tojo, Y., Dairoku, H., & Hasegawa, T. (2004). Reflexive orienting in response to eye gaze and an arrow in children with and without autism. *Journal of Child Psychology and Psychiatry*, 45(3), 445–458.

Smith, I. M., & Bryson, S. E. (1994). Imitation and action in autism: A critical review. *Psychological Bulletin*, 116(2), 259–273.

Southgate, V., & Hamilton, A. F. (2008). Unbroken mirrors: challenging a theory of autism. *Trends in Cognitive Sciences*, 12(6), 225–229.

Southgate, V., Senju, A., & Csibra, G. (2007). Action anticipation through attribution of false belief by 2-year-olds. *Psychological Science*, 18(7), 587-592.

Usui, S., Senju, A., Kikuchi, Y., Akechi, H., Tojo, Y., Osanai, H., & Hasegawa, T. (2013). Presence of contagious yawning in children with ASD spectrum disorder. *Autism Research and Treatment*, 2013, Article ID 971686, 1-8.

von Grünau, M., & Anston, C. (1995). The detection of gaze direction: A stare-in-the-crowd effect. *Perception*, 24(11), 1297–1313.

Wallace, S., Coleman, M., Pascalis, O., & Bailey, A. (2006). A study of impaired judgment of eye-gaze direction and related face-processing deficits in autism spectrum disorders. *Perception*, 35(12), 1651–1664.

Effectiveness of a Nursery School Teacher Training Program in Providing Interventions and Supports for Children with Developmental Disorders

Junichi Yamamoto and Atsuko Matsuzaki

Several studies have reported that the number of children with developmental disorder is increasing (Ministry of Education, Culture, Sports, Science, and Technology of Japan, 2014). Correspondingly, the Japan Nursery Association (2010) noted that 54.2 percent of nursery schools accepted developmentally delayed children and 13 percent of the schools had more than 10 children who need special care. However, teachers reported that they had not received sufficient training to support those children. The Japan Nursery Association (2010) concluded that developing a training program for teachers was an urgent issue.

As part of a national commitment to the increased number of children with developmental disorder, every prefecture and designated cities across the country established regional support centers based on Services and Supports for Persons with Disabilities Act (Ministry of Health, Labour and Welfare in Japan, 2005). Children and their families are able to receive special support at the centers, and the number of children who use the centers has increased (Information Center for Persons with Developmental Disabilities, 2011). However, despite the serious responsibilities of teachers working at the centers, an evidence-based training program for teachers has not yet been established.

Evidence has demonstrated that outcomes for children with developmental disorder are improved by early intervention based on applied behavior analysis (ABA). ABA produces great improvements in communication, social functions, and play skills for children with autism spectrum disorders (e. g., Dawson et al., 2012; Lovaas, 1987; Sallows & Graupner, 2005; Smith, Groen, & Wynn, 2000), as well as for children with other disabilities (e.g., Clark-Bischke & Crowley, 2011; Feeley & Jones, 2006). However, many of those intervention programs require very intensive and long-term one-to-one sessions with certified therapists. It is difficult to implement these intervention programs in the Japanese welfare/education system because of the lack of skilled therapists, time constraints, and economic cost.

Therefore, the authors examined the conditions that maximized intervention effects with less-intensive and short-term interventions. We developed an intervention program called the "Keio Early Intervention Program (KEIP)" that can be applied in several different settings in Japan (Yamamoto & Matsuzaki, 2010; Yamamoto & Matsuzaki, 2014a, 2014b). The program features (a) focusing on five modules of early communication development: attention, joint attention, imitation, receptive language, and expressive language; (b) supporting the child's strengths rather than his/her weaknesses; (c) modifying the child's daily life to maximize opportunities for children to receive the intervention; and (d) a fidelity scale that ensures the quality of the therapist's intervention.

After we demonstrated the effects of the program for a child with autism (Matsuzaki & Yamamoto, 2012), we developed a training program so that more teachers could use the intervention program (Matsuzaki & Yamamoto, 2015). One way to implement the intervention program was by engaging nursery school teachers who already have the general knowledge and skills related to child development.

Several studies have demonstrated the effects of teacher training in preschool, inclusion classes, and special education settings. In Japan, Tanaka et al. (2011) reported the effects of nursery teacher training on the design of intervention plans for children with developmental disorder. Fifteen nursery school teachers received four 3.5 hour sessions on the basic principles of ABA, a method of functional assessment, planning behavioral support, and implementing the program for children with behavioral problems. Consequently, the teachers improved their skills for coping with behavioral problems in a simulated case. The teachers also reported that the skills they learned were effective for increasing desired behaviors and reducing unwanted behaviors in children.

Rose and Church (1998) reviewed intervention studies and suggested that training sessions alone did not affect teachers' intervention skills, but that training packages including feedback procedures had stronger effects on their skills. Casey and McWilliam (2008) examined the effects of graphical feedback on teachers acquiring the techniques of incidental teaching (McGee & Daly, 2007), one of several naturalistic ABA strategies using daily routines as an opportunity to learn conversational language. Twenty-one teachers participated in the study. They received a one- to two-hour lecture and one hour of classroom practice, which allowed the teachers to have immediate feedback and suggestions on site. Then they received graphical feedback on an incidental teaching checklist three days a week for about 20 to 50 sessions. As a result, teachers increased their usage of incidental teaching during and after the intervention. However, despite the study's strengths, changes in the children were not assessed.

The purpose of this study was to establish a short-term teacher training program and assess its effects. The training program consisted of a 90-minute lecture and five 30-minute on-the-job training (OJT) sessions to increase teachers' individual intervention skills as assessed by a fidelity scale. The primary goals were to (a) assess teachers' acquisition of intervention skills and (b) evaluate changes in children resulting from the training program. All procedures were performed at the teachers' and children's school facilities. Utilizing these facilities' familiar environments and materials would facilitate teachers' use of their newly acquired teaching skills in their everyday teaching.

1. METHOD

1.1 *Participants*
Three female teachers participated in this study. Teacher A worked at a private nursery school, and Teachers B and C worked at a regional support center. Usually, teachers at nursery schools teach basic communication skills, social skills, and self-care through daily routines and play to children between the ages 0–6. Teachers at regional support centers teach

communication skills and self-care skills to children with developmental disorder in small-group or one-to-one settings. All three teachers were in their 20s, had national licenses in early childhood education, and had between three and six years of experience (mean = 4.3). They had not studied ABA prior to the study, and neither facility had incorporated ABA into its daily teaching.

The child participants were three boys with developmental disorders in communication. The children were between two to six years old (mean = 4.5) at the beginning of the study. Prior to this study, the Kyoto Scale of Psychological Development 2001 (KSPD; Ikuzawa, Matsushita, & Nakase, 2002), a commonly administered standardized scale in Japan, was conducted to assess the children's physical-movement, cognitive-adaptive, and language-sociability functioning.

Koichi (2 years, 1 month) attended the private nursery school where Teacher A worked five days a week. He has a mild intellectual disability. He had several one-word expressions in his vocabulary, such as "give me," "more," and "please," but he did not speak more than two-word sentences. Although he was very social and friendly most of the time at the nursery school, he often threw tantrums when other people could not understand his speech. His KSPD score yielded a mental age of 1 year 9 months (developmental quotient (DQ): 80).

Ryota (5 years, 9 months) and Takashi (6 years, 2 months) both visited the regional support center twice a week where Teachers B and C worked. They had been diagnosed with autism by pediatricians not related to this study. According to the criteria set by the Childhood Autism Rating Scale (CARS; Schopler, Reichler, & Renner, 1988), both children were considered to be in the severely autistic range, scoring 46 and 50, respectively.

Ryota's KSPD score yielded a mental age of 3 years, 8 months (DQ: 61). He expressed his desires with one-word expressions, such as "book," "go," or "card," and usually repeated the words until his requests had been answered. He also often produced jargon, especially when he did not know the words for what he wanted to express. His receptive language skills were limited to simple directions, and he usually responded to questions with echolalia.

Takashi's KSPD score yielded a mental age of 2 years, 7 months (DQ: 48). He had verbal imitation skills for up to two-word phrases, but he rarely produced spontaneous verbal utterances. He tended to respond to questions with echolalia, and usually took an adult's hand when he needed help with a task. Teachers at the regional support center reported that he often screamed, bit his wrists, hit his head, covered his ears, and cried aloud. Teachers were often unable to identify the causes of the tantrums, but assumed that noise, temperature, hunger, or sleepiness might have been involved.

This study was approved by the research ethics committee at the authors' home institution (No.11054), and the children's teachers and parents provided written consent.

1.2 *Settings and Materials*

All phases, from baseline through three-month follow-up, were held in a one-to-one setting at the facilities where the teachers taught. Each teacher was assigned one of the children (Koichi with Teacher A, Ryota with Teacher B, and Takashi with Teacher C) according to their administrators' requests. The rooms used for the sessions were about 15 m^2 and contained a child-sized table, chairs, and age-appropriate toys and materials. The teachers and a supervisor (the second author, described in the procedure section) selected the toys and materials such as cards, puzzles, coloring books, and teaching aids. All sessions were video recorded with a digital video camera with surrounding microphones for feedback and assessment purposes.

1.3 *Procedures*

1.3.1 Baseline

Ryota and Takashi had been receiving one-to-one teaching for about 15 minute per week for about a year with the participating teachers at the regional support center. To evaluate the baseline, the supervisor video-recorded these teaching sessions for 20 minute and 40 minute, respectively. Koichi had not received any special instruction at the nursery school, so the one-to-one setting was new to both the teacher and the child. To evaluate a baseline, Teacher A was instructed to interact with Koichi to establish his communication behaviors as much as possible in a one-to-one setting using toys, puzzles, bubbles, and modeling clay for 20 minute. All the interactions were video recorded and split into 10-minute segments as probes.

1.3.2 Intervention

The intervention consisted of (a) a 90-minute didactic lecture and (b) 30-minute OJT sessions once a week for five consecutive weeks. The second author is a clinical developmental psychologist with over 10 years' experience in working with children with developmental disorders. She had also intensively practiced ABA intervention strategies under the first author for one year and worked as a supervisor in this study.

Teachers received a 90-minute lecture at their facilities and were introduced to (i) the basic principles of ABA, such as three-term contingency, functional assessment, and task analysis; (ii) intervention techniques such as prompt-fading, time delay, and shaping; (iii) knowledge of the five modules of early communication development, attention, joint attention, imitation, receptive language, and expressive language; and (iv) intervention skills to establish communication behaviors. The intervention skills included 15 items: five items for antecedents, six items for target behaviors, and four items for consequents in the three-term contingency. Table 1 shows each item of the intervention skills as the KEIP fidelity scale for teacher training.

Thirty-minute OJT sessions were held for five consecutive weeks for each pair of participants, and the first 10 minute of each session were used as the assessment probe. The target behaviors for the children were selected from the KEIP checklist (explained in the dependent measures section) by teachers and the supervisor. The activities, such as puzzles, blowing bubbles, modeling clay, or play shopping, were selected according to the child's interests. On the first training session, the supervisor led most of the session to model teaching skills such as getting the child's attention, enhancing the child's motivation, choosing target behaviors, providing opportunities to elicit verbal utterances, and giving functional reinforcement. On the second and third sessions, the supervisor first prompted verbal utterances and desired communication behaviors from the child, and then handed him over to the teacher to continue to work on these skills.

Table 1 KEIP fidelity scale for teacher training

	Antecedents
1	Use appropriate vocal tones, speed, dynamics, and/or timing to get the child's attention.
2	Use exaggerated facial expressions or gestures.
3	Get the child's attention before giving instructions.
4	Use toys selected by the child.
5	Give clear instructions.
	Target behavior
6	Follow the child's interests and set the target tasks within the activity.
7	Teach the target behavior joyfully to maintain the child's motivation.
8	Mix learned tasks and target tasks within the activity.
9	Give sufficient modeling for tasks.
10	Repeat learning cycles (ABC) for teaching new tasks.
11	Provide appropriate prompts for acquisition tasks.
	Consequents
12	Give reinforcement immediately after the response.
13	Give reinforcement clearly.
14	Give reinforcement approximating the target behavior.
15	Give reinforcement using a variety of stimuli (expressions, gestures, toys, activities, foods, or drinks).

During those sessions, the supervisor performed several ABC cycles and supports, which were (A) providing modeling or a verbal instruction as the antecedents, (B) facilitating the appropriate teaching behavior, and (C) giving performance feedback as the consequent. More specifically, the supervisor instructed the teacher to focus on target teaching behaviors to promote child target behavior and provided information about results on the behavior. When the teachers did not perform well, the supervisor provided modeling or verbal instruction and demonstrated application of the skills and/or points of observation. During the fourth and fifth sessions, the teachers primarily led the sessions, and the supervisor provided immediate feedback on the teacher's skills, target behaviors, and activities.

1.3.3 Follow up

Follow-up sessions were scheduled three months after the last training session. The setting and procedures were identical to those of the baseline phase. The observations were made for 20 to 30 minutes and split into 10-minute segments as probes.

1.4 *Dependent measures*
1.4.1 Teacher outcomes

Fidelity of implementation. The teacher's intervention skills were evaluated using the KEIP fidelity scale (Table 1) for teacher training on each video probe. The fidelity scale consisted of 15 items, evaluated on a 5-point Likert scale from 1 (very poor) to 5 (very good). The total points were divided by the maximum possible score of 75 and multiplied by 100 to represent the fidelity scores for the assessment. The criterion for the fidelity score was set at 80 percent.

1.4.2 Child outcomes

Language and early communication skills. Language development was measured using the Japanese MacArthur Communicative Developmental Inventory (JCDI; Ogura & Watamaki, 2004), which is standardized and designed to assess early communication developments. The JCDI consisted of two tests, "Language and Gestures" and "Vocabulary and Grammar." In this study, the "Language and Gestures" scale was used and the total numbers of production, gesture, and comprehension subscales were used as the scores. The parents were asked to answer a series of questions before and after the intervention.

Early communication skills were measured by the KEIP checklist (Yamamoto & Matsuzaki, 2010). The list consisted of seven modules of early communication development, including attention, joint attention, imitation, gesture, receptive language, expressive language, and social interaction. Each module consisted of 11 to 24 items, a total of 89 items. The parents were asked to rate each item using the following scale: Behaviors the child did often received a plus, behaviors the child did not do received a minus, and behaviors the child did occasionally received a plus/minus. For analysis purposes, responses were recorded to a 3-point scale (minus = 0; plus/minus = 1; plus = 2), and the total number was used as the overall score.

Social and challenging behaviors. To assess changes in the children's social and communication behaviors, each video probe was evaluated for four behaviors: (a) attention, (b) social interaction, (c) functional verbal utterances, and (d) challenging behaviors. Attention was measured using the attention category of the child behavior rating scale (CBRS; Mahoney & Wheeden, 1998). The attention category consisted of four items: attention to activities, persistence, involvement, and cooperation. Each item was evaluated on a 5-point Likert scale ranging from 1 (very low) to 5 (very high). The average of the items was used as the attention score.

Social interaction was measured by the initiation category of the CBRS (Mahoney & Wheeden, 1998). The initiation category consisted of three items: initiating activities, joint attention, and affect. Each item was evaluated on a 5-point Likert scale ranging from 1 (very low) to 5 (very high). The average of the items was used as the social interaction score.

Functional verbal utterances were defined as verbalizations that (a) were initiated by the child without an adult model, (b) were relevant to the interaction, and (c) contained a phonetically correct approximation of the word or word combination (adapted from Koegel, O'Dell, & Dunlap, 1988; Vismara, Colombi, & Rogers, 2009). Functional verbal utterances within each 10-minute period were counted.

Challenging behaviors were also counted. These included occurrences of predefined behaviors within each 10-minute period, such as (a) screaming, (b) hitting himself or others, (c) pushing others, or (d) throwing or upsetting materials.

1.5 Study design

A non-concurrent multiple baseline design across participants (Watson & Workman, 1981) was used to measure teacher outcome and pre-post design was used for child outcome. For the children's communication behaviors, the average of the first two probes of the baseline phase was used as the baseline score for each child; the average of the probes of the fourth and fifth sessions (the last two sessions) of the intervention phase was used as the intervention score; and the average of the first two probes of the three-month follow-up phase was used as the follow-up score.

1.6 *Inter-observer reliability*
1.6.1 Fidelity of implementation
Inter-observer reliability for the fidelity scale was 36 percent across teachers. Prior to the study, the supervisor and a research assistant practiced coding with video recorded sessions that had not been taken for assessment purposes. After practicing coding until reliability was at 90 percent or higher for the three probes, the actual coding for the study started. Following Vismara et al. (2009), agreement was defined as both coders' scores being within one point on the Likert scale for each item. The mean inter-observer agreement was 99.2 percent with a Cohen's kappa of .97 (Cohen, 1968).

1.6.2 Children's social and communication behaviors
Inter-observer reliabilities obtained for the children's communication behaviors were 36 percent across children. Agreement for attention and social interaction were defined as both coders' scores being within one point on the Likert scale for each item. The mean inter-observer agreement was 100 percent for attention, 100 percent for social interaction, 78 percent for functional verbal utterances, and 100 percent for challenging behaviors.

2. RESULTS

2.1 *Teacher outcomes*
2.1.1 Fidelity of implementation
Figure 1 shows the fidelity scores across teachers. None of the teachers met the criterion (80 percent) at baseline (the average of baseline probes were 50 percent, 54.7 percent, and 55.3 percent, respectively, for Teachers A, B, and C). Teacher C met the criterion at the third training session, and Teachers A and B at the fourth training session. Once the teachers met

the criterion, they were able to maintain this improvement through the three-month follow-up phase.

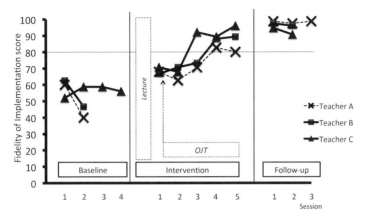

Figure 1 Teachers' fidelity scores across baseline, intervention, and three-month follow-up phases. The horizontal line indicates the criterion for the fidelity of implementation (80 percent). The OJT started after a 10-min assessment period during the first session of the intervention phase, which is represented by the arrow in the figure.

2.2 *Child outcomes*

2.2.1 Language and early communication skills

Figure 2 shows the data for each subscale of the JCDI across children. All children increased their scores for speech production on the JCDI, with Koichi increasing from 63 to 205, Ryota from 292 to 384, and Takashi from 123 to 157. Scores for comprehension also increased from 245 to 285 for Koichi, from 398 to 427 for Ryota, and from 140 to 176 for Takashi. Scores for use of gesture also increased from 50 to 61 for Koichi, from 49 to 53 for Ryota, and from 25 to 29 for Takashi. Thus, the changes for Takashi were smaller than those of the other two children.

On the KEIP checklist, all children increased their scores after the intervention. Specifically, Koichi increased his score from 126 to 170, Ryota from 125 to 149, and Takashi from 91 to 114. The maximum possible score is 178.

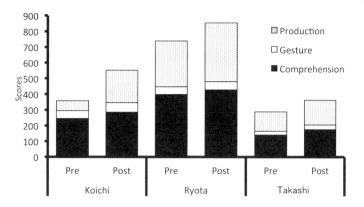

Figure 2 Scores of "Language and Gestures" in the Japanese MacArthur communicative developmental inventory (JCDI) scale of the children.
The totals of production, gesture, and comprehension subscales were used as the scores.

2.2.2 Social and communication behaviors

Table 2 shows averaged scores of CBRS for each phase across children. All children demonstrated an increase in attention scores after the intervention. Between the intervention and the three-month follow-up, Koichi made gains and Takashi maintained prior gains. Although Ryota's score decreased in the follow-up, this score was still higher than his baseline score.

For the social interaction, all children showed increases in scores of CBRS after the intervention. The trend between the intervention and follow-up phases was similar to that for the attention scores; Koichi made gains and Takashi maintained prior gains. Ryota's score decreased in the follow-up; however, this score was still higher than his baseline score.

For functional verbal utterances, Koichi and Ryota increased their scores in the intervention, while Takashi displayed a slight decrease. However, all numbers in the follow-up phases were higher than those in the baseline.

Koichi and Ryota did not show any challenging behaviors in any of the phases. Takashi screamed and bit his wrist 4, 7, 13, and 0 times, respectively, during the four 10-minute baseline probes. After the second intervention session, Takashi did not show any further challenging behaviors, including during the three-month follow-up phase.

Table 2 Children's behavioral changes across baseline, intervention, and 3-month follow-up phases

	Child	Baseline	Intervention	3-Month follow-up
Attention	Koichi	4.1	4.3	5.0
	Ryota	3.4	4.3	3.5
	Takashi	2.8	3.8	3.8
Social Interaction	Koichi	1.8	4.5	5.0
	Ryota	2.8	4.0	3.0
	Takashi	1.8	3.3	3.3
Functional Verbal Utterances	Koichi	14.5	31.5	45.0
	Ryota	19.5	32.5	37.0
	Takashi	6.0	4.5	18.0
Challenging Behaviors	Koichi	0.0	0.0	0.0
	Ryota	0.0	0.0	0.0
	Takashi	5.5	0.0	0.0

Note   The baseline score represents the average of the first two probes, the intervention score represents the average of the last two probes, and the three-month follow-up score represents the average of the first two probes of the phases.

3. DISCUSSION

This study evaluated the effects of short-term teacher training in an early childhood education setting by measuring three teachers' acquisition of intervention skills and the subsequent outcomes of three children with disorder in communication development.

Results indicated that the teachers' intervention skills on the fidelity scale slightly increased after the 90-min lecture, but none of them reached the criterion level of 80 percent from the lecture alone. As OJT sessions proceeded, all teachers showed improvements in skills that improved child attention, social interaction, and communication behaviors. Teachers maintained their fidelity scores through the rest of the intervention phase, as well as in the three-month follow-up phase. This suggests that the lecture was not sufficient for teachers to gain competence in intervention skills and that several feedback sessions were necessary. This finding is consistent with previous studies (Rose & Church, 1998). However, the training program in this study improved teachers' intervention skills within a much shorter period of time compared with the previous studies (Casey & McWilliam, 2008, 2011; Kohler, Anthony, Steighner, & Hoyson, 2001). One reason could be that we employed OJT as a feedback procedure. In the OJT sessions, the teachers observed modeling of the intervention skills as many times as needed. Then teachers imitated these skills immediately after observing them being modeled with the same child for the same activity and situation. Teachers easily understood the procedure and function of the intervention skills. Another reason for the program's effectiveness is that we clarified 15 specific target behaviors for teachers in the fidelity scale. These skills are applicable to various settings, tasks, and levels of child development. Repeating many ABC cycles, observing modeling, practicing, and receiving knowledge of results, enabled the teachers to acquire the specific intervention skills within just five 30-minute OJT sessions.

We provided a questionnaire to ask teachers their opinions about the training program during the last training session, and all teachers reported that the program was very helpful in providing knowledge and skills through interaction with the children. The teachers' administrators reported that the teachers tended to generalize the acquired skills to their work with other children and also applied them to group settings after the training. One unique aspect of this study was that all procedures were administered at the facilities in which the teachers and children worked and studied. Ecologically valid interventions, such as utilizing the participants' environments, might encourage and motivate teachers to integrate their newly acquired skills into their daily teaching settings.

In terms of child outcomes, all children increased their scores on all subscales of the JCDI and on the KEIP checklist. Their frequency of functional verbal utterances increased after the intervention and showed further increases in the three-month follow-up period. However, the rates of the gain varied among the children. Koichi's gains were larger than those of the other two children. One reason could be because Koichi attended the nursery school five days a week, whereas Ryota and Takashi attended only two days a week. Thus, Koichi had more opportunities to interact with his teacher (Teacher A). If this was the reason for the improvement, training nursery school teachers could have very significant effects. The other reason could be that Koichi's attention skills were better compared with those of the other children. Attention skills are among the foundations for learning more complex behaviors (Mahoney, Perales, Wiggers, & Herman, 2006); therefore, Koichi might have been able to acquire communication skills more efficiently than others.

Only Takashi displayed challenging behaviors such as hitting his head, biting his arms, and screaming frequently. These behaviors decreased dramatically to zero after the intervention, and this improvement was maintained in the follow-up phase. His teachers also reported that his challenging behaviors noticeably decreased in a group setting as well. Conceivably, this decrease in challenging behaviors might be related to an increase in functional verbal utterances. In related a study, Durand and Carr (1991) succeeded in reducing challenging behaviors with communication training, and they theorized that communication skills replaced challenging behaviors as functionally equivalent responses. In addition, Vismara et al. (2009) noted that the low level of disruptive behaviors may have been facilitated by the motivational components within naturalistic play routines. Further investigation is needed to determine the relationship between communication development and challenging behaviors.

As mentioned at the beginning, the number of children with developmental disorder and the number of nursery schools accepting those children have dramatically increased in Japan (Japan Nursery Association, 2010). Teachers strongly expressed the need for special training to support those children, so a great demand exists for the development of an effective teacher training program (Japan Nursery Association, 2010). The results of this study suggested the feasibility of the short-term teacher training program. As the number of teachers who use evidence-based intervention skills in their daily work increases, so will the number of children who will have learning opportunities during their daily routines regardless of location, time, or geographical restrictions. We believe that this study could be the start of a major step to providing a support system for children with developmental disorder and their families.

Our next challenge is disseminating the laboratory-based training program to community settings so that teachers can use the ABA-based intervention strategies in their daily work. Developing training protocols and a dissemination system must be the key for the success of the program. The training protocol should include a manual, target tasks, implementation strategies, and case examples. More importantly, we have to develop a system to train the trainers. The authors have started studies of a train-the-trainer (TTT) model for such specialists as clinical developmental psychologists, clinical psychologists, speech-language-hearing therapists, and special education teachers to train practitioners of the next generation. We continue studying the dissemination of ABA-based intervention strategies so that persons working with children in the community can receive the evidence-based training program beyond administrative and/ or geographical boundaries.

ACKNOWLEDGEMENTS

The affiliations of the authors are Keio University. This study was supported by Japan Science and Technology Agency (JST), CREST and a Grant-in-Aid for Scientific Research (B) No. 26285213 by Japan Society for the Promotion of Science (JSPS). We greatly thank the teachers, children, and parents for their participation.

REFERENCES

Casey, A. M. & McWilliam, R. A. (2008). Graphical feedback to increase teachers' use of incidental teaching. *Journal of Early Intervention*, 30(3), 251-268.

Casey, A. M., & McWilliam, R. A. (2011). The characteristics and effectiveness of feedback interventions applied in early childhood settings. *Topics in Early Childhood Special Education*, 31(2), 68-77.

Clark-Bischke, C., & Crowley, E. (2011). Applied behavior analysis and students with visual impairments: A literature review. *Research & Practice in Visual Impairment & Blindness*, 4(1), 2-14.

Cohen, J. (1968). Weighted kappa: Nominal scale agreement provision for scaled disagreement or partial credit. *Psychological Bulletin*, 70(4), 213-220.

Dawson, G., Jones, E. H., Merkle, K., Venema, K., Lowy, R., Faja, S., & Webb, S. J. (2012). Early behavioral intervention is associated with normalized brain activity in young children with autism. *Journal of the American Academy of Child & Adolescent Psychiatry*, 51(11), 1150-1159.

Durand, V., & Carr, E. G. (1991). Functional communication training to reduce challenging behavior: Maintenance and application in new settings. *Journal of Applied Behavior Analysis*, 24(2), 251-264.

Feeley, K. M., & Jones, E. A. (2006). Addressing challenging behavior in children with Down syndrome: The use of applied behavior analysis for assessment and intervention. *Down Syndrome Research & Practice*, 11(2), 64-77.

Ikuzawa, M., Matsushita, Y., & Nakase, A. (Eds.) (2002). *Kyoto scale of psychological development 2001*. Kyoto, Japan: Kyoto International Social Welfare Exchange Centre.

Information Center for Persons with Developmental Disabilities (2011). *The number of children with developmental disabilities used support center for developmental disabilities*. Retrieved from http://www.rehab.go.jp/ddis/

Japan Nursery Association (2010). *Survey of intervention for children with development delay*. Retrieved from http://www.nippo.or.jp/research/pdfs/2009_01/2009_01.pdf

Koegel, R. L., O'Dell, M., & Dunlap, G. (1988). Producing speech use in nonverbal autistic children by reinforcing attempts. *Journal of Autism and Developmental Disorders*, 18(4), 525-538.

Kohler, F. W., Anthony, L. J., Steighner, S. A., & Hoyson, M. (2001). Teaching social interaction skills in the integrated preschool: An examination of naturalistic tactics. *Topics in Early Childhood Special Education*, 21(2), 93-103.

Lovaas, O. (1987). Behavioral treatment and normal educational and intellectual functioning in young autistic children. *Journal of Consulting and Clinical Psychology*, 55(1), 3-9.

Mahoney, G., & Wheeden, C.A. (1998). Effects of teacher style on the engagement of preschool-aged children with special learning needs. *Journal of Developmental and Learning Disorders*, 2, 293-315.

Mahoney, G., Perales, F., Wiggers, B, & Herman, B. (2006). Responsive teaching: Early intervention for children with Down syndrome and other disabilities. *Down Syndrome Research and Practice*, 11(1), 18-28.

Matsuzaki, A. & Yamamoto, J. (2012). The effects of early intervention program on preverbal communication in a child with autism: Developmental and behavioral analysis with the multiple-baseline design. *The Japanese Journal of Special Education*, 49(6), 657-669.

Matsuzaki, A. & Yamamoto, J. (2015). The effects of a teacher training program: Dissemination of evidence-based intervention techniques to the community. *Journal of Special Education Research*, 52(5), 359-368.

McGee, G. G., & Daly, T. (2007). Incidental teaching of age-appropriate social phrases to children with autism. *Research & Practice for Persons with Severe Disabilities*, 32(2), 112-123.

Ministry of Education, Culture, Sports, Science, and Technology in Japan (2014). *Survey about special education*. Retrieved from http://www.mext.go.jp/a_menu/

shotou/tokubetu/material/1348283.htm

Ministry of Health, Labour, and Welfare in Japan (2005). *Services and Supports for Persons with Disabilities Act.* Retrieved from http://www.mhlw.go.jp/topics/2005/02/tp0214-1c.html

Ogura, T. &.Watamaki, T. (2004). *The Japanese MacArthur communicative development inventory.* Kyoto, Japan: Kyoto International Social Welfare Exchange Centre.

Rose, D. J., & Church, R. J. (1998). Learning to teach: The acquisition and maintenance of teaching skills. *Journal of Behavioral Education,* 8(1), 5-35.

Sallows, G., & Graupner, T. (2005). Intensive behavioral treatment for children with autism: Four-year outcome and predictors. *American Journal on Mental Retardation,* 110(6), 417-438.

Schopler, E., Reichler, R.J., & Renner, B.R. (1988). *The childhood autism rating scale (CARS): For diagnostic screening and classification of autism.* Los Angeles, US: Western Psychological Services.

Smith, T., Groen, A. D., & Wynn, J. W. (2000). Randomized trial of intensive early intervention for children with pervasive developmental disorder. *American Journal of Mental Retardation,* 105(4), 269-285.

Tanaka, Y., Mitamura, T., Noda, W., Baba, C., Shimazaki, T., & Tanaka-Matsumi, J. (2011). Effects of applied behavior analysis workshops on support behaviors of supervising teachers of nursery schools for children with developmental disabilities. *Behavioral Science Research,* 49(2), 107-113.

Vismara, L.A., Colombi, C., & Rogers, S.J. (2009). Can one hour per week of therapy lead to lasting changes in young children with autism? *Autism: The International Journal of Research & Practice,* 13(1), 93-115.

Watson, P. J., & Workman, E. A. (1981). The non-concurrent multiple baseline across-individuals design: An extension of the traditional multiple baseline design. *Journal of Behavior Therapy and Experimental Psychiatry,* 12(3), 257-259.

Yamamoto, J. & Matsuzaki, A. (2010). *Keio Early Intervention Program 2010: A treatment manual.* Tokyo, Japan: Keio University.

Yamamoto, J. & Matsuzaki, A. (2014a). Developing an early intervention program. *Japanese Journal of Clinical Psychology,* 14(3), 361-366.

Yamamoto, J. & Matsuzaki, A. (2014b). A comprehensive intervention program for developing communication based on applied behavior analysis: Keio Early Intervention Program. *Health Science for Children,* 14(1), 23-29.

Japanese Children's Use of Function Morphemes during Language Development
—

Etsuko Haryu and Sachiyo Kajikawa

Function morphemes such as determiners (demonstratives, definite, and indefinite articles, etc.), particles (case-marking devices known as *joshi* in Japanese), and verb suffixes should play an important role in children's language acquisition, since they appear at the edge of syntactic boundaries. Although children frequently omit function morphemes from their early speech (Brown, 1973), recent studies have demonstrated that children are indeed sensitive to these elements from very early on. That is, children learning English, French, or German clearly represent some determiners at 6 to 8 months of age (Hallé, Durand, & de Boysson-Bardies, 2008; Höhle & Weissenborn, 2003; Shi, Marquis, & Gauthier, 2006; Shi, Werker, & Cutler, 2006), use them as a cue to word segmentation by 11 months of age (Höhle & Weissenborn, 2000; Shi, Cutler, Werker, & Cruickshank, 2006; Shi & Lepage, 2008), and syntactically categorize nouns by attending to preceding determiners around the age of 15 months (Höhle, Weissenborn, Kiefer, Schulz, & Schmitz, 2004; Shi & Melançon, 2010).

In the present article, we report our research on Japanese children's use of function morphemes in segmenting and syntactically categorizing adjacent words. Unlike previously researched languages, function morphemes do not precede but rather follow content words in Japanese. A case particle follows a noun to indicate the grammatical relation (or case) of the preceding noun to the predicate. A verb suffix appears immediately after a verb to mark the preceding verb for tense, aspect, negation, and so on. In the following sentence (a), a subject-marking particle *ga* marks the preceding noun *inu* 'dog' as a subject. Another particle *o* indicates that the preceding noun *booru* 'ball' is an object of the predicate verb *oikake-ta* 'chased.' The verb suffix-*ta* in (a) marks the preceding verb *oikake* 'chase' for past tense, and another suffix-*teiru* in (b) marks the same verb for the present progressive aspect.

(a) *Inu   ga   booru   o   oikake-ta.*
    dog   SUB[i]   ball   OBJ[ii]   chased
    'A dog chased a ball.'

(b) *Otokonoko   wa   inu   o   oikake-teiru*
    boy   TOP[iii]   dog   OBJ   is chasing
    'As for the boy, he is chasing the dog.'

i   Subject marker
ii   Object marker
iii   Topic marker

What is interesting for Japanese is not only that function morphemes follow content words, but also that case particles that attach to nouns are often omitted in casual speech, especially when the grammatical relation of the preceding noun to the predicate can be easily inferred from the context. Pertaining to the above sentence (a), Japanese-speaking adults may say "*Inu ga booru _ oikake-ta*" or "*Inu _ booru _ oikake-ta*," omitting the object-marking particle *o*, the subject-marking particle *ga*, or both. Analyses of 25 Japanese mothers' speech to their 6- to 15-month-old infants have indicated that the subject-marking particle *ga* was dropped an average of 35 percent of the time, and that the object-marking particle *o* was omitted an average of 91 percent of the time (Kajikawa & Haryu, 2008). Cook also found that a Japanese mother omitted the subject-marking particle *ga* and the object-marking particle *o* in 16 percent and 82 percent of their potential contexts, respectively, in her speech to her two-year-old child (Cook, 1985).

This extensive omission of particles appears to have two consequences, which differentiate Japanese from previously studied languages. First, the frequent omission of particles may lower the frequency with which

Japanese-learning children hear particles in speech input, which may make it difficult for them to learn to use particles. As a result, Japanese-learning children may require more time to become able to use function morphemes in segmenting and syntactically categorizing adjacent words compared with English-, French-, and German-learning children.

Second, the co-occurrence relationship between content words and function words is predicted to be stronger for verbs than for nouns in Japanese. This is because case particles are often omitted in casual speech whereas a verb never appears without a verb suffix in utterances. This fact contrasts with previously studied languages, English, French, and German. In these languages, it has been reported that the co-occurrence relationship between determiners and nouns is stronger than that between pronouns and verbs (Höhle, Weissenborn, Kiefer, Schulz, & Schmitz., 2004; Shi & Melançon, 2010). Accordingly, French- and German-learning children around the age of 15 months successfully categorized nouns by attending to preceding determiners, while they failed to syntactically categorize verbs using preceding pronouns as cues (Höhle, Weissenborn, Kiefer, Schulz, & Schmitz, 2004; Shi & Melançon, 2010).

Keeping these facts in mind, we investigated Japanese children's use of function morphemes in segmenting and syntactically categorizing adjacent words. In Study 1 (Haryu & Kajikawa, 2016), we explored the use of function morphemes in word segmentation by children learning Japanese by focusing on the subject-marking particle *ga*. The reason for focusing on this particle is that we found that it occurred most frequently among the particles attaching to nouns in 20 Japanese mothers' speech to their 10- to 15-month-old children (Haryu & Kajikawa, 2015a). In Study 2 (Kajikawa & Haryu, 2008), we examined Japanese-learning children's knowledge that case particles can be omitted. In Study 3 (Haryu & Kaji kawa, 2015b), we investigated whether Japanese-learning children begin to use verb suffixes to syntactically categorize verbs earlier than they use particles to syntactically categorize nouns. Based on these results, we discuss what property of input languages may affect the ease with which children learn to use function morphemes to segment and syntactically categorize adjacent words.

1. Study 1: Word segmentation using the subject-marking particle *GA*

From what age do Japanese-learning children use the subject-marking particle *ga* to segment an adjacent word from fluent speech? To explore this problem, we tested 10-, 12-, and 15-month-olds using a modified procedure of habituation. The experiment consisted of a habituation phase and a test phase. During the habituation phase, children heard a standard passage (noun standard passage, see Table 1; A) comprising two sentences, in each of which a target nonsense word appeared always followed by the particle *ga*. During the test phase that began immediately after habituation, children were tested in two types of test trials, word-particle test trials and isolated-word test trials. That is, children heard speech segments consisting of the target word and the particle *ga* (e.g., *X-ga*) during the word-particle test trial, while they heard isolated target words (e.g., *X*) during the isolated-word test trial. Note that the target word was always followed by the particle *ga* in the standard passage during the habituation phase. If children rely on transitional probability to segment a word from fluent speech, they should regard the word-particle sequence (e.g., *X-ga*) as one word. As a result, the isolated words should be unexpected for the children and they should attend to the isolated target words longer than to the word-particle speech segments during the test phase. However, if the children do recognize the particle *ga* and successfully separate the target word from the following particle in the standard passage, the isolated target words should be more expected than the word-particle speech segments. Therefore, the children should attend longer to the word-particle speech segments than to the isolated words during the test phase.

Japanese-learning 10-, 12-, and 15-month-olds took part in the experiment. Figure 1 depicts the mean listening times for children of each age group during the isolated-word and word-particle test trials. Ten-month-olds listened longer to the isolated words than to the word-particle speech segments, whereas 15-month-olds demonstrated the reverse pattern. Twelve-month-olds did not respond differently to the two types of test stimulus. Statistical analyses confirmed this impression.

224

Table 1 Stimulus materials used in Studies 1 and 3.

A.	Noun standard passage used in Studies 1 and 3

Kore	*wa*	*X* [i]	*ga*	*sukina*	*kai.*
This	TOP [ii]	X	SUB [iii]	like	shell

'This is the shell that X likes.'

X	*ga*	*yorokobu*	*to ii*	*ne*
X	SUB	be pleased with	hope that	sentence-final particle

'I hope that X is pleased with (it).'

B.	Verb standard passage used in Study 3

Min-na	*issyoni*	*X-tteiru*
Everybody	together	is X-ing

'Everybody is X-ing together.'

X-tteiru	*no*	*wa*	*dare?*
X-ing	that	TOP	who

'Who is that X-ing?'

C.	Noun test passage used in Study 3

X	*o*	*goran?*
X	OBJ [iv]	look

'Look at (the) X'

X	*wa*	*dokoni*	*iru?*
X	TOP	where	is

'Where is (the) X?'

D.	Verb test passage used in Study 3

X-ranai	*no?*
X-not	sentence-final particle

'Why don't you X?'

X-ru	*no*	*wa*	*doo?*
X	that	TOP	how about?

'How about X-ing?'

i A disyllabic nonsense word was used here.
ii TOP = Topic marker
iii SUB = Subject marker
iv OBJ = Object marker

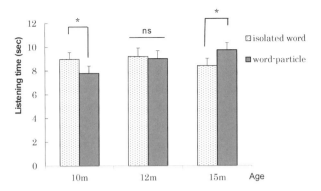

Figure 1   Mean listening times for children of each age group (error bars indicate standard errors) during isolated-word test trials and word-particle test trials in Study 1.
*p <.05

Ten-month-olds demonstrated longer listening times in the isolated-word test trials than in the word-particle test trials, which indicated that isolated words were unexpected for 10-month-olds, probably because they segmented the word-particle sequence as a word from the standard passage by relying on transitional probability. In contrast, 15-month-olds attended longer to the word-particle speech segments than to the isolated words, indicating that the word-particle speech segments were more unexpected than the isolated target word as a word that should be segmented from the standard passage. This suggests that 15-month-olds successfully separated the target word from the particle in the standard passage. Twelve-month-olds did not demonstrate clear preference for one type of test stimulus over the other. However, we should not conclude that 12-month-olds have no idea about particles when comparing their responses with those of 10-month-olds. Probably, 12-month-olds begin to recognize particles, although their knowledge of particles is not sufficiently strong to lead them to think that segmenting the word-particle sequence as a word from the passage is unreasonable.

The results suggest that at 15 months of age Japanese-learning children use the particle *ga* as a more important cue than transitional probability during word segmentation. This age is not very early when we consider that French-, English-, and German-learning children use determiners to segment words by 11 months at the latest (Höhle & Weissenborn, 2000; Shi, Cutler, Werker, & Cruickshank, 2006; Shi & Lepage, 2008). This relative delay observed for Japanese-learning children should be attributed to the properties of Japanese particles. As mentioned previously, Japanese particles do not precede but rather follow nouns and are often omitted. However, with regard to the first factor, i.e., word order, a previous study has demonstrated that even 8-month-olds are already familiar with the relative order of function morphemes (frequent elements) and content words (infrequent elements) in the language they are learning (Gervain, Nespor, Mazuka, Horie, & Mehler, 2008). Given this, the word order in which function morphemes follow content words in Japanese should not make children's learning of particles extremely difficult.

The second characteristic, the frequent omission of particles, appears to lower the frequency with which Japanese-learning children hear particles in speech input and to make it difficult for them to learn particles. However, corpus analyses have indicated that Japanese children hear the high-frequency particle *ga* as frequently as French-learning children hear the high-frequency determiner *des* (indefinite plural article "some"). In the Japanese mothers' speech to three children aged 16 to 23 months (Aki, Ryo, and Tai corpora, Miyata, 2004a, 2004b, 2004c in the CHILDES database, MacWhinney, 2000; Oshima-Takane, MacWhinney, Sirai, Miyata, & Naka, 1998), the percentage of use of the particle *ga* was 0.89 percent (490 of 55,204 morpheme tokens), whereas that for the frequent determiner *des* was 0.69 percent (20 of 2,901 word tokens) in French-speaking mothers' speech to two children from 14 to 21 months (Shi & Lepage, 2008). Considering that French-learning children begin to demonstrate the ability to use the determiner to segment an adjacent word at eight months (Shi & Lepage, 2008), frequency cannot explain why Japanese-learning children require so much time to learn to use particles to segment adjacent words.

As a factor that makes it difficult for Japanese children to learn to use particles, we may rather consider the fact that case particles rarely appear at utterance edges. For example, the subject-marking particle *ga* usually not only follows a noun but also is followed by a predicate verb. This fact should make the learning of the particle difficult, given the finding that infants recognize words positioned at an utterance boundary more easily than those positioned in the middle (Seidl & Johnson, 2006). Furthermore, the fact that the noun-particle phrase does not appear without being followed by a predicate led us to adopt a procedure in the present experiment that required the children to extract a word preceding the particle from a sentence. This procedure is slightly different from that of previous studies which required children to extract a target word from a speech segment consisting of a determiner and the target word (Shi, Cutler, Werker & Cruickshank, 2006; Shi & Lepage, 2008). This change of procedure in the present experiment may also have made the segmentation task more difficult for Japanese children. However, at the same time, the procedure enabled us to identify the age at which Japanese-learning children establish a robust ability to use particles in word segmentation. From this point of view, we might expect that 15-month-olds learning Japanese have a more advanced understanding of particles that extends beyond just using them to segment words from fluent speech. For example, 15-month-olds may already know that the subject-marking particle *ga* can be omitted from a sentence without making much difference to its meaning. In the next section, we describe a study that explored this question (Kajikawa & Haryu, 2008).

2. STUDY 2: CHILDREN'S KNOWLEDGE THAT PARTICLES CAN BE OMITTED

In order to examine whether Japanese-learning children know that the particle *ga* can be omitted from a sentence, we compared their responses to a sentence change in which the subject-marking particle *ga* was omitted with a change in which the subject-marking particle was replaced with a non-particle syllable. Specifically, we first habituated Japanese-learning 15-month-olds to a standard sentence containing *ga*: "*Rume* (subject noun) *ga* (subject-marking particle) *muwa-tteiru* (is *muwa*-ing) *yo* (sentence-final particle)," in which *rume* (subject noun) and *muwa* (verb) were nonsense words. The standard sentence was repeatedly presented until the children were fully habituated, as indicated by a decline in listening time. During a test phase immediately following habituation, the children heard 1) the standard sentence, 2) the particle-dropped sentence, i.e., "*Rume_ muwa-tteiru yo*," and 3) the particle-replaced sentence in which the particle *ga* was replaced with the non-particle syllable *ki*, i.e.,

"Rume-**ki** muwa-tteiru yo." If children successfully detect the change of a syllable in a sentence, they should demonstrate longer listening times to the particle-replaced sentence than to the standard sentence. In addition, if children know that omission of a particle affects neither word boundaries nor the sentence meaning, they should not react much to the particle-dropped sentence. That is, listening times for the particle-dropped sentence should not differ from those for the standard sentence. However, if children lack knowledge about omission of particles, they should listen to the *ga*-dropped sentence longer than to the standard sentence. The results (Figure 2; graph (A)) suggested that 15-month-old children know that the particle *ga* can be omitted. Children listened significantly longer to the *ga*-replaced sentence compared with the standard sentence. However, listening times for the *ga*-dropped sentence did not differ from those for the standard sentence.

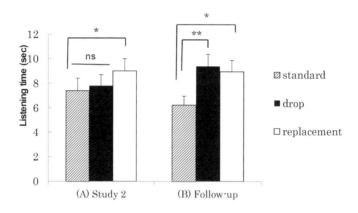

Figure 2 Mean listening times (error bars indicate standard errors) for the standard, dropped, and replaced test sentence in Study 2 in which 15-month-olds were habituated to a sentence including the subject-marking particle *ga* graph (A), and a follow-up study in which children were habituated to a sentence without the particle graph(B).
*p <.05, ** p <.01

In a follow-up experiment, we examined whether children of the same age could detect the dropping of a syllable from a sentence. This time, we habituated the children to another standard sentence that included a non-particle syllable *ki* instead of the particle *ga*, "Rume-ki muwa-tteiru yo." During the test phase, we observed the children's responses to 1) the standard sentence, 2) the syllable-dropped sentence, i.e., "Rume_ *muwa-tteiru yo,"* and 3) the sentence in which the non-particle syllable *ki* was replaced with the particle *ga*, i.e., *"Rume-ga muwa-tteiru yo."* Figure 2; graph (B) shows the results of this follow-up experiment. Statistical analyses indicated that listening times for the syllable-dropped sentence were as long as those for the syllable-replaced sentence, both of which were significantly longer than listening times for the standard sentence. These results indicated that 15-month-olds successfully detected not only a change of syllable but also its complete omission from the sentence.

Taking these results together, 15-month-olds did not react to dropping of the particle *ga*, not because they did not detect the omission, but rather because they knew that dropping a particle does not make much difference in terms of the original meaning of the sentence. Children learning Japanese appear to take much time to learn to use particles to successfully segment adjacent words, as demonstrated in Study 1. However, by the time children are able to do so, they also understand that the particles can be omitted without substantially changing the sentence meaning and word boundaries.

3. STUDY 3: SYNTACTIC CATEGORIZATION OF NOUNS AND VERBS

Studies 1 and 2 demonstrated that 15-month-olds learning Japanese not only use the subject-marking particle *ga* to segment adjacent words from fluent speech, but also know that the particle can be omitted without making much difference to the sentence meaning. Given that function morphemes appear at the edge of syntactic boundaries in utterances, however, they should serve not only as a cue to word boundaries but also as a cue to the syntactic categories of adjacent words. For example, a determiner *the* in English is likely to indicate that the following word is a noun and the noun may be preceded by another determiner in another utterance. Likewise, pronouns precede verbs. For example, in French, a verb may be preceded by a pronoun *il* 'he' in one utterance, and may be preceded by another pronoun *elles* 'they' in another utterance.

Previous studies have demonstrated that French- and German-learning children around the age of 15 months succeeded in syntactically categorizing nouns by attending to preceding determiners while at the same time they failed to syntactically categorize verbs using pronouns as cues. These asymmetrical results were thought to be due to the fact that the co-occurrence relationship between nouns and determiners is stronger than that between verbs and pronouns in these languages. Höhle, Weissenborn, Kiefer, Schulz, & Schmitz, (2004) analyzed a German corpus of child-directed speech and found that the indefinite article *ein* 'a' is followed by a noun 71 percent of the time, whereas the pronoun *sie* 'she' is followed by a verb only 31 percent of the time. Furthermore, in the child-directed speech of French-speaking mothers, determiners were followed by a noun 71 percent of the time, whereas pronouns were followed by verbs 59 percent of the time (Shi & Melançon, 2010).

In Japanese, case particles indicate that the preceding word is a noun while verb suffixes indicate that the preceding word is a verb. For example, in the sentence (a), the word *inu* 'dog' that was followed by the subject-marking particle *ga* is a noun and in different utterances it may be followed by another particle such as an object marker *o* or a topic marker *wa*. A verb *oikake* is followed by a verb suffix-*ta* in (a) while it is followed by another verb suffix-*teiru* in (b). What is interesting for Japanese is that the co-occurrence relationship between content words and function morphemes is stronger for verbs than for nouns. This is because case particles are often omitted in casual speech while a verb never occurs without a verb suffix in an utterance. If the strength of the co-occurrence relationship matters, as discussed in previous studies, Japanese children should become able to syntactically categorize verbs earlier than nouns. Therefore, in Study 3, we investigated Japanese-learning children's use of function morphemes (particles and verb suffixes) to syntactically categorize nouns and verbs.

For this purpose, we assigned 15-month-olds either to the noun or to the verb condition. The procedure consisted of a habituation phase and a test phase. During the habituation phase, children in the noun condition were habituated to a noun standard passage (see Table 1; A), and those children in the verb condition to a verb standard passage (Table 1; B). In the noun standard passage, the target nonsense word was always followed by the particle *ga*. In the verb standard passage, the target word was always followed by a verb suffix-*tteiru*, which was the most frequent of the verb suffixes used in Japanese mothers' speech to their 10- to 15-month-old children (Haryu & Kajikawa, 2015a). During the test phase immediately after their habituation, children in both conditions were presented with two types of test passage, a noun test passage (Table 2; C) and a verb test passage (Table 2; D). Both test passages consisted of two sentences. In the noun test passage, the target word was followed by the object-marking particle *o* in one sentence and by the topic-marking particle *wa* in the other sentence. In the verb test passage, the target word was followed by a verb suffix-*ru* (conclusive) in one sentence and by another suffix-*ranai* (negative) in the other sentence. If children syntactically categorize the target word as a noun during the habituation phase, they should be surprised to hear the verb test passage. That is, they should listen to the verb test passage for longer than the noun test passage. If they syntactically categorize the target word as a verb, they should demonstrate the reverse pattern.

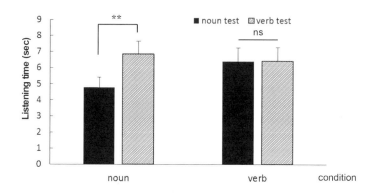

Figure 3 Mean listening times to the noun and verb test passages (error bars indicate standard errors) for the noun and verb conditions in Study 3.
** $p < .01$

As Figure 3 demonstrates, 15-month-olds in the noun condition listened to the verb test passage longer than the noun test passage. In contrast, the children in the verb condition listened to the noun test passage for approximately the same length of time as the verb test passage. These results indicate that Japanese 15-month-olds can syntactically categorize a novel word into a noun class by attending to following particles. However, they are not yet able to use verb suffixes to syntactically categorize verbs.

The results may be deemed quite astonishing, considering that the co-occurrence relationship between a content word and an adjacent function morpheme should be stronger for verbs than for nouns in Japanese. However, a further analysis of Japanese mothers' speech to their children (Haryu & Kajikawa, 2015a) indicated another possible factor that makes verb categorization more difficult than noun categorization for Japanese-learning children. In the mothers' speech, the mean number of different verb suffixes that followed a verb is 1.08 while the average number of different particles that followed a noun is 1.37. This means that a particular verb is almost always followed by a particular verb suffix. Such occurrence patterns of verb suffixes may make it difficult for children to separate a verb from the following suffix and to learn that a word followed by a particular verb suffix may be followed by a different verb suffix in a different utterance. This explanation remains speculative since the speech sample analyzed by Haryu and Kajikawa (2015a) is not large and is based mainly on describing pictures. In future research, the distributional properties of function morphemes should be investigated in more detail as well as under different circumstances.

4. GENERAL DISCUSSION

In the present article, we reported our research that examined Japanese children's use of function morphemes during language development. By 15 months of age, Japanese-learning children come to rely on particles more heavily than transitional probability for segmenting words from fluent speech. This timing is not early compared with English-, French-, and German-learning children who begin to use determiners to segment adjacent words before their first birthday (Höhle & Weissenborn, 2000; Shi, Cutler, Werker, & Cruickshank, 2006; Shi & Lepage, 2008). However, this delay observed for Japanese-learning children cannot be attributed to the low frequency with which they hear the particle in the input. The frequency of the particle *ga* in Japanese mothers' speech to their children was comparable to that of a high-frequency determiner *des* in

French-speaking mothers' speech to their children. Instead, another possibility was discussed: The fact that Japanese case particles rarely occur at utterance edges may make learning them difficult.

Although Japanese-learning children take a long time to become able to use particles to segment words from fluent speech, at the age of 15 months they also know that the particle can be omitted without changing the meaning of a sentence. Furthermore, they use particles to syntactically categorize adjacent word into noun classes, although they still fail to syntactically categorize verbs by attending to following verb suffixes. This asymmetry concerning the ability of syntactic categorization has also been observed for German- and French-learning children (Höhle Weissenborn, Kiefer, Schulz, & Schmitz, 2004; Shi & Melançon, 2010), which means that the co-occurrence relationship between function morphemes and content words cannot explain the relative ease of noun categorization to verb categorization: The co-occurrence relationship is stronger for nouns than for verbs in German and French, whereas it is stronger for verbs than for nouns in Japanese. Preliminary analyses of Japanese mothers' speech to their children (Haryu & Kajikawa, 2015a) suggested that the pattern of distribution rather than simple frequency of occurrence of function morphemes may matter in children's learning of syntactic categorization. This hypothesis remains to be explored in future research.

At any rate, data from children learning various languages would potentially reveal what property of the language input affects children's learning of function morphemes and how the knowledge of function morphemes in turn guides their learning of other aspects of language. The present research extended knowledge of children's use of function morphemes during language development by investigating children learning Japanese.

Acknowledgements

We are very grateful to infants and their parents who participated in the experiments. This work was supported by the JSPS KAKENHI Grant Number 25285183.

References

Brown, R. (1973). *A first language*. Cambridge, MA: Harvard University Press.

Cook, H. M. (1985). Frequency of nominal markers in the speech of a Japanese child and his caretakers: A case study. *Descriptive and Applied Linguistics*, 18, 13–24.

Gervain, J., Nespor, M., Mazuka, R., Horie, R., & Mehler, J. (2008). Bootstrapping word order in prelexical infants: A Japanese-Italian cross-linguistic study. *Cognitive Psychology*, 57, 56–74.

Hallé, P. A., Durand, C., & de Boysson-Bardies, B. (2008). Do 11-month-old French infants process articles? *Language and Speech*, 51, 23–44.

Haryu, E., & Kajikawa, S. (2015a). Functional morphemes in Japanese mothers' speech input to their infants. *Bulletin of the Graduate School of Education the University of Tokyo*, 54, 279–284.

Haryu, E., & Kajikawa, S. (2015b). Japanese infants' use of functional morphemes in syntactic categorization. *Poster presented at the Workshop on Infant Language Development 2015*. Stockholm, Sweden.

Haryu, E., & Kajikawa, S. (2016). Use of bound morphemes (noun particles) in word segmentation by Japanese-learning infants. *Journal of Memory and Language*, 88, 18-27.

Höhle, B., & Weissenborn, J. (2000). The origins of syntactic knowledge: Recognition of determiners in one year old German children. In C. Howell, S.A. Fish, & T. Keith-Lucas (Eds.), *BUCLD 24 Proceedings*, 418–429. Sommerville, MA: Cascadilla.

Höhle, B., & Weissenborn, J. (2003). German-learning infants' ability to detect unstressed closed-class elements in continuous speech. *Developmental Science*, 6, 122–127.

Höhle, B., Weissenborn, J., Kiefer, D., Schulz, A., & Schmitz, M. (2004). Functional elements in infants' speech processing: The role of determiners in the syntactic categorization of lexical elements. *Infancy*, 5, 341–353.

Kajikawa, S., & Haryu, E. (2008). Nyuji ni okeru joshi 'ga' no ninshiki. [Recognition of a function morpheme, ga, in infants]. *Tamagawa Daigaku Nokagaku Kenkyujo Kiyo*, 2, 13–21.

MacWhinney, B. (2000). *The CHILDES Project: Tools for analyzing talk. 3rd ed. Vol. 2. The Database*. Mahwah, NJ: LEA.

Miyata, S. (2004a). Japanese: Aki Corpus. Pittsburgh, PA: Talkbank. 1-59642-055-3.

Miyata, S. (2004b). Japanese: Ryo Corpus. Pittsburgh, PA: Talkbank. 1-59642-056-1.

Miyata, S. (2004c). Japanese: Tai Corpus. Pittsburgh, PA: Talkbank. 1-59642-057-X.

Oshima-Takane, Y., MacWhinney, B., Sirai, H., Miyata, S., & Naka, N. (1998). *CHILDES for Japanese. Second Edition*. The JCHAT Project Nagoya: Chukyo University.

Seidl, A., & Johnson, E. K. (2006). Infant word segmentation revisited: Edge alignment facilitates target extraction. *Developmental Science*, 9, 565-573.

Shi, R., Cutler, A., Werker, J.F., & Cruickshank, M. (2006). Frequency and form as determinants of functor sensitivity in English-acquiring infants. *Journal of Acoustical Society of America*, 119, EL61-67.

Shi, R., & Lepage, M. (2008). The effect of functional morphemes on word segmentation in preverbal infants. *Developmental Science*, 11, 407–413.

Shi, R., Marquis, A., & Gauthier, B. (2006). Segmentation and representation of function words in preverbal French-learning infants. In D. Bamman, T. Magnitskaia, & C. Zaller (Eds.), *BUCLD 30 Proceedings*, 549–560. Sommerville, MA: Cascadilla.

Shi, R. & Melançon, A. (2010). Syntactic categorization in French-learning infants. *Infancy*, 15, 517–533.

Shi, R., Werker, J.F., & Cutler, A. (2006). Recognition and representation of function words in English-learning infants. *Infancy*, 10, 187–198.

Communicative Behavior of ASD and Typically Developing Children in Japan and China

Miki Kakinuma and Kayoko Uemura

There is growing evidence that neurodevelopmental disorders such as autistic spectrum disorders (ASD), which are biologically based yet diagnosed by behavioral criteria, are treated differently across cultures and ethnic groups (Mandell et al., 2009; Matson et al., 2011). The question is, are children with ASD, despite the neurological dysfunction, actually exhibiting different types of communication disorders, or are they treated differently due to the cultural expectation of communicative behavior? For example, children with ASD is known to have difficulties making eye contact during requests for assistance (Phillips, Baron-Cohen, & Rutter, 1992), but eye contact may not be the primary means of seeking help in some Eastern cultures, while in some Western cultures it is (Friedlmeier & Trommsdorff, 1999). Therefore, in some Eastern cultures, children with ASD may not experience as many difficulties due to their lack of eye contact in social situations.

Some studies suggest that the cultural values and expectations mentioned above may lead to differences in prevalence rates of ASD (see the review by; Norbury & Sparks, 2013). More Blacks and Asian/Pacific Islanders were identified as "autistic" than Hispanics or American Indians (Dyches, Wilder, Sudweeks, Obiakor, & Algozzine, 2004). Studies based on reports of ASD by parents or teachers in several countries show that the difficulties children with ASD face in daily life differ across cultures (Chung et al., 2012; Horovitz, Matson, Rieske, Kozlowski, & Sipes, 2011;

Matson et al., 2012). These studies indicate that children with ASD have different types of difficulties, but it is not clear whether some cultures are less concerned with autistic traits or the behaviors of ASD actually differ as the result of their upbringing.

Freeth, Sheppard, Ramachandran, and Milne (2013) used the Autism-spectrum Quotient (AQ) (Baron-Cohen, Wheelwright, Skinner, Martin, & Clubley, 2001) to survey the expression of autistic traits in general populations in Western and Eastern cultures, and showed that Eastern cultures had higher scores in four out of five subcategories; that is, more autistic-like behaviors are considered culturally typical. Their result suggests that culture has an effect on behavior and cognitive processes. Even though AQ is a widely used measure, a limitation of this study is that it used a self -reported questionnaire and not a direct comparison of ASD persons across cultures.

Until recently, we could only speculate about these differences in behavioral patterns. Rogoff (2003) suggested that even an infant's autonomy, such as the age which it sleeps for eight uninterrupted hours or becomes toilet trained differs across cultures. Advances in technologies allow us to focus on cultural differences at neural network levels. For example, cultural differences are observed even in neural networks involved in simple visual and attentional tasks (Hedden, Ketay, Aron, Markus, & Gabrieli, 2008). If experiences after birth influence the behavior at neural network levels, it is possible that differences in the communicational behavior of children with ASD exist as well.

In order to find out whether reported differences in behavior are due to the cultural norms or social interactions persons with ASD experience in the cultural framework, direct comparison is needed. Unfortunately, many studies are based on interviews of or questionnaires to parents, teachers, or other professionals and not direct comparisons of children with ASD. Thus, the differences are based on the cultural filters of the educators/parents who answered the questionnaires. Conducting direct comparisons of clinical samples in two different cultures and also within the same cultural framework may answer this question.

One of the measures used for the diagnosis of ASD, the Diagnostic and Statistical Manual of Mental Disorders Fifth Edition (American Psychiatric Association, 2013), suggests that even though cultural factors may affect the recognition of ASD, children with ASD are "markedly impaired against the norms of the cultural context."

The need to understand the cultural differences of children with ASD is increasing, particularly in multicultural societies or non-Western cultures, for diagnostic purposes (Mandy, Charman, Puura, & Skuse, 2014). In the U.S., Hispanic populations are known to be slow to recognize ASD, possibly due to differences in social sensitivities. Comparing ASD populations in different cultures may shed some light on the neurological impairment of the disorder.

Mothers play an important role in children's language acquisition and aspects of social cognitive development such as acquisition of theory of mind (Baron-Cohen, Leslie, & Frith, 1985; Koyasu, 2000; Premack & Woodruff, 1978; Wellman, 1990). Both language acquisition and theory of mind development occur at about the same stage of development, but the timing does differ across cultures (Liu, Wellman, Tardif, & Sabbagh, 2008). These differences indicate that even though language acquisition or theory of mind development are important aspects of human development, the content and timing of development is somewhat dependent on the environment the child is placed in. In cases of severe social deprivation, children are known to have delays in language as well as social cognition development (Nelson et al., 2007).

ASD is a communication disorder, and mothers of children with ASD are known to have difficulties establishing joint attention or obtaining cooperative behavior. Some of the children do learn to use language, and at some stage of their development, pass the false belief test. Do they learn because their disabilities are less severe or because they had better education opportunities?

Social norms are usually transmitted from adults to children in a society. When the child is young, primarily the main caretakers do the job. Parents teach their children how to behave, what is expected, and what is wrong. Children learn what is good and what is bad by daily experiences as well as by observing how parents behave in socially conflicting situations.

Kuhl et al. (2006) showed that children as young as 12 months can discriminate the sounds of their mother tongue. Kinzler and Spelke (2011) showed that between 2.5 and 5 years, children learn to express social preferences for individuals of their own race. Even though the development of social cognitions such as theory of mind is constant across cultures, there are some age differences (Liu, Wellman, Tardif, & Sabbagh., 2008). These results suggest that children are actively acquiring social values during daily interactions with their caretakers. Based on that assumption, we set up an experiment in which a mother and child in different cultures talk about drawings of mildly conflicting social situations to examine how the transmission takes place (Kakinuma, Uemura & Jing, 2006). By age 3, mother and child have established a relationship with the mother teaching social lessons by encouraging child to participate in story-telling sessions that are constant across cultures. Some cultural differences were observed in the contents of the story as well as how they tell the story.

In this study, we directly compared the mother-child interactions of both ASD and typically developing (TD) children in Japan and China to see how social experiences and neurological dysfunctions affect the contents of stories told by children with ASD. Their communicative behaviors, including pointing and turn-taking, information processing styles, and interpretation of the mildly conflicting situations were analyzed. The mothers' behaviors and interactions with the child were also analyzed. Determining how story telling patterns in ASD differ from those of TD may indicate how the experiences affect the development of children with ASD.

Our hypothesis, based on existing studies of ASD, was that communicative styles would be similar across cultures, although demonstrating some communicative awkwardness. We also assumed that there would not be many cultural differences for mothers of children with ASD who are dealing with children with distinct impairments in communication.

1. METHOD

1.1 *Participants*

One hundred and twenty four children participated in this study. There were 68 from Japan and 56 from China ranging from 3 to 12 years of age

(Table 1 shows sample characteristics). Children with ASD were divided into two groups, young ASD (yASD; 3–6 years old) and older ASD (oASD; 7–12 years old).

Table 1 Participants

	TD	Young ASD	Older ASD
Japan	50	10	8
China	32	10	14

Children with ASD were assessed at specialist clinics or pediatric units at university hospitals. Those with IQ >80 participated. ASD diagnoses were assigned based on parent report, direct observation in a clinic, IQ tests, and some theory of mind tests. In this study, all participants receiving a diagnosis of autistic disorder, Asperger's disorder, or pervasive developmental disorder not otherwise specified were classified as having ASD. TD children were in the mainstream education system, and parents were not concerned about their general development. Chinese participants resided in Guangzhou area and Japanese participants resided in Tokyo, Yamagata, Yamaguchi, and Okinawa. Clinical psychologists or pediatricians collected data on both Japanese and Chinese samples.

The ethical committees of hospitals and universities from which participants were recruited reviewed and approved this study.

1.2 Procedure
Children and their mothers were presented with two drawings of minor interpersonal conflicts and were asked to talk about them together (see Figures 1 and 2). The pictures were handed to the mothers in random order (Wakabayashi, Fernald, & Kakinuma, 1999). The first picture depicted a scene of a child crying and another child facing the crying child. On the ground, close to the children is something that looks like a broken stick. The second picture depicted a child on a ladder reaching for something in a cupboard. One of the bowls is shown as falling off the shelf. Facing away from the child in the kitchen is a woman wearing an apron.

The researcher explained the purpose of the study, and the session was video- and audiotaped with the mother's consent. The stories were transcribed and then translated into Japanese by a bilingual Chinese person living in Japan. Both Japanese and Chinese texts are used as a reference in the analysis.

Figure 1 Drawing of "Crying boy"

Figure 2 Drawing of the "Kitchen" story

1.3 *Analysis*

Video data were analyzed using the PTS113 coding system (DHK, Japan). Coding categories were the durations of pointing and talking using two pictures by both mothers and children. Pointing here is defined as touching the picture with the tip of the index finger. The contents of speech of the ladder picture (Figure 2) were analyzed with a focus on which area the conversation was based on. The picture was divided into two areas, the front area of the picture with the boy and the back area with the woman. The script was analyzed by which area was talked about and who selected the area to talk about. For example, if the mother started talking about the boy in the front and then talked about the woman in the back, that was counted as one shift by the mother. If the child was talking about the boy, and mother started talking about the woman, that was also counted as one shift by the mother (see Table 2 for the coding example).

Table 2 Coding example of "Kitchen" story

MOM: Here, mom is doing chores, and the boy is doing something.	(back area)
What is he up to?	(front area)
CHILD: Well	
MOM: He wants this, here	
CHILD: This?	
MOM: Yes	
CHILD: Dumplings	
MOM: The boy, while mom is here	(back area)
tried to take the dumpling, and	(front area)
CHILD: The dish broke	

2. RESULTS

2.1 Pointing duration

The mean durations of pointing per minute (Figure 3) were subjected to a mixed-design ANOVA with three factors (country, group, and mother/child). There was a significant interaction for three factors ($F(1,114) = 4.56$, $p<.05$). Post-hoc tests revealed that (1) Chinese mothers pointed longer than Japanese mothers; however, there were no differences between Chinese and Japanese children in the pointing durations, (2) Chinese mothers pointed longer than their children, and Chinese mothers in the yASD group pointed longer than those in the TD group, and (3) Japanese mothers in the TD group pointed longer than their children.

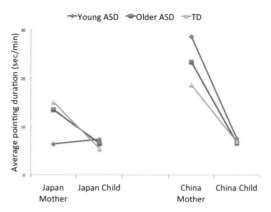

Figure 3 Durations of pointing

2.2 *Talking duration*

The mean durations of talking per minute (Figure 4) were analyzed using a mixed-design ANOVA with three factors (country, group and mother/child). There was a significant interaction between country and mother/child factors (F(1,114) = 10.06, p<.01). Post-hoc tests revealed that (1) Chinese mothers talked longer than Japanese mothers; however, there were no differences between Chinese and Japanese children in talking durations, (2) Chinese and Japanese mothers talked longer than their children, and (3) there were no group (yASD/oASD/TD) differences in both countries.

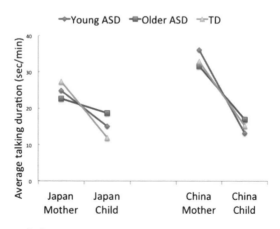

Figure 4 Durations of talking

2.3 Shifting areas of interest

The mean number of times that mothers and their children changed the subject is shown in Fig. 5. We performed a mixed-design ANOVA with three factors (country, group and mother/child) and found a significant interaction between country and mother/child factors ($F(1,114)=6.62$, $p<.05$). Post-hoc tests revealed that (1) Chinese and Japanese mothers more frequently changed the subject than their children, and (2) although there was no difference between Chinese and Japanese children, Chinese mothers changed the subject more frequently than Japanese mothers.

We also found a significant interaction between country and group (TD/ASD) factors ($F(1,114) = 6.10$, $p<.05$). Post-hoc tests revealed that (1) the Chinese ASD group changed the subject more frequently than the Japanese ASD group; however, there was no difference between Chinese and Japanese TD groups, (2) the Japanese TD group more frequently changed the subject than the Japanese ASD group, and the Chinese ASD group more frequently changed the subject than the Chinese TD group.

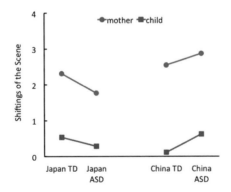

Figure 5 Freguencies of scene shifting

3. Discussion

3.1 Role of mothers

Our previous studies of the contents of mother-child talks indicated that despite the cultural differences in the interpretation of the situation, mothers used the opportunity to teach social lessons to their children (Kakinuma, Uemura & Jing, 2006). The results of this study also revealed that mothers made efforts to send social messages to their children. Mothers talked longer than children, shifted the focus of attention, and pointed more. The exception is the frequency of pointing by Japanese mothers of yASD.

3.1.1 Cultural differences

Cultural differences were observed in mothers' behavior. That is, Chinese mothers talked and pointed longer than Japanese mothers. These results suggest that by pointing and shifting the attention to different aspects of the drawings, mothers were using the opportunity to teach children how to interpret socially conflicting situations and how to deal with them. Chinese mothers teach directly, while Japanese mothers "provide exposure to adult values and install a readiness on the part of the child to imitate, accept, and internalize such values" (Hess & Azuma, 1991).

3.1.2 Mothers of children with ASD

In both countries, mothers of yASD differed from TD or oASD mothers in pointing duration. ASD mothers behaved differently to shift the focus of attention as well. Chinese mothers pointed and shifted topics more and Japanese less, suggesting that mothers of ASD tend to overdo what is expected in their culture. This tendency was particularly clear for the pointing of Japanese mothers of yASD. Rather than teaching, Japanese mothers allow children to explore on their own, and this tendency may be more pronounced in yASD.

3.2 *Children with ASD*

No cultural or group differences were observed in pointing or talking duration of children. One cultural difference observed in ASD was the frequency of shifting of the area of interest. Chinese children with ASD shifted back and forth more often, possibly because Chinese mothers of children with ASD shifted back and forth more often. The same tendency, for the child's behavior to be influenced by mother's behavior, was observed in Japanese ASD.

A direct comparison of children with ASD across cultures revealed that some communicative behaviors can be affected by interactions with others. Just as children with ASD can acquire language, some communicative skills, such as turn taking and selecting the topics to focus on, may be acquired. Future studies are needed to investigate the implication of this result.

Despite the fact children with ASD are known to have difficulties in pointing, the pointing frequencies of ASD and TD children did not differ in either culture. One possible reason for this is that the functions of pointing, such as declarative, imperative, informative (Liszkowski, Carpenter, Striano, & Tomasello, 2006), or other, were not differentiated in this study. Individuals with ASD have difficulties in fixating their eye gaze (Dalton et al., 2005), and children with ASD may be using their fingers to keep their attention on what they are talking about (Klin, Jones, Schultz, Volkmar, & Cohen, 2002). Further analyses are needed to differentiate the functions of pointing by children with ASD.

3.3 *Plasticity of ASD*

Direct comparison of children with ASD in the two cultures revealed the plasticity of communicative development, as well as areas of solid deficits that may be difficult to modify. Comparison of ASD and TD children within a culture indicate that mothers tend to overdo in an attempt to overcome the child's deficits. As is suggested by DSM-5, the basic difficulties of ASD remain across cultures, but our results show that in some areas, there is room for change. With the development of devices such as the portable eye tracker, we may be able to investigate the basic deficits and identify areas that can be modified.

The lesson of this study is that cultural comparisons can lead to understanding of the mechanism of neural deficits such as ASD and allow us to look for further possible interventions.

References

American Psychiatric Association. (2013). *Diagnostic and statistical manual of mental disorders* (5th ed.). Washington, D.C.

Baron-Cohen, S., Leslie, & A.M., Frith, U. (1985). Does the autistic child have a "theory of mind"? *Cognition 21*, 37–46.

Baron-Cohen, S., Wheelwright, S., Skinner, R., Martin, J., & Clubley, E. (2001). The autism-spectrum quotient (AQ): Evidence from Asperger syndrome/high-functioning autism, males and females, scientists and mathematicians. *Journal of Autism and Developmental Disorders*, 31(1), 5–17.

Chung, K.-M., Jung, W., Yang, J.-w., Ben-Itzchak, E., Zachor, D. A., Furniss, F., & Barker, A. A. (2012). Cross cultural differences in challenging behaviors of children with autism spectrum disorders: An international examination between Israel, South Korea, the United Kingdom, and the United States of America. *Research in Autism Spectrum Disorders*, 6(2), 881–889.

Dalton, K. M., Nacewicz, B. M., Johnstone, T., Schaefer, H. S., Gernsbacher, et al. (2005). Gaze fixation and the neural circuitry of face processing in autism. *Nature Neuroscience*, 8(4), 519–526.

Dyches, T. T., Wilder, L. K., Sudweeks, R. R., Obiakor, F. E., & Algozzine, B. (2004). Multicultural issues in autism. *Journal of Autism and Developmental Disorders*, 34(2), 211–222.

Freeth, M., Sheppard, E., Ramachandran, R., & Milne, E. (2013). A cross-cultural comparison of autistic traits in the UK, India and Malaysia. *Journal of Autism and Developmental Disorders*, 43(11), 2569-2583.

Friedlmeier, W. & Trommsdorff, G. (1999). Emotion regulation in early childhood: A cross-cultural comparison between German and Japanese toddlers. *Journal of Cross-Cultural Psychology*, 30(6), 684–711.

Hedden, T., Ketay, S., Aron, A., Markus, H. R., & Gabrieli, J. D. (2008). Cultural influences on neural substrates of attentional control. *Psychological Science*, 19(1), 12–17.

Hess, R. D., and Azuma, H. (1991). Cultural support for schooling: Contrasts between Japan and the United States. *Educational Researcher*, 20(9), 2–9.

Horovitz, M., Matson, J. L., Rieske, R. D., Kozlowski, A. M., & Sipes, M. (2011). The relationship between race and challenging behaviours in infants and toddlers with autistic disorder and pervasive developmental disorder-not otherwise specified. *Developmental Neurorehabilitation*, 14(4), 208–214.

Kakinuma, M., Uemura, K., and Jing, J. (2006). Joint storytelling as an opportunity for cultural learning (1): A comparison of Japanese, Chinese and US styles. *Human Developmental Research*, 20, 13–22. (in Japnese)

Kinzler, K. D., and Spelke, E. S. (2011). Do infants show social preferences for people differing in race? *Cognition*, 119(1), 1-9.

Klin, A., Jones, W., Schultz, R., Volkmar, F., & Cohen, D. (2002). Visual fixation patterns during viewing of naturalistic social situations as predictors of social competence in individuals with autism. *Archives of General Psychiatry*, 59(9), 809-816.

Koyasu, M. (2000). Kokoro no riron: Kokoro o yomu kokoro no kagaku (Theory of mind: A science of reading mind). Iwanami Shoten.

Kuhl, P. K., Stevens, E., Hayashi, A., Deguchi, T., Kiritani, S., & Iverson, P. (2006). Infants show a facilitation effect for native language phonetic perception between 6 and 12 months. *Developmental Science*, 9(2), F13–F21.

Liszkowski, U., Carpenter, M., Striano, T., and Tomasello, M. (2006). 12-and 18-month-olds point to provide information for others. *Journal of Cognition and Development*, 7(2), 173–187.

Liu, D., Wellman, H. M., Tardif, T., & Sabbagh, M. A. (2008). Theory of mind development in Chinese children: A meta-analysis of false-belief understanding across cultures and languages. *Developmental Psychology*, 44(2), 523.

Mandell, D. S., Wiggins, L. D., Carpenter, L. A., Daniels, J., DiGuiseppi, C. et al., J. A. (2009). Racial/ethnic disparities in the identification of children with autism spectrum disorders. *American Journal of Public Health*, 99(3), 493.

Mandy, W., Charman, T., Puura, K., & Skuse, D. (2014). Investigating the cross-cultural validity of DSM-5 autism spectrum disorder: Evidence from Finnish and UK samples. *Autism*, 18(1), 45–54.

Matson, J. L., Worley, J. A., Fodstad, J. C., Chung, K.-M., Suh, D. et al. (2011). A multinational study examining the cross-cultural differences in reported symptoms of autism spectrum disorders: Israel, South Korea, the United Kingdom, and the United States of America. *Research in Autism Spectrum Disorders*, 5(4), 1598–1604.

Matson, J. L., Worley, J. A., Kozlowski, A. M., Chung, K.-M., Jung, W., & Yang, J.-w. (2012). Cross cultural differences of parent reported social skills in children with autistic disorder: An examination between South Korea and the United States of America. *Research in Autism Spectrum Disorders*, 6(3), 971–977.

Nelson, C. A., Zeanah, C. H., Fox, N. A., Marshall, P. J., Smyke, A. T., & Guthrie, D. (2007). Cognitive recovery in socially deprived young children: The Bucharest Early Intervention Project. *Science*, 318(5858), 1937–1940.

Norbury, C. F., and Sparks, A. (2013). Difference or disorder? Cultural issues in understanding neurodevelopmental disorders. *Developmental Psychology*, 49(1), 45.

Phillips, W., Baron-Cohen, S., & Rutter, M. (1992). The role of eye contact in goal detection: Evidence from normal infants and children with autism or mental handicap. *Development and Psychopathology*, 4(3), 375–383.

Premack, D., Woodruff, G. (1978). Does the chimpanzee have a theory of mind? *Behavioral and Brain Sciences*, 1, 515–526.

Rogoff, B. (2003). *The cultural nature of human development*. Oxford University Press.

Wakabayashi, T., Fernald, A., & Kakinuma, M. (1999). What, how and why?: Japanese and American mothers' questions in joint storytelling sessions. Paper presented at the 2001 Biennial Meeting of the Society for Research in Child Development,

Minneapolis, MN.

Wellman, H. M. (1990). *The child's theory of mind*. MIT Press.

Where Developmental Psychology Meets the Law: Forensic Interviews with Witnesses and Alleged Child Victims

Makiko Naka

In this chapter, I will describe how developmental psychology contributes to forensic practice, especially in investigative interviews with witnesses and alleged child victims. First I will describe my area of research and how I got involved with this fascinating topic. Then I will review three studies we have conducted on memory and communication in children that are relevant to investigative interviews, and then describe a scientifically sound method of interviewing, i.e., the forensic interview of children. I will also describe the development of a training program and the current state of child interviews in Japan.

My research area is developmental cognitive psychology. One of the research topics I studied was how children learn functional words such as numerical classifiers in daily conversation (e.g., Naka, 1999). While studying the topic, I was impressed by how caretakers lead children to learn new vocabulary. Typically, caregivers talk a lot while maintaining a conversation with a child who talks less (asymmetry of conversation) and expose them to words in the so-called *zone of proximal development*. In such conversations, the acquisition of numerical classifiers proceeds from the use of general classifiers, *ko* or *tsu*, which can be used for any object or event, followed by the use of more specific classifiers such as *mai* for thin objects and *hon* for long objects. Mothers adjust the use of numeral classifiers to their child's acquisition level. A mother of a two-year old child would use *ko* for plates, but the mother of a three- or four-year old child would use *mai* instead, without realizing which classifier she was using. If a child makes errors in using classifiers (e.g., "I have two *mai* spoons," which should be counted using *hon*), the mother would not say "No, you should not count them using *mai*"). Instead she just says, "Yes, right, you have two-*hon* spoons." Again, caretakers do not seem to be aware of using different classifiers but subtly introduce the next level of classifiers. I was struck by how such coordination helps children acquire the complex use of numerical classifiers in a relatively short period of time.

1. A CASE

Sometime during the 1990s, I received a phone call from a lawyer asking for an expert opinion on eyewitness testimony given by a child with learning difficulties. From a piece of information that the child wrote in her journal, the child's caregiver suspected she was being molested by a familiar person who lived nearby. Being anxious, the caregiver asked the child a number of questions with a tape recorder running, thinking the tape could be used as evidence.

Later, I was asked to listen to the audiotape and give an opinion on whether the child's testimony was credible. The credibility of a child's testimony heavily relies on how it is elicited. Listening to the conversation, I was surprised how similar the skills were to those used to help children learn vocabulary, i.e., a caregiver talks a lot, introducing new information, and leading the child to learn, which, however, could harm the accuracy of child's testimony. The beginning of their conversation was like this (description of the incident and situations changed to preserve anonymity, but the wording of utterances as shown.)

Mother: Were (you) hit by X?
Child: ... [silence]
Mother: Were (you) hit?
Child: [silence]
Mother: You didn't tell me that. Is there time (you were) hit?
Child: [silence]

Mother: But (inaudible)?

Child: [silence]

Mother: Think hard and tell the truth.

Child: [silence]

Mother: Think. (You) shouldn't be like "(you) choose to tell this and choose not to tell this." You should tell the truth. You should say you don't know if you don't know.

Child: [silence]

Mother: I cannot understand. So…

Child: [silence]

Mother: (You) really were hit, weren't you?

As soon as the tape recorder was turned on, mother introduced the crucial information, namely the suspect's name (X) and suspected event (hitting). She presented the information repeatedly in the form of leading questions, and finally reached a conclusion by herself without hearing anything from the child ("(You) really were hit, weren't you?") As such, throughout the conversation, the child spoke little, whereas the mother talked a lot (asymmetry).

The conversation was about 40 minutes long. It contained 1125 utterances that covered 55 topics, which could be categorized as central (topics related to the suspected abuse), peripheral (events contingent on the suspected abuse, such as reporting to a police officer), and unrelated (unrelated topics such as comments on the weather.) Looking at who started these topics, we found the parent started 22 central topics, nine peripheral topics, and six unrelated topics. On the other hand, the child started three central topics, one peripheral topic, and 14 unrelated topics. The child did not start or follow the central topic. Rather, she seemed to escape from them into unrelated topics, but the caregiver always took her back and continued the conversation by introducing what seemed to be important to the caregiver.

For instance, one of the central topics was whether the alleged abusive act hurt, and it was repeated six times during the conversation. Each of the six conversations could be paraphrased like this:

MOTHER: Didn't it (suspected abusive act) hurt?

Child: It didn't hurt.
Mother: Didn't it hurt?
Child: No.

The child said "No" five times, but one time, she asked her mother whether it would hurt (child: "Would it hurt?") and the mother said "Yes." Although the child never said it hurt during this conversation with her mother, in the next conversation with a police officer, she changed her words to "It hurt a little." The child might have changed her mind to disclose this after the conversation with the worried parent, but another interpretation is that the child changed her response in accordance with her parent. The repeated questions might have contaminated her memory, or the repeated questions might have made the child think that she had to change her answer.

2. BACKGROUND OF REPEATED QUESTIONS

After this case, I saw many other cases in which a child was asked the same questions many times during an interview and across interviews (Naka, 2001). I conjecture there are several reasons that make repeated questioning necessary.

First, when the Child Abuse Act was passed in 2000, it stated that "a child who *was* abused must be reported" (Section 6). Although the phrase was amended to "a child who *was suspected of being* abused" in 2004, the case described above suggests that many people still feel they have to make sure that a child really was abused before reporting to professionals.

Second, we do not have a multidisciplinary approach toward the alleged victims. Institutions work individually rather than cooperatively. Therefore, even if a child was referred, they have to be interviewed by different agents: social workers at the Child Guidance Center, doctors and nurses at the hospital, police officers, and then prosecutors.

Third, because Japanese criminal court proceedings are traditionally based on documents rather than live testimony (Shinomiya, 2009), our criminal procedures require very precise documentation of an incident, including specific temporal and spatial information about an incident. If there is a contradiction, the child is repeatedly interviewed in order to resolve the contradiction (or change his/her statement). A police officer once told me that in difficult cases, it is necessary to interview a child six to seven times, each interview taking three to four hours. The same procedure may occur at the prosecutor's office, too, because they need to make their own documents as well. Kuraishi and Iwasa (2009) report that a child may be interviewed several to ten times before she/he goes to court.

Finally, it is important to note that there are no formal/official guidelines for videotaping interviews with a child witness. A child's statement is written down in the first-person form, even though the information is actually elicited through questions and answers. Because there is no objective recording of what the child said and the accuracy of the statement depends on how it is written, it is difficult to verify the statements, and thus the child is asked questions whenever necessary.

3. EFFECTS OF REPETITION OF QUESTIONING

3.1 *Pragmatics*

How does repeated questioning within and across interviews affect a child's testimony? First, repeated questioning affects the accuracy of the information. One aspect of this is associated with social pressure that a child may experience during an interview, or the pragmatics (the knowledge on social language use) that a child may have. Siegal (1996) construed there must be some rationale to understand a question. If a child is asked to answer the same question twice, the child might assume the first answer was wrong or not good enough and that he/she should change the answer.

Indeed, Sasaki and Naka (2014) have shown that children use such pragmatics to understand the meaning of an interviewer's utterances. In this study, children were shown pictures depicting objects and asked the rough or precise number, length, color, or location of the objects. For instance, first- and fourth-grade children were shown a sheet of paper with a number of dots and instructed "Tell me the approximate [number of dots]" or "Tell me the precise [number of dots]." When the instructions were given as a between-participant variable, i.e., a child was given either of the instructions, the precision (grain size) of answers by the first-grade children did not change between the conditions, although some differences were found for the fourth-grade children. However, when the instructions were given within participants, i.e., each child was given two instructions (the order was alternated), then even younger children changed the level of preciseness of their report for numerical tasks. The findings suggest that creating a contrast between the two instructions helps them comprehend the meanings of utterances. Nevertheless, if an inadvertent contrast is created by asking the same question repeatedly, it may harm the accuracy of a child's report.

3.2 Memory contamination

Repeated questioning could also reduce the accuracy of a report. A body of research has shown that misleading information given after an event in the form of a text (e.g., a story book), statement, or questions affects the accuracy of the memory. In the second or third interviews, a blended memory would be retrieved rather than the original memory (Metcalfe, 1990). The tendency to accept information from others, or suggestibility, is known to be more prominent in young children than in older children and adults. Schacter, Kagan and Leichtman (1995) hypothesized that development of the prefrontal lobe may be associated with suggestibility, and Shing et al. (2010) showed that episodic memory emerges in the preschool period and develops across childhood to adolescence from a neuropsychological point of view.

In one study that we conducted, second- and fifth-grade children were shown a film clip and asked to remember the material using one of four different techniques (Naka, 2012). Because the purpose of this experiment was to see the effect of different methods of recollection in the first place on the subsequent recollections, children were assigned to one of four experimental conditions: (a) children were instructed to write what they saw on a sheet of paper (free recall); (b) they were instructed to close their eyes for one minute and visualize what they saw, and then to write what they remembered on a sheet of paper (imagining); (c) they were asked to answer WH questions (i.e., when, where, who, etc.), which contained some inaccurate information (questioning); or (d) they were interviewed by an interviewer who asked open-ended questions ("Tell me what you saw.") and follow-up probes ("Then what happened?") before asking closed questions (interviewing).

The interviewing condition produced accurate information three times more than the other conditions. The questioning condition (c) produced the least information because children gave no more information than that necessary to answer the questions. There was an interaction between age and instruction, showing that older children produced a greater amount of accurate information using the free recall, imagining, and interviewing conditions than for the questioning condition. The imagining condition was effective only with older children, suggesting that the use of such a retrieval strategy requires metacognitive skills, a strategic component suggested by Shing et al. (2010).

Immediately after the first recollection, children were given a recognition test in order to determine the effect of first recollection on the second recollection (i.e., the recognition test). They heard verbal descriptions of 20 scenes, and for each scene, they were instructed to decide whether they "saw it with their own eyes," "did not see," or "do not know." Out of 20 items, 15 were false statement such as "the girl was wearing a white shirt" when in reality "the girl was wearing a red parka." The younger children made "I saw it" judgments about false scenes more often than the older children (4.77 vs. 3.01.) We also found was that younger children produced a greater number of false recollections in the imagining and questioning conditions (5.68 and 5.48, respectively), suggesting again that the intrusion of misinformation was more likely to occur with young children regardless of the source, i.e., the child's own imagination or the information provided via questions. The results showed the first recollection affected the later recollection.

After a few days, children were given two more occasions to remember, i.e., a free recall test and the same recognition test described above. Although no difference was found in free recall between the four conditions, the number of "I saw it" judgments increased by 39 percent in the recognition test, especially for the questioning condition. The results indicate that early reminiscing affected the later recollection.

3.3 Lack of awareness

One may think the suggestibility is restricted to young children. However, let us give one more example of the effect of suggestive questions (Naka, Sugiura, Hiroi, Shiratori, Nishida, and Nishino, 2008). In this study, junior high school students and university undergraduates participated. Participants were asked to attend a survey on Saiban-in Seido (the lay judge system, which was about to be introduced into the Japanese Criminal Court system), and were invited to visit a law firm in pairs.

While they were answering a questionnaire, an incident (actually fake) occurred. A lawyer came into the office stating his name and the purpose of his visit, i.e., a legal consultation for children, but the woman at the reception desk said he had come at the wrong time. This made the lawyer angry. He shouted at the receptionist and made a phone call, asked for his own office clerk and scolded him, rang off, and left the office with a "director" of the firm. Afterwards, the director interviewed each participant, one by one, on the incident.

Fourteen questions were asked, ten of which were followed by misleading information. For instance, a misleading conversation went as follows:

INTERVIEWER: What color suit was he wearing?
PARTICIPANT: Gray, maybe.
INTERVIEWER: Wasn't it navy? (misleading)
PARTICIPANT: I don't know but er, maybe navy.
INTERVIEWER: Was it possibly navy?
PARTICIPANT: Yes.

We counted the number of answers that participants changed in accordance with the director's utterance. On average, junior high students changed 22 percent of their answers, and undergraduates changed 24 percent of them, which is not a significant difference. After the interview, we told the participants that the incident was a fake, apologized to them, and asked them to answer a questionnaire on the interview. This questionnaire was to assess their awareness of the suggestive nature of the interview. The questionnaire included such questions as "Were you affected by the interviewer's questions?," "Were you mislead?," and "Did you say anything that was not true?" Participants were to choose "Yes,"

"No," or "Don't know." On average, 45 percent of undergraduate students said "No" to these questions, whereas 82 percent of junior high students did so, showing younger participants were not aware they actually had been misled and had given wrong answers. It was notable that in free answer section of the questionnaire, undergraduates wrote that they wanted to talk freely rather than being asked many questions, whereas younger participants said they liked being asked questions and some said they wanted to be asked even more questions.

4. EMOTIONAL ASPECT

So far we have considered the cognitive aspect of the effect of repeated questions/interviews. Yet another important aspect is the emotional effect. It is difficult to find literature on this topic, perhaps because it is considered to be obvious. One report I found was written by Fulcher (2004). Based on her experience as a clinical psychologist and her own experience after a serious car accident, she described how repeated interviews by medical and legal personnel affected her mental state and development of post-traumatic reactions. She wrote "a relatively large number of victims become progressively more agitated and exhibit increasing rates of post-traumatic symptoms … in an almost arithmetic accumulation after sequential interviews …" (Fulcher, 2004). Indeed, a police officer who often interviews victims told me that as the number of interviews increased, the more often the victim showed psychosomatic symptoms, such as headache and stomachache, and anxiety. Such victims would say, the police officer reported, "A victim's feelings are never understood by those who have not had such an experience", and may retract their accusation.

5. FORENSIC INTERVIEWS

After many cases in which inappropriate interviews led to wrongful accusations and false charges on one hand and putting child victims at risk on the other, scientifically more sound methods of interviewing children were developed (e. g., Poole, and Lamb, 1998). Such interviews are called "forensic interviews" or "investigative interviews" and are widely used in the U.S., U.K., Israel, Oceania, and Nordic countries.

The aim of the forensic interview is to elicit as much accurate information as possible from children and at the same time minimizing the traumatizing effect of being interviewed. There are quite a few variants of the interview protocols across jurisdictions, but it commonly emphasizes the use of open-ended questions to elicit free narratives from children and to maximize the child's motivation and ability to talk. Also, it is flexibly structured: (1) introducing and describing the purpose of the interview, (2) establishing ground rules such as telling the truth, saying "I don't know/understand" when one doesn't know/understand, (3) building rapport to to help the child feel comfortable, (4) helping the child practice talking about his/her episodic memory, (5) transitioning to the substantive phase, i.e., the incident in question, and (6) closing the interview by thanking the child, asking if he/she has questions, providing a name for further contact, etc. (Home Office, 1992, 2002; Lamb, Orbach, Hershkowitz, Esplin, and Horowitz, 2007; Lamb, Hershkowitz, Orbach, and Esplin, 2008; Poole, and Lamb, 1998).

In 2008, supported by the Japanese Science and Technology Agency and a Grant-in-Aid from the Japanese Ministry of Education, Culture, Sports, Science and Technology, we opened the Hokkaido University Support Office for Forensic Interviews in the Faculty of Literature at Hokkaido University, in Sapporo, Japan, and started a training course on forensic interviews based no the NICHD protocol (Lamb et al., 2007). The training consists of lectures on cognitive development, especially memory and suggestibility in children, past cases where problematic interviews hindered fair listening, and development of forensic interviews. Then we practice collecting information with input-free (i.e., open-ended) questions, and introduce the structure of the forensic interview described above. Trainees practice conducting interviews using a scenario as well as a real child (who participated in a particular activity beforehand about which he/she is interviewed), which are videotaped and then reviewed (Naka, 2014, 2015). We conducted evaluative studies on the training course and found the training increased the use of open-ended questions, which produced a greater amount of speech by interviewees while the interviewing time remained the same (Naka, 2011).

6. THE CURRENT STATUS OF INTERVIEWING

As the number of referrals to the Child Guidance Center has increased, the importance of testimony and statements by children have been recognized (Ministry of Health, Labour and Welfare, 2012). The number of Child Guidance Centers that use the forensic interview technique with alleged victims of sexual abuse has increased from 8 percent in 2007 to 41 percent in 2010 to 78 percent in 2011 (Yamamoto, 2012, 2013). The number of participants in our training program increased from 21 in 2008 to more than 1000 in 2015. Over four-thousand professionals have attended our training course so far.

One of the problems in our legal system is that videotaped interviews conducted by social workers do not have evidential value because of the hear-say rule. Exceptions to the hear-say rule are interviews conducted by police officers and prosecutors. Because of this, and because the lack of multi-disciplinary approach, even if a child is given a videorecorded interview at a Child Guidance Center, she/he must be interviewed again by police officers and then prosecutors.

However, there have been increasing number of cases in which the prosecutor conducted the interview in an early stage of the procedure in order to minimize the number of interviews. Because prosecutors make the final decisions about whether or not a case goes to court, this may be a breakthrough for child witnesses. In one case, a child was seriously injured by a caretaker and brought to a hospital. A doctor informed us, so we coordinated a forensic interview: A prosecutor conducted an interview with a child, and other professionals, i.e., medical doctors, social workers, police officers, and clinical psychologists monitored and supported the interview as back staff (professionals who monitor the interview via closed circuit video). By this procedure, the child was saved from repeated interviews by different professionals. Besides these practices, very recently, the Ministry of Health, Labour and Welfare, the National Police Agency, and the Supreme Public Prosecutors Office jointly announced that they promote the multidisciplinary interviews with alleged child victims (Asahi Shimbun, 2015). This is a huge step. We do hope such an approach will be realized in the near future. Research and practice in developmental psychology can be an important key to making this happen.

REFERENCES

Asahi Shimbun (2015). Gyakutai utagawareru ko no choshu o ipponka: Jiso, Kensatsu, Keisatsu ga renkei. Nov. 2, 2015. http://www.asahi.com/articles/ASHC176VWHC1 ULOB00Q.html accessed on Nov. 2, 2015. [Joint interviews with alleged child abuse victims: The multi disciplinary alliance of the Child Guidance Center, the Police, and the Public Prosecutors Office].

Fulcher, G. (2004). Litigation-induced trauma sensitisation (LITS): A potential negative outcome of the process of litigation. *Psychiatry, Psychology and Law, 11*, 79–86.

Home Office. (1992). *Memorandum of good practice on video recorded interviews with child witnesses for criminal proceedings.* London: The Stationery Office. [Naka, M., and Tanaka, S. (2007). Kodomo no shiho mensetsu: Bideo rokuga mensetsu gaidorain [Child forensic interview: A guideline for video recorded interview] Tokyo: Seishin Shobo]

Home Office. (2002). *Achieving the best evidence in criminal proceedings: Guidance for vulnerable and intimidated witnesses, including children.* London: Home Office Communication Directorate.

Kuraishi, T., and Iwasa, K. (2009). Ano hito wo uttaetai to omottara: Kimeru mae ni shitte hoshii tetsuzuki to nagare [If you are planning to sue someone: Procedures and processes to know before making decisions]. Osaka Bar Association.

Lamb, M. E., Hershkowitz, I., Orbach, Y., and Esplin, P. W. (2008). *Tell me what happened: Structured investigative interviews of child victims and witnesses.* Chichester: Wiley and Sons.

Lamb, M. E., Orbach, Y., Hershkowitz, I., Esplin, P. W., and Horowitz, D. (2007). A structured forensic interview protocol improves the quality and informativeness of investigative interviews with children: A review of research using the NICHD Investigative Interview Protocol. *Child Abuse and Neglect*, 31, 1201–1231.

Metcalfe, J. (1990). Composite holographic associative recall model (CHARM) and blended memories in eyewitness testimony. *Journal of Experimental Psychology: General*, 119, 145–160.

Ministry of Health, Labour and Welfare (2012). *On the guideline of how to respond to child abuse.* http://www.mhlw.go.jp/stf/houdou/2r9852000002fxos-att/2r9852000002fy23.pdf (Accessed on September 1, 2012)

Naka, M. (1999). The acquisition of Japanese numerical classifiers by 2-4-year-old children: The role of caretakers' linguistic inputs. *Japanese Psychological Research*, 41, 70–78.

Naka, M. (2001). Child interview in court: A case study of lawyerese. *Japanese Journal of Law and Psychology*, 1, 80–92. (In Japanese)

Naka, M. (2011). The effect of forensic interview training based on the NICHD structured protocol. *Japanese Journal of Child Abuse and Neglect*, 13, 316–325. (In Japanese)

Naka, M. (2012). The effect of different ways of interviewing on children's reports and subsequent memories of an eye-witnessed event. *Japanese Journal of Psychology*, 83, 303–313. (In Japanese)

Naka, M. (2014). A training program for investigative interviewing of children. In R. Bull (Ed.) *Investigative Interviewing.* (pp. 103-122). New York: Springer.

Naka, M., Sugiura, H., Hiroi, R., Shiratori, Y., Nishida, M., and Nishio, Y. (2008). Workshop report: Interviews with young offenders. *Japanese Journal of Law and Psychology*, 7, 70–72. (in Japanese)

Naka, M. (2015). Interviews with victims and witnesses of crime in Japan: Research and practice. In D. Walsh, G. E. Oxburgh, A. D. Redlich, and T. Myklebust (Eds.) *International developments and practices in investigative interviewing and interrogation, Volume 1: Victims and witnesses.* (pp. 43-57). U.K.: Routledge.

Poole, D. A., and Lamb, M. E. (1998). *Investigative interviews of children: A guide for helping professionals.* Washington D.C.: American Psychological Association.

Sasaki, S., and Naka, M. (2014). Development in skills to report with different grain size: "Roughly" and "exactly." *Japanese Journal of Psychology*, 84, 585-595. (in Japanese)

Schacter, D. L., Kagan, J., and Leichtman, M. D. (1995). True and false memories in children and adults: A cognitive neuroscience perspective. *Psychology, Public Policy, and Law*, 1, 411–428.

Shinomiya, S. (2009). Saiban-in-saiban to hotei gijutsu: Sono rinen to arikata (The mixed tribunal system and law and psychology). *Gendai no Esprit.* Okada, Y., Fujita, M., and Naka, M. (Eds.) *Saibanin seido to hoshinrigaku.* Tokyo: Gyosei.

Shing, Y. L., Werkle-Bergner, M., Brehmer, Y., Müller, V., Li, S. C., and Lindenberger, U. (2010). Episodic memory across the lifespan: The contributions of associative and strategic components. *Neuroscience and Behavioral Reviews*, 34, 1080–1091.

Siegal, M. (1996). Conversation and cognition. Gelman, R. (Ed), and Kit-Fong, T. (Ed).

Perceptual and cognitive development. Handbook of perception and cognition (2nd ed.). (pp. 243–282). San Diego: Academic Press, Inc.

Yamamoto, T. (2012). Kateinai seiboryoku higaiji (jido gyakutai, jido poruno, to) no hakken, shien ni okeru kaku kankei kikan no taio to renkei ni kansuru chosa kenkyu [Survey on actions and cooperation of relevant organizations in finding and supporting the victimized children in intra-familial sexual abuse [child abuse and child pornography]. Tokyo: Kodomo Mirai Zaidan.

Yamamoto, T. (2013). Kodomo kara no uttae o kiku: Seido toshite no shihomensetsu o jitsugensuru tame ni [Hearing what a child says]. Paper presented at JaSPCAN, Matsumoto, Nagano. Dec. 13-14. 2013.

Index

A

ABC cycles and supports 209
absence of the father 8
abuse in family-oriented nursing care 15
academic journal for qualitative
    research 86
accommodative strategy 167, 181
accuracy of child's testimony 252
acquisition of grammar 48
acquisition of numerical classifier 251
acquisition of various rule 48
aggression 70, 71
aging process 143
alleged child victim 262
allomothering 28
androgyny 12
anticipatory look 195
applied behavior analysis (ABA) 122
argument structur 51
Asperger syndrome 195
Asperger's disorder 241
assimilative strategy 167, 181, 182
asymmetry of conversation 251
asymmetry of syntactic categorization 234
at-home husband stress syndrome 11
attachment 64, 65, 98
attention to the eye 189
atypical mutual gaze behavior 190
autism spectrum disorder (ASD) 68, 121,
    189, 237
Autism-spectrum Quotient (AQ) 238
autonomy 23, 25–28
averted gaze 190

B

background of repeated question 254
baseline 207
behavioral intervention 122
Better Broadcasting for Children
    Project 41
Binet, Alfred 36

biological concept 130
biological thought 129
body temperature 74
breakdown of the "feminization of
    carework" 14
breastfeeding 22
Broca area 120
building-up strategy 155
burden of long-term care 13

C

Canada's National Longitudinal Study of
    Children and Youth 41
career planning 11
care for parent 13
case particles rarely appear at utterance
    edges 227
category analysis 92
causality 151
change detection paradigm 121
change in man 11
change in women's identity 6
Child Guidance Center 261
child negativism 25
childrearing anxiety 7
child's naive theory 150
cognition 33
cognitive and behavioral
    development 105
cognitive neuroscience technique 113
cohort effect 184
collaborative inquiry learning 159
communicative skill 247
communicative style 240
companionship 28
concept-based learning 157
conflict 24
conflicting emotional information 68, 69
consolation 70
consumer 152
contagious yawning 189, 194

265

co-occurrence relationship matters 231
co-sleeping 24
credibility of child's testimony 252
cross mind-body interdependence 135
crying 68
cultural filter 238

___

D
dannyu 27
demise of filial piety 13
demographic factor 3
demographic revolution 5
developmental behavioral genetic
    study 100
developmental disorder 203
developmental trajectory 118
Dewey, John 35
Diagnostic and Statistical Manual of
    Mental Disorders Fifth Edition
    (DSM-5) 238
diffusion tensor imaging (DTI) 113
digestion 143
direct gaze 190
disappointing gift 73
dissatisfaction with husband 9
dissemination of training program 217
divorce in middle-aged couple 10
domain-specific knowledge 129
dropping of the particle *ga* 230
dual-process model 166, 167

___

E
economics 151
economic understanding 153
effect of different methods of
    recollection 256
effect of repeated questions 255, 259
electroencephalograph (EEG) 114
Elementary Education Act 34
emotional effect 259
emotion-focused coping 72
emotion-regulation 73
envy 71
excessive investment in a few
    children 16

executive function 44
extended post-retirement 11
eye contact 237
eye-tracking 191

___

F
facial expression 65–67
false belief 189
false belief test 194
falsified emotion 69
fear response to stranger 64
feasibility of short-term teacher training
    program 217
feeding 22, 24
feminization of labor 8
fidelity scores across teachers 212
field research in action 86
fixed word order 53, 54
food intake 141
forensic interview 260
formal/official guideline 255
free recall 256
frontier of qualitative research 92
frontier spirit 93
function morpheme 221, 227
functional cerebral lateralization 114
functional connectivity analysis 126
functional magnetic resonance imaging
    (fMRI) 113
functional NIRS (fNIRS) 113
functional verbal utterance 211
fusiform gyrus 192

___

G
gaze cueing effect 190
gaze direction 197
gender-based difference 58
gender-based linguistic form 57
gender socialization 59
genetic epistemology 37
grammatical development 55
Grounded Theory (GT) 90
groundwork for qualitative research 84
gustatory sensibility 143

H

Hall, Stanley 34
Hatano, Giyoo 38
Hatano, Kanji 38
health maintenance 141
hear-say rule 261
hemispheric specialization 114
honorific language 56
human capital network 101
humble language 56

I

immune system 143
immunization 180, 181, 183
importance of "myself" 7
independence of children 15
independence of parent 15
inferiority 71
intellectual development 98
intellectually gifted child 40
intelligence quotient (IQ) 36
intelligence test 36
interactive knowledge 89
inter-observer reliability 212
intervention program 204
investigative interview with
    witnesses 251
isolated-word test trial 224
issues regarding resource investment 10

J

James, William 34
Japan Environment and Children's Study
    (JECS) 104
Japanese Association of Educational
    Psychology 44
Japanese child's use of function
    morpheme 233
Japanese MacArthur Communicative
    Developmental Inventory
    (JMCDI) 210
Japanese Psychological Association 35, 44
Japan Society of Developmental
    Psychology 44

K

Keio Early Intervention Program
    (KEIP) 204
Keller, Helen 38
Kido, Mantaro 39
kimochishugi 75
KJ method 90
kowakare 28
Kubo, Yoshihide 37
Kyoto Institute for the Blind and
    Dumb 39

L

lack of awareness 258
lack of eye contact 237
laterality index 118
life satisfaction 170, 176, 177, 179, 183, 185
lifespan perspective 83
local knowledge 87
longest parent-child relationship 12
Longitudinal Study of Australian
    Children 41
Longitudinal Study by Ochanomizu
    University 101
Longitudinal Survey in the Twenty-first
    Century 104

M

maintenance of life 140
mathematical understanding 153
Matsumoto, Matataro 35
media usage 101
memory contamination 256
mental state 129
mind-body distinction 131
mindset of researcher 81
mirror neuron system 193
misleading information 256, 258
Miyake, Koichi 36
model of self-regulation strategy 166
modified GT approach (M-GTA) 91
moral transgression 132
mother-child interaction 240
mother's unemployment 7
Motora, Yujiro 35

267

M-shaped labor force curve 20
multicultural society 239

N
National Assessment of Academic
    Ability 42
near-infrared spectroscopy (NIRS) 113
neonate NIRS study 123
NHK 100
noun modification 48
nursing care 14

O
oddball paradigm 116
omission of particle 222
on-the-job training (OJT) 205
organ intentionality 140
overgeneralization of modification rule 50

P
particle *ga* 226
particle-dropped sentence 228
particle *no* error 49
particle-replaced sentence 228
passive viewing 193
pervasive developmental disorder not
    otherwise specified (PDD-NOS) 241
physical development 100
Piaget, Jean 37
pioneer of Japanese qualitative research 85
play context 59
pointing 243
polite language 55
politeness register 56
positivity bias 67
postpositional particle 48
pragmatics 255
pre-action phase 181, 182, 185
pre-operational stage 129
pre-post design 211
pretend play scenario 57
problem-focused coping 72
procedure of habituation 224
process-oriented knowledge 88

producer viewpoint 152
prolongation of life expectancy 10
prolongation of lifespan 4
proportional reasoning 154
prosocial behavior 70
proximal parenting style 28
psychogenic illness 133
psychological essentialism 138
psychosomatic causality 135
purpose of woman's life 6

Q
qualitative description 83
qualitative reasoning 154, 155
quantitative reasoning 154

R
recurrent physical symptom 144
regulation of emotion 72
regulator and facilitator style of
    parenting 26
rejection of mother 23
reproductive revolution 5
role of mother in child's language
    acquisition 239
Rousseau, Jean-Jacques 33
rule-governed learning 51

S
self-regulation 168, 181
self-regulation strategy 167, 169, 174,
    176–180, 182–184
separation from mother 74, 75
sequence analysis 92
short-term teacher training program 205
signal-driven hypothesis 119
signal-driven lateralization 115
Simon, Théodore 36
skin conductance response (SCR) 192
smile and fearful expression 64
social and challenging behavior 211
social and communication behavior 214
social cognition 189
social cognitive development 239

social deprivation 239
socialization of polite linguistic form 57
social pressure 255
social science researcher 83
somatosensory process 125
speech perception 121
spontaneous false belief test 195
spontaneous theory of mind 197
stare-in-the-crowd effect 191
strategy change 161
subject-marking particle *ga* 222, 224
suggestibility 256, 258
Sullivan, Anne 39
Suzuki, Harutaro 37
sympathy 70
systemic knowledge 87

———

T
Tanaka, Kan'ichi 37
teacher's intervention skill 210, 215
teleology 138
temperament 64, 98
Terman, Lewis 36
theory of mind 43, 239, 240
theory-theory 141
Tokyo Metropolitan Institute of
    Gerontology 100
Tokyo Teen Cohort Study 101
training course on forensic interview 260
training program 216
training protocol 218
train-the-trainer (TTT) model 218
Trajectory Equifinality Model (TEM) 93

transitive verb 51
transmission of vital force 140
turn taking 247
twin 100
typically developing children (TDC) 121,
    190

———

U
UK Millennium Cohort Study 41
unit strategy 156, 157

———

V
verb island hypothesis 54
verb suffix *ta* 222
vitalism 139
vitalistic causality 137
vocalization 67, 68
Vygotsky, Lev Semenovich 82

———

W
Wallon, Henri 82
weaning 22, 27
western style parent-child
    relationship 15
WH questions 256
wider variety of viewpoint 83
Wundt, Wilhelm 34
word order of argument 52
word-particle sequence 226
word-particle speech segment 226
word-particle test trial 224

Frontiers in Developmental Psychology Research:
Japanese Perspectives

—

発行
2016年7月22日 初版1刷

定価
5000円＋税

編者
© 一般社団法人 日本発達心理学会

監修者
岩立志津夫・子安増生・根ケ山光一

発行者
松本功

ブックデザイン
小川順子

印刷・製本所
亜細亜印刷株式会社

発行所
株式会社 ひつじ書房

〒112-0011 東京都文京区千石2-1-2 大和ビル2階
Tel.03-5319-4916
Fax.03-5319-4917
郵便振替00120-8-142852
toiawase@hituzi.co.jp
http://www.hituzi.co.jp/

ISBN 978-4-89476-798-0　C3011

造本には充分注意しておりますが、落丁・乱丁などがございましたら、小社かお買上げ
書店にておとりかえいたします。ご意見、ご感想など、小社までお寄せ下されば幸いです。